Microwave Cooking in 3 speeds

•LOW •MEDIUM •HIGH

from **Frigidaire**
Division of General Motors

All recipes in this cookbook are designed for microwave cooking.
They have been carefully selected and written by the Home
Economics Department, Frigidaire Division, General Motors Corporation.

*Pictured on the front cover: Barbecued Country Ribs (page 131);
Corn in the Husk (page 207)*

Pictured on the back cover: Swedish Fruit Soup (page 89)

ISBN: 0–385–13233–6
Library of Congress Catalog Card Number 77–76585

Frigidaire
Home Environment Products

Frigidaire Division
General Motors Corporation
300 Taylor St.
Dayton, Ohio 45442

Area Code (513) 445-5000

Dear Homemaker,

Welcome to **Microwave cooking in 3 speeds,** from Frigidaire. Whether you're cooking for one or for a crowd, we know you'll use your microwave oven often.

We've prepared this cookbook especially for you. Do read the introductory chapters first. They contain information you should know before you start—information about dishes and utensils, microwave time, and food handling techniques.

Then start enjoying the food you can prepare with your microwave oven. We suggest that you try some of the simple breakfast, lunch, and dinner recipes in the *Getting Started* chapter to help you get the feel of microwave cooking. Then you are on your own; explore the recipe chapters for your family favorites as well as new taste treats.

The recipe chapters include microwave time for basic foods—those foods you already know how to prepare without a recipe—as well as recipes developed especially for microwave cooking.

We're confident that you will enjoy using these recipes and that you, your family, and guests will soon be enjoying microwaved foods.

Virginia Stacy

Virginia Stacy

Director of Home Economics
Frigidaire Division
General Motors Corporation

Symbols used in the recipes

 These recipes are easy to prepare.

 These recipes have instructions for making the food ahead of time and freezing it for later use.

 These recipes are made with store-purchased convenience foods.

 These recipes serve one or two people.

Table of Contents

Microwave Cooking

An exciting adventure awaits you

Remember the excitement the first time you stood around a bonfire as a child? What fun it was to watch the grownups roast hot dogs, corn on the cob! And the greatest part of all—you were allowed to toast your own marshmallows with mom or dad standing nearby. Well, it's time to relive that excitement.

Microwave cooking is an exciting adventure. Everything about it—the speed, the simple cooking techniques, the variety of cook-and-serve utensils, the taste treats—will fill you with awe. Never before have you experienced anything quite like microwave cooking; it's different from the bonfire, different from the charcoal grill, different from the conventional range.

Soon you will be using your microwave oven throughout the day—breakfast, lunch, dinner, and snacks. You'll wonder how you ever got along without it. It's a cooking accessory, adding a whole new world of versatility to your kitchen.

However, remember that your microwave oven won't do everything; it's not a replacement for other appliances. You'll probably still prefer to use the conventional oven for loaves of golden brown bread and for light and fluffy souffles; the conventional broiler for seared steaks. And the microwave oven cannot replace the electric coffeemaker or toaster.

Because microwave cooking is so different, take time to read the introductory chapters in this book. Become familiar with microwave do's and don'ts, time variables, and food handling techniques. And by all means practice. Don't be upset if the first recipes you try are less than perfect. (Remember your first experiences with conventional cooking?) Miracles will happen with microwave cooking; give yourself time to develop a few new cooking skills.

Once you become comfortable with your microwave oven and this cookbook, you may wish to venture on to other microwave cookbooks available in bookstores. Check the introductory information in these books for the cooking watts (also known as output power) of the microwave oven that was used to test the recipes. If the power differs from your microwave oven, adjust microwave time accordingly. Reduce time if the power of your oven is greater; add more time if your power is less.

Recipes in this book were tested in microwave ovens with a nominal rating of 675 watts of cooking power.

Microwave speeds. In conventional cooking, you adjust the controls to suit the food. For instance, you select a higher surface unit setting to boil water than you do to warm milk. You set the oven for 325°F, or 375°F, or whatever temperature is specified in the recipe.

Likewise, your microwave oven offers multi-speed flexibility. Check the *Use and Care Instructions* supplied with your microwave oven for specifics about these speeds.

The recipes in this cookbook give microwave times in Low, Medium, or High, whichever of these speeds best suits the food.

Lobster Tails (page 154)

How microwaves cook

Microwaves cause food to produce heat, cooking itself

Bonfires, charcoal grills, gas and electric ranges all use a different fuel source to produce heat. The heat moves through the air to the outer layer of food; then the heat slowly penetrates deeper into the food, cooking its center.

Microwave ovens don't produce heat; instead they cause the food itself to produce heat. To understand this principle, let's follow the path that microwaves take within the oven as they are generated, reflected, transmitted, and absorbed. You can trace this path in the illustration of a vegetable casserole in a microwave oven.

Generated. Just as a light bulb generates light waves, the magnetron tube generates microwaves. The microwaves travel through a channel across the top of the oven and then strike a slowly rotating fan, called the stirrer.

Reflected. The stirrer reflects the microwaves, causing them to bounce into the oven at numerous angles. As the waves strike the metal oven interior —walls, ceiling, bottom, and door screen—they are reflected again, bouncing back into the oven cavity. (The microwaves cannot escape through the perforated metal door screen. You might think of them as being too fat to get through the holes.)

Transmitted. In the illustration a vegetable casserole is in the oven. As the microwaves approach the glass dish and lid, they don't bounce. Instead, the glass transmits the microwaves; the microwaves pass through the glass, into the food.

Absorbed. The vegetables then absorb the microwaves. The microwaves cause the molecules in the food to vibrate back and forth 2450 million times each second. The friction from all of this molecular movement produces heat which, in turn, cooks the vegetables.

You are already familiar with other methods of using friction to generate heat. On a cold day you rub your hands together very quickly to warm them up. Likewise, food molecules in a microwave oven rub together and produce the heat which cooks the food.

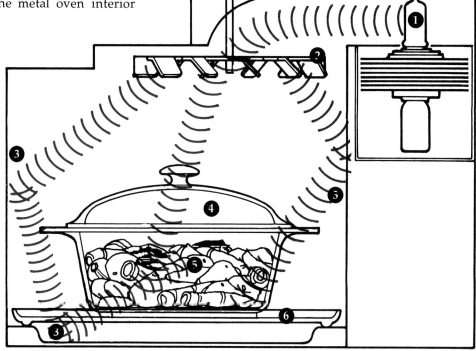

Magnetron tube **1** *generates microwaves.*

Stirrer **2** *and metal oven interior* **3** *reflect microwaves.*

Glass casserole dish and lid **4** *transmit microwaves.*

Food **5** *absorbs microwaves.*

Glass tray **6** *raises food off of metal oven floor; transmits microwaves, allowing them to bounce off the floor and cook the bottom layer of food.*

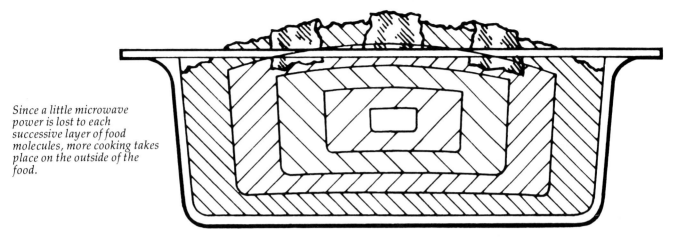

Since a little microwave power is lost to each successive layer of food molecules, more cooking takes place on the outside of the food.

Microwaves penetrate the food from all sides

In your conventional oven, the air heats up first. Then the hot air heats up the oven walls, the utensil, and then the outer layers of food. Finally, the heat moves from the hot outer layers of food inward, cooking the food's center.

In your microwave oven, the microwave energy does not heat up the air, oven walls, nor the utensil. Instead, the food molecules absorb the energy, causing friction. This in turn produces the heat which cooks the food, as explained before.

However, more cooking takes place on the outer layers of food, as illustrated in the cross section of a meat loaf. This is because the outer layers of food receive the most microwave power; each successive layer of food receives less and less. In other words, the microwaves cause less friction and, therefore, less heat and less cooking in the center of the food than in the outer layers. The center of food cooks—partly due to the limited amount of microwave energy, and partly due to the heat that moves from the hot layers of food inward.

Notice the degree of cooking along the bottom edge of the meat loaf. In order for microwaves to bounce (reflect) off the bottom of the oven and enter the food, the food cannot sit directly on the metal oven floor. It must be raised up; some space is needed for bouncing to occur.

Your microwave oven is equipped with a removable glass tray, a sealed-in ceramic shelf, or some other nonmetallic surface that transmits microwaves. If this nonmetallic tray in your oven is removable, be sure it is in place before you begin to cook. See the *Use and Care Instructions* for your microwave oven for specifics.

How to select cooking utensils

Use utensils that transmit microwaves

The covered glass casserole dish that was used to cook the vegetables (see page 2) transmits microwaves. In other words, the glass does not interfere with the microwave energy. Instead the microwaves pass through the glass and go directly to the food.

Use the chart on the next three pages to help you select appropriate utensils. Many utensils transmit microwaves and can be used in the microwave oven. These utensils may be made of glass, glass-ceramic, paper, plastic, and other nonmetallic materials.

Do not use utensils that reflect microwaves

The stirrer and metal oven interior (see page 2) reflect microwaves. They change the direction of microwaves, bouncing the energy off of the metal surface. Never put any metal in your microwave oven. (Exception: see Shielding, page 12.)

Metal utensils. If food were in a metal pan—stainless steel, aluminum, copper, cast iron, etc—the metal barrier would keep the microwaves from entering the food. This could cause product damage and unsatisfactory cooking results.

- The microwaves would strike the metal pan and keep bouncing in the oven. This could cause the magnetron tube to overheat; possible damage to the tube could occur.
- Food would cook unevenly because the microwaves could not enter the food through the metal pan. The uncovered top layer of food would become overdone; the bottom, sides, and center would remain uncooked.

Metal parts. If a glass or glass-ceramic utensil has metal parts (such as gold or silver decorative paint, a metal handle, or gold/silver printing on the underside of the utensil), do not use the utensil in the microwave oven. The metal will cause arcing, a static discharge of electricity, within the oven cavity. Sparks will fly.

Examples of materials that cause arcing are:
- Metal parts on glass and glass-ceramic utensils
- Staples used on tea bags, straw baskets, etc

- Metal ties used to close a plastic bag
- Metal stirring spoon accidentally left in the casserole
- Aluminum foil improperly used for shielding (see page 12)

Invisible metallic content. Some dishware has metallic content. Do not use Centura® Dinnerware, Corelle® Livingware cups with closed handles, or melamine plastic dishware.

If in doubt about other utensils, use the Dish Test (see page 7).

Do not use these utensils in an operating microwave oven

> Do not use the following utensils in an operating microwave oven. Depending on the utensil, they may produce adverse effects. They may become damaged; they may prolong cooking; they may cause a fire or explosion; they may permanently damage the magnetron tube. See specifics for each item, pages 4 to 7.

- Metal cookware and bakeware (stainless steel, aluminum, copper, cast iron, etc)
- Aluminum foil (exception: see Shielding, page 12)
- Foil trays, (frozen dinner, pot pie, etc)
- Dinnerware and glassware with metallic trim or signature
- Plastic, glass, china, or pottery with invisible metallic content
- Crystal, cut glass, antique glassware
- Lids, handles, etc with metal parts
- Metal spoons, forks, etc
- Conventional meat or candy thermometer (see page 13 for out-of-the-oven technique)
- Metal skewers
- Metal ties to close a plastic or paper bag
- Metal staples
- Bottles, jars with restricted openings

Utensils for Microwave Use

Material	Typical Brandnames	Typical Shapes	Limitations
Heat-resistant glass, including see-through and opaque varieties	Pyrex® brand Ovenware Creative Glass® Fire King® Cookware Corelle® Livingware (among others)	Baking dishes Cake dishes Pie plates Loaf dishes Covered casseroles Custard cups Measuring cups Wide-mouth jars Mixing bowls Dinnerware	Remove metal handles, lids, and other parts. Don't use glass with decorative gold or silver trim or other unremovable metal parts. Do not use Pyrex® brand Rangetop Ware, Beverage Servers, or Serving Pitchers & Flasks. Do not use bottles with narrow openings, such as soft drink bottles and salad dressing bottles. The restricted opening will prevent steam from escaping; the bottle may explode.
China, Pottery	French Chef by Marsh Industries Temper-ware by Lenox® (among others)	Dinnerware Serving platters Serving bowls Mixing bowls Ovenproof casseroles	Do not use china with gold or silver decorative trim or signature (printing on underside). Do not use if utensil has unremovable metal parts. If in doubt, check manufacturer's instructions. If still in doubt, use the Dish Test, page 7.
Glass-ceramic ovenware	Corning Ware® Cookware Cookmates® Cookware Centura® Cook 'n Serve Companions (among others)	Assorted casseroles Saucemakers Skillets Baking dishes	Remove metal handles, lids, and other metal parts. Do not use Corning Ware® Beverage Makers. Do not use utensil if it has unremovable metal parts.
Glass-ceramic dinnerware	Centura® Dinnerware (among others)	Plates Saucers Bowls Serving pieces	Do not use Centura® Dinnerware; it has a metallic content. If in doubt, check manufacturer's instructions. If still in doubt, use the Dish Test, page 7.

Chart continued on next page

Utensils for Microwave Use, *continued*

Material	Typical Brandnames	Typical Shapes	Limitations
Paper	ScotTowels® Napkins Kleenex® Towels, Napkins Cut-Rite® Wax Paper (among others)	Paper plates Paper bowls Napkins Paper towels Hot cups Cardboard containers Waxed paper	Use for short-term cooking only; prolonged cooking can cause paper to scorch or burn. Paper can become soggy if food is moist or greasy.
Paper cooking bags Plastic cooking bags	Green Giant Frozen Vegetables Seal-a-Meal Bags™ Cooking Magic™ bags Reynolds Brown-In-Bag® (among others)	Boilable plastic bags Roasting paper bags	Do not use foil-lined paper bags. The foil will reflect the energy away from the food, preventing cooking and possibly damaging the magnetron tube. Do not use metal ties; use string instead. The metal will cause sparks, possibly igniting the paper or plastic bag. To prevent a pressure buildup, pierce several holes in paper or plastic bags, or cut an X in plastic bags.
Plastic film	Glad® Wrap Saran Wrap™ Handi-Wrap® (among others)	Cut to fit; use as a cover	Use some brands for a short time only, for instance to cover foods you are reheating. Some films may become sticky and difficult to remove; others may shrink. Pierce the film for steam to escape, or cover loosely. Do not remove until steam has escaped to avoid burning your fingers.
Plastic dishes Plastic bowls	Cool Whip® tubs Nu-Maid® tubs (among others)	Variety of sizes and shapes	Use for short time only, for instance to reheat foods. Use stronger plastics that can withstand the heat from the food; do not use plastics that cannot withstand heat. Tupperware® is not recommended for microwave use by the manufacturer. Do not use any plastic to reheat or cook dense foods, meat sauces, and gravies. These foods can become hot enough to damage the plastic. If food is frozen, use plastic container only until you can transfer the food to another utensil. Do not use plastics with metallic content, such as melamine plastic dishware. If in doubt, check manufacturer's instructions. If still in doubt, use the Dish Test, page 7.

Chart continued on next page

Utensils for Microwave Use, *continued*

Material	Typical Brandnames	Typical Shapes	Limitations
Styrofoam	Assorted	Variety of sizes and shapes	Use for a short time only—for instance to boil water or heat bread. Do not use for long-term cooking, as in a casserole.
Straw Wood	Assorted	Bread baskets Paper plate liners Wooden bowls Wooden skewers	Use for a short time only. After repeated, prolonged exposure to microwave energy, the wood or straw may have lost all of its moisture and will begin to crack/split.
Glass-ceramic skillets with coated bottoms	Frigidaire Browning Skillet Corning® Browning Skillet	Covered skillets	Follow manufacturer's instructions carefully. Bottom of skillet has a special coating to absorb the microwaves; it becomes very hot, up to 600° F. Use oven mitts after preheating the empty skillet. Place preheated skillet on a trivet, not a countertop.
Special microwave utensil	Frigidaire Microwave Oven Roasting Rack Micro-Ware™ Roasting Rack by Anchor Hocking	Nonmetallic roasting rack	Follow manufacturer's instructions. Place rack in glass dish. Place meat on top of rack. Juice will drain below the level of the food. Baste off juice occasionally so it doesn't slow the cooking process. Can substitute an inverted saucer if: • Saucer can withstand high temperatures • Saucer can withstand weight of food • Saucer is appropriate for microwave use

Dish Test

Certain plastics (such as melamine) and certain glass-ceramic dishes/utensils (such as Centura® Dinnerware) contain invisible metallic substances. Do not use these in the microwave oven. They may prolong cooking time. They may be damaged by microwave energy. They may permanently damage the magnetron tube.

If you are uncertain about using a certain dish, perform the following dish test:

1. Fill a glass measuring cup with approximately eight ounces of cool water. Place the container of water on the dish being tested.

2. Microwave on High for 1¼ minutes.

3. Check the dish and water when time is up.

If	Then
A. Cool dish, very warm water	Dish is ok for microwave use.
B. Warm edges of dish, warm water	Dish can be used only for short-term reheating; don't use at all, if possible.
C. Hot dish, lukewarm water	**Do not use the dish.**

How to select microwave time

With conventional cooking, an extra minute or two of cooking won't ruin most foods. But with the speed of microwave cooking, an extra minute may be quite critical.

Most foodloads cook much faster—up to 75% faster—in the microwave oven than conventionally. However, a few foods take about the same amount of time—rice and pasta, for instance, which need time to rehydrate.

Until you get the feel of microwave cooking, check the basic recipes and charts in this cookbook for suggested microwave times and speeds. Set the Timer for the minimum amount of time; then check the food. You can always microwave the food for a few minutes longer if required; but you can't easily correct overdone food, if at all.

Microwave times in the recipes are approximate

The microwave times in this cookbook, and in other cookbooks, are not exact. Variables in the food, electrical supply, altitude, and microwave speed all affect the actual amount of time needed.

Volume of food. More food takes longer to cook than less food. In general, if you double the quantity of food, increase microwave time by slightly less than double.

Density of food. Denser food, such as meat, takes longer to cook than an equal weight of porous food, such as bread.

Moisture in food. Food with a high moisture content takes longer to cook than an equal weight of food with less moisture.

Sugar/Fat in food. Food with a high sugar or fat content heats and cooks quicker than food with less sugar or fat.

Temperature of food. Colder ingredients take longer to reach cooking temperatures than do those at room temperature. In general, microwave times in this cookbook are based on fresh ingredients at refrigerated temperatures, shelf ingredients at room temperatures, and frozen foods at 0° to -5° F.

Electrical supply. The electrical voltage supplied to your house may not be the same as for another part of the city, state, or country. And your house power supply may fluctuate throughout the day, an extreme example being brownouts. Allow more time if the voltage to your house is low.

Altitude. If you live in high altitudes, increase microwave time slightly.

High, Medium, Low speeds. Depending on many variables, including the model of your microwave oven, you may have to adjust microwave time for one speed but not the others. For example, you may find that one speed generally cooks faster or slower than the microwave time specified in the recipes, while the other two speeds run true to recipe time. Adjust microwave time accordingly. (See the *Use and Care Instructions* supplied with your microwave oven for more specifics.)

Rules of thumb for selecting microwave time

1. Set the Timer for the minimum amount of time given in the recipes; then check the food. Continue to microwave if more cooking is needed.

2. If you double the recipe, increase microwave time by slightly less than double.

3. Remember that actual microwave time increases with the quantity of food. This concept is completely different from conventional cooking; in a conventional oven you could prepare a roast and baked potatoes simultaneously without changing the time required for each item. Not so with microwave cooking. Not only would microwave time increase, but cooking results would be unpredictable. Microwave energy would be attracted to the food with the higher moisture, fat, or sugar content. One food may overcook, while the other remains underdone.

   However, you can reheat a complete meal for one—meat, vegetable, and potato, for instance—all together at one time.

4. To adapt conventional recipes, start with these generalized formulas. Adjust time to suit the particular recipe.

   ¼ of conventional time = Microwave on High
   ⅓ of conventional time = Microwave on Medium
   ½ of conventional time = Microwave on Low

Many of the food handling techniques that you use conventionally can still be used with microwave cooking. Many others are unique. Discussed in this chapter are the techniques you will be using before, during, and after microwave time, as well as a few additional techniques.

Before microwave time

Cut the food into uniform pieces

For more even cooking results, cut up meats, vegetables, and other ingredients into pieces that are similar in size and shape (for instance, for casseroles, stews, pot roasts, etc).

If an ear of corn is much larger than the others, for instance, cut it in half.

Do not add salt to some uncooked foods

Salt foods after microwave time for a more satisfactory food product, unless otherwise specified in the recipe.

- If salt is sprinkled on foods such as vegetables before microwave time, the food will get a spotted appearance.
- If salt is sprinkled on meats, poultry, etc, it tends to draw the natural moisture out of the food during the microwave process, resulting in dry meat.
- Add salt to casseroles, breads, and other mixtures before microwave time, as you normally would.

Of course, you may add other seasonings—pepper, herbs, spices—to any food before microwave time.

Add ingredients to improve the color of some cooked food

Food slowly browns when it bakes in a conventional oven. Food quickly browns when intense heat is applied to the surface of the food, as in conventional broiling and frying.

For most microwave cooking, neither long microwave time nor intense heat is present; browning does not occur. (The exceptions—browning skillet, large roasts, and turkey—are noted below.) Following are a few suggestions to improve the color of some cooked food.

Baked goods—such as breads, cakes, pastry shells, cookies—will not brown in the microwave oven. Try one of the following tips:

- Select recipes with dark ingredients: wheat flour, brown sugar, chocolate, and the like.
- Add food coloring to a light mixture, for instance to pastry dough.
- Use a topping (cinnamon-nut topping, for instance) on the uncooked batter.
- Frost the finished product.

For meats, poultry, etc, you may prefer to:

- Brush the exterior with a dark seasoning mixture, such as Kitchen Bouquet, a gravy mix, or dry onion soup paste. Or use a jelly glaze.
- Use the Frigidaire Browning Skillet accessory to sear the meat with intense heat.
- Team up your conventional range (to brown the meat quickly) with your microwave oven (to finish the cooking).

For turkey, large roasts, etc, browning may occur if microwave time is long enough. The fats melt, baste the meat, and become very hot. This hot layer of fats causes browning.

Allow a means for steam to escape

During microwave cooking, foods start to steam quite readily. If steam is trapped inside food or in the cooking dish, pressure builds up. Then the food may erupt and/or the untensil's cover may blow off. To avoid these eruptions:

- Using a knife or fork, prick several holes in the skin of acorn squash, potatoes, apples, tomatoes, and other foods with a skin or membrane.
- Remove eggs from the shell. Using the tines of a fork, carefully pierce the yolk membrane.
- Prick holes in the plastic film (Saran Wrap™, Glad® Wrap, etc) that is used to cover a dish, to wrap a sandwich, etc.
- Loosely tie a plastic or paper cooking bag with string. Do not use metal ties; arcing will occur. The paper bag may ignite.
- Cut an X in some sealed plastic bags (such as with some frozen vegetables).
- Prick several holes in the top surface of other sealed plastic bags (such as with some frozen casseroles). This will prevent the sauce from spilling out but will allow steam to escape.
- Open sealed jars, containers. Let plastic lids rest lightly on the bowls; do not snap into place.
- Most lids supplied with casserole dishes can be used as normal. They are tight-fitting in that they help retain the steam inside the casserole; but they do not form an airtight cover. Enough steam will escape to prevent a pressure buildup.

Arrange food items in the dish, or arrange several small dishes in the oven

Some food arrangements allow more even cooking than do others. In general, spread the foodload throughout the oven, with the least amount of food in the center of the arrangement as possible. Expose the surface area of the food within a larger amount of oven space. These techniques will distribute the food within the pattern of microwaves.

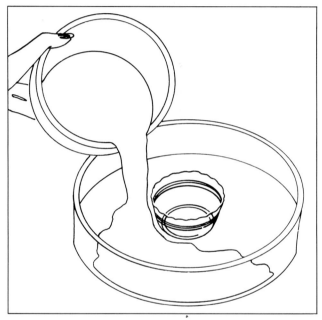

Place an empty custard cup or juice glass, upright, in the center of a baking dish. Pour the batter around the cup.

Place an empty custard cup or juice glass, upright, in the center of a baking dish. Pour the batter (for instance, cornbread or nutbread) into the dish, letting it flow around the cup. Leave the empty cup in place during microwave time. This technique permits the batter to cook more evenly. Otherwise, the edges of the food may finish cooking long before the center.

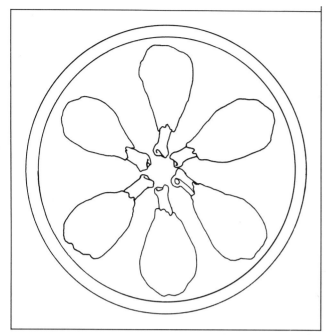

Arrange thicker pieces/parts of food toward the outside of the dish.

Arrange items in the cooking dish with thicker pieces/parts toward the outer edges of the dish, as shown in the illustration of chicken legs.

Arrange individual items in a circle; leave the center of the circle empty.

Arrange cupcakes, baking potatoes, custard cups, etc in a circle with at least one inch separating them. Don't place a food item in the center of the circle; leave it empty.

Cover the food to steam it and/or to avoid spatters

According to the recipe, many foods should be covered. Covering helps to hold some steam and heat around the food, speeding the cooking process. It also minimizes oven cleanup due to spattering.

To help retain some steam and heat inside the dish:
● Use the lid supplied with the dish, if appropriate for microwave use. To prevent a pressure buildup, don't snap plastic lids into place.
● Cover the dish with plastic film; pierce holes in the film for excess steam to escape.
● Place a saucer on top of the cooking utensil.

To help prevent spatters:
● Use any of the covers specified above.
● Use paper towels, paper napkins, waxed paper, etc.

During microwave time

Use caution; cooking utensils become hot

During microwave time, the food gets hot and conducts some of this heat to the cooking utensil. As you remove the utensil from the oven to stir the food etc), always wear oven mitts. Place the utensil on a trivet or hot pad.

> Always wear dry fire-resistant oven mitts that protect all fingers and hands. Moist or damp oven mitts on hot surfaces may result in burns from steam. Do not use a towel or bulky cloth, nor a pot holder that does not protect all fingers.

> After removing a hot utensil from the microwave oven, place it on a trivet or hot pad. Do not place the hot cooking utensil on the countertop, table, or other surface that may be damaged by heat.

Turn the food over, stir it, or rotate the dish occasionally

Interrupt the microwave time, and turn over or stir the food as specified in the recipe. This results in more even cooking results by redistributing the food-load within the pattern of microwaves. Stirring also helps to equalize temperatures, mixing hotter portions of the food with cooler portions.

If you cannot stir or turn over the food, such as a cake, rotate the dish a quarter turn occasionally during microwave time.

Baste off juice and excess moisture

Use a spoon or baster to remove excess moisture as it accumulates in the cooking utensil, as with meats and poultry.

- Excess moisture absorbs microwave energy, slowing down the cooking process.
- Moisture, juice, and fat will spatter.
- Spattering may continue after you stop the microwave oven if the liquid is hot enough. Hot spatters can cause burns.

Shielding: Use only as directed

For large turkeys and large roasts that require prolonged microwave time, the fats melt, baste the meat, and become very hot. This hot layer of fat causes browning. Thin food surfaces, if uncovered, may overcook before thicker portions are done.

To prevent this form of overcooking, use this shielding technique:

1. Use on large poultry and roasts only.
2. Use small pieces of aluminum foil to shield wing tips, leg bones, tip of breast bone, and thin areas of large roasts. Apply foil during the second quarter of microwave time.
3. Keep most of the food surface uncovered, allowing microwaves to enter the thick parts of the food. Otherwise, the aluminum foil will reflect too many microwaves, causing an overload of energy and possible damage to the magnetron tube.
4. Arrange poultry and meat so the foil does not touch the metal oven interior. Otherwise, arcing or pitting will occur during microwave time.

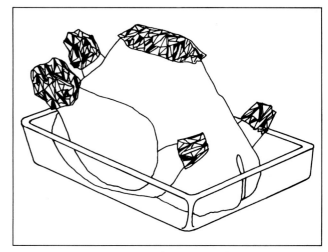

Shielding: Use small pieces of aluminum foil to cover certain areas of a turkey or large roast. Use only as directed.

Use a meat/candy thermometer as directed

To use a meat thermometer that is specifically designed for use in an operating microwave oven, follow manufacturer's instructions. A Frigidaire Microwave Thermometer is available from your Frigidaire Dealer at extra charge.

To use a conventional meat or candy thermometer:

1. Stop the microwave oven. Remove the food to a counter.
2. Insert the thermometer, and wait for the pointer to stabilize.
3. Check this temperature against the temperature specified in the recipe. If specified temperature has not been reached:
   - Remove the thermometer.
   - Return the food to the microwave oven.
   - Restart for additional microwave time.

> Never use a conventional meat/candy thermometer in an operating microwave oven; neither the metal trim nor the temperature-indicating chemical (usually mercury) should be exposed to microwaves. Use the out-of-the-oven technique, above.

After microwave time

Allow standing time, as specified in the recipe

Remove food while it is slightly underdone. Allow standing time, as specified in the recipe or chart. Cooking will continue during this period. As temperatures equalize, the internal temperature of meat will continue to rise.

If food does not finish cooking as completely as you prefer, return it to the microwave oven briefly. (Remove conventional meat thermometer first.) Underdone food is correctable.

Resist the temptation to microwave food to desired doneness. The food may be overdone at the end of standing time. Overdone food is not correctable.

The length of standing time varies with the food and the recipe. Some foods, such as vegetables, may require only a moment or two. Others, such as meats, may require up to 20 minutes. See individual recipes or charts for guidelines.

Allow for this standing time as you schedule foods in and out of the microwave oven.

Additional techniques

Reheat leftovers

After a meal, package remaining food in suitable materials for the refrigerator or freezer. Package food items in bulk to serve at another family meal; or portion the foods into individual packets for quick single-serving meals.

Refrigerate or freeze the packaged food immediately. If the food is to be stored for longer than two days, freeze it.

To reheat refrigerated foods, place the food in a container suitable for the microwave oven. Microwave on High, covered, until reheated, stirring once. Do not overcook; food may dry out.

To reheat frozen foods, see the *Defrosting Foods* chapter.

Prepare foods in advance

At times you may find it convenicnt to prepare food in advance and then refrigerate or freeze the food until needed.

- While all the ingredients are out, mix up a double batch of meat loaf, family casserole, etc. Prepare one for now; freeze the other for later.
- Take advantage of spare time, and prepare a casserole for an upcoming busy day.
- To reduce last-minute party preparations, make the food in advance and freeze it until needed.

Depending on the recipe, you may:

- Mix all ingredients, and freeze the food uncooked. Later thaw the food; then cook it.
- Mix up partial ingredients and freeze. Later thaw the food; then continue with the recipe.
- Prepare the dish, and cook it until slightly underdone. Later thaw the food; then finish cooking it.

Freezer wrap. Wrap the food in an appropriate freezer wrap—one that is airtight, moistureproof, and vaporproof. Consider using a material that is also appropriate for microwave use. Freeze the food immediately.

Microwave instructions. Thaw and reheat/cook the food in separate operations. See the *Defrosting Foods* chapter for more information.

Getting Started

Using menus in this chapter

Now you're ready to use your microwave oven—and to enjoy it! We've prepared this chapter to get you off to a good start. It contains menus for simple breakfasts, lunches, and dinners.

These menus will let you experience the variety of foods you can quickly and easily prepare in the microwave oven—from-scratch dishes to cook; frozen convenience foods to thaw and reheat; instant-type food to prepare in the serving dishes; sweet rolls to reheat.

In addition, a step-by-step procedure for each menu will help you have all food items ready to serve at the same time.

Planning meals on your own

Selecting foods. Start with simple foods to get the feel of microwave cooking and to practice some of the basic microwave techniques. Next, progress at your own speed, preparing other simple foods with familiar results.

Then you're ready to experiment—to try new foods and some of the more challenging recipes. Use the following chart to help you select foods as you progress from simple ones to those requiring more microwave know-how.

Level one
 	
Simple foods to get the feel of microwave cooking
	Heat-and-serve foods, such as
	    Sweet rolls
	    Canned foods
	    Baby foods
	Instant-type foods, such as
	    Coffee, tea
	    Soup mix
	    Cereals
	Frozen convenience foods
	Packaged mixes, such as
	    Box dinners
	    Cakes
	    Puddings
	Easy-to-prepare foods, such as
	    Fish
	    Bacon
	    Baked potatoes
	    Vegetables, fresh and frozen
	    Sandwiches

Level two Foods with simple recipes, familiar results	Casseroles Sauces Chicken pieces in a sauce Meat loaf Stuffed peppers Stuffed cabbage rolls
Level three Foods that require some microwave experience; and foods that have microwave limitations	Meats Poultry From-scratch breads and cakes Party foods

Developing a time schedule. Since microwave times are so much faster than conventional times, you may find that your sequence of preparing a meal might change. It doesn't take as long to microwave the meat and vegetables; but setting the table and preparing the salad take just as long as before. Soon you'll develop your own time schedule—one that suits you.

If things get behind schedule, for instance if the food is cooked but the table isn't set, relax. Take your time and set the table. Just before it's time to serve the food, you can always return it to the microwave oven until hot.

On some occasions the microwave oven can help you out of a time jam.

● If unexpected visitors arrive, you can use the microwave oven to defrost and prepare additional food to supplement the planned menu.

● If dinner must be served earlier than expected, you can transfer foods from the conventional range to the microwave oven to speed up the cooking process.

Using other appliances too. Remember that your microwave oven is not a replacement for the conventional range or other cooking appliances. Use it to help you with meal preparations, but don't feel that you have to do all the cooking in it.

Some items—such as vegetables—you may prefer to microwave almost always. Others—such as steaks—you can prepare either way but you may prefer to do conventionally. Still others—such as toast—you must always prepare conventionally.

Then again, your day's schedule may change the way you would normally prepare the food. For instance, if you are using the conventional oven to bake yeast bread, you might decide to prepare other items conventionally also—making double use of the oven.

In other words, recognize that the microwave oven can be an advantage—or a disadvantage—as you prepare a meal. Use it, use conventional cooking appliances, use both. Use whichever appliance best suits the food, your preferences, and your schedule.

Handling latecomers. If a family member is detained but the meal is ready, you will find the microwave oven to be quite convenient.

● Serve now, reserving a plate of food for the latecomer. Wrap and refrigerate the individual's dinner. Later, simply reheat the meal-on-a-plate in the microwave oven, and serve hot.

● Or delay the entire meal until later. Cover all foods, and refrigerate them. When the latecomer arrives, reheat the foods in the microwave oven. Then serve a hot meal to the entire family.

Handling special diets. The microwave oven also helps prepare special diets (low calorie, low fat, no sugar, etc). Simply prepare the diet food items in the microwave oven. Since an individual portion of food cooks so quickly, everyone can still sit down and eat together.

Breakfast for 1

Fruit Juice
Danish Pastry
page 35

Quick-cooking Oatmeal
page 167

Instant Coffee or Tea

1. Pour juice.
2. Prepare oatmeal in serving bowl. Microwave. Set aside, covered.
3. Microwave water in mug. Stir in instant beverage. Serve.
4. Microwave sweet roll. Serve.
5. Uncover cereal. Serve.

Lunch for 1

Instant Soup Mix
page 184

Hot Dog
page 171

Fresh Fruit

Soft Drink

1. Prepare soup in serving bowl. Microwave. Set aside, covered.
2. Place wiener in bun. Wrap loosely in paper napkin. Microwave.
3. Serve soup and hot dog together.
4. Later serve fruit and soft drink.

Dinner for 1

Lasagna (frozen)
page 225

Spinach Salad

Vanilla Ice Cream
with Hot Fudge Sauce
page 181

Iced Tea

1. Prepare Hot Fudge Sauce ahead of time; refrigerate. (Or use store-purchased sauce.)
2. Microwave lasagna fifteen minutes before serving time.
3. Wash spinach leaves, and prepare salad. Add dressing just before serving.
4. Prepare iced tea. Serve.
5. Serve lasagna when hot.
6. Later microwave a portion of Hot Fudge Sauce for a few seconds. Serve over ice cream.

Breakfast for 4

Baked Grapefruit
page 86

Bacon
page 128

Scrambled Eggs
page 61

Toast

Perked Coffee

Milk

1. Twenty minutes before serving time, start to perk coffee.

2. Microwave bacon. While bacon is cooking, prepare eggs. Remove bacon when done. Set aside.

3. Microwave eggs. While eggs are cooking, prepare grapefruit. Remove eggs from oven. Set aside, covered.

4. Microwave grapefruit. Start toast. While grapefruit is baking, season eggs and stir once. Serve, topped with bacon strips.

5. Butter toast. Pour milk. Remove grapefruit from oven and serve.

Lunch for 4

Egg Drop Soup
page 189

Tuna Boats
page 175

Vanilla Pudding
with Peach Slices
page 100

Milk

1. Make ahead vanilla pudding from packaged mix. Place in individual serving dishes, and cover. Refrigerate.

2. Start Egg Drop Soup about fifteen minutes before serving.

3. While chicken stock is heating, make tuna mixture.

4. Stir cornstarch mixture and salt into chicken stock. While continuing to heat the soup, fill buns with tuna mixture.

5. Remove soup from the oven. While heating sandwiches, stir egg into soup and serve. Serve sandwiches when heated. Pour milk.

6. Later arrange peach slices on pudding. Serve.

Dinner for 4

Flounder in Herbs
page 149

Peas and Carrots
page 197

Baked Potatoes
page 210

Tossed Salad

Butter Brickle Peach Cake
page 71

Perked Coffee

Milk

1. Prepare Butter Brickle Peach Cake early in the day.

2. Make salad ahead of time (except dressing). Cover and refrigerate.

3. Microwave frozen Peas and Carrots. Set aside, covered.

4. While Peas and Carrots are cooking, prepare baking potatoes. Microwave potatoes as soon as Peas and Carrots are done. Perk coffee.

5. Prepare Flounder in Herbs while baking potatoes. Remove potatoes when done. Set aside. Microwave flounder.

6. Toss salad while reheating Peas and Carrots for 1 to 2 minutes. Serve salad, fish, and vegetables. Pour beverages.

7. Later microwave individual servings of Peach Cake for 15 seconds each, if you wish to serve them warm.

Appetizers

Successful parties don't just happen. But watch how easily they will happen when you combine your natural flair for throwing parties with piping hot appetizers from your microwave oven.

Imagine your guests' eyes when you take a plate of food out of the refrigerator, pop it into the microwave oven, and then serve piping hot hors d'oeuvres! Imagine the raves about the food, the compliments about your talents as host/hostess. Imagine—all of this because of your Frigidaire Microwave Oven.

Make your selection of party foods from the many recipes in this chapter: toppings to melt on crackers; cereal/pretzel mixes to eat by the handful; meat shrimp tidbits to spear with woodenpicks; seafood delicacies to eat with cocktail forks.

Many of these foods can be prepared early in the day and refrigerated, or early in the week and frozen. For cracker-bottom appetizers, refrigerate/freeze the topping separately to prevent the cracker from becoming soggy. Assemble and heat at party time.

For finger foods such as Walnut Bacon Crisps, and for woodenpick foods such as Sweet-Sour Meatballs, freeze the food in the serving dish. Select a dish that does not have metal trim, and fix the food as you would serve it—even with a paper lace doily under the food if appropriate. Then wrap the dish with a material that is suitable both for the freezer and for the microwave oven; freeze the food. At party time, just heat and serve.

When the gang drops in unexpectedly, toast nuts or freshen potato chips in the microwave oven for a quick snack. Or open the container of already-prepared Cocktail Nibbles, heat, and serve.

Microwave most appetizers on High—those that require only a minute or two in the oven, and those longer-cooking foods that are sturdy. Microwave delicate appetizers, such as cheese, on Medium. Microwave on Low those appetizers that should simmer to develop flavor.

Popcorn: Do not pop popcorn in any microwave oven. Use a conventional method instead. Popping corn in the microwave oven is similar to operating an empty oven; since the small kernels cannot absorb enough of the microwave energy in the oven, energy may be reflected back to the magnetron tube, damaging it. Moreover, if you attempt to pop corn in a paper bag, the kernels may become hot enough to ignite the paper.

Clockwise from center: Hot Cheese Dip (page 20), Foxy Franks (page 26), Herbed Shrimp (page 25), Toasted Nuts (page 20)

Hot Cheese Dip

Clams, green pepper, and onions perk it up

Pictured on page 18

¼ large green pepper, minced
½ bunch green onions, minced
2 jars (5 oz each) very sharp cheese spread
1 can (7 oz) minced clams, drained
2 to 4 dashes hot pepper sauce
Garlic powder to taste

Corn chips

1. Combine all ingredients except corn chips in a 1½-quart glass casserole.

2. Microwave on Medium, uncovered, for 4 minutes, or until cheese melts, stirring twice.

3. Serve very hot with crisp corn chips for dippers.

Toasted Nuts

Crisp and delicious hors d'oeuvre

Pictured on page 18

1½ cups shelled nuts

1. Spread nuts on paper plate or shallow dish.

2. Microwave on High for 3 to 5 minutes, stirring twice.

Tuna Curry Fondue

Easy appetizer or supper dish; makes 3 cups

1 package (8 oz) cream cheese

1 can (6½ oz) tuna, drained and flaked
1 can (10½ oz) cream of chicken soup
2 tablespoons instant minced onion
¼ teaspoon curry powder

Bread chunks, crackers, or toast

1. Place cream cheese in a 1½ quart glass casserole. Microwave on Low for 2 minutes or until softened.

2. Blend in remaining ingredients. Microwave on Medium, covered, for 8 minutes, stirring once.

3. Serve with bread chunks or crackers; or spoon over toast as a main dish.

Cocktail Nibbles

8 cups of a bite-size snack to keep on hand

1 small box (9 or 10 oz) thin pretzel sticks
1 can (6¾ oz) cocktail peanuts
1 can mixed nuts or cashews
2 cups wheat cereal squares
2 cups rice cereal squares
2 cups donut-shape oat cereal

¾ cup butter or margarine
3 tablespoons Worcestershire sauce
1 teaspoon garlic salt
1 teaspoon onion salt
1 teaspoon celery salt

1. Combine first 6 ingredients in a large glass bowl. Set aside.

2. Combine remaining ingredients in a 2-cup measure. Microwave on High for 1 minute or until melted.

3. Pour over cereal mixture. Mix well until coated. Microwave on High for 8 minutes. Mix thoroughly after each 2 minutes.

4. Cool and store in a plastic or tin container with tight-fitting lid.

Curried Shreddies

Serve warm or cold

1 box (7¼ oz) spoon-size wheat cereal squares

½ cup butter or margarine
¾ teaspoon curry powder
½ teaspoon onion salt
¼ teaspoon ginger

1. Place cereal in an 8x8x2-inch glass dish; set aside.

2. Put butter and seasonings in a small glass dish. Microwave on High, covered, for 1 to 2 minutes or until butter is melted.

3. Stir and pour over cereal. Toss until well coated.

Bread Spreads

16 finger sandwiches from the holiday roast

4 slices white bread
2 tablespoons mayonnaise

4 slices cooked turkey or ham
4 slices Cheddar cheese

1. Remove crusts from bread. Spread mayonnaise on bread slices.

2. Place meat on bread. Top with cheese. Cut into quarters. Place on paper plate.

3. Microwave on High for 2½ to 3 minutes, or until cheese melts.

Tip: *Substitute tuna for meat.*

Ham Nibbles

Bite size, makes 20 treats

1 cup ground or minced cooked ham
3 tablespoons mayonnaise
2 teaspoons prepared mustard

1 package Melba toast rounds
1 can rolled anchovies

1. Mix together ham, mayonnaise, and mustard.

2. Spread mixture on toast rounds. Place rolled anchovy in center of each round. Arrange 10 nibbles on a plate at a time.

3. Microwave on High for 1¼ minutes. Repeat for remaining nibbles. Serve hot.

Bubbly Beer Balls

Top 36 crackers with this cheese-caraway-beer mixture

1½ ounces cream cheese
2 tablespoons butter or margarine
2 cups shredded Cheddar cheese
½ cup flour
⅓ cup beer
½ teaspoon caraway seed
½ teaspoon dry mustard

36 crackers

1. Place cream cheese and butter in a bowl. Microwave on High for 30 seconds or until softened. Blend in remaining ingredients except crackers.

2. Microwave on Medium for 3½ minutes, or until cheese is melted and mixture is smooth. Stir every minute. Cool.

3. Form into 36 balls, about ½ inch in diameter. Place each ball on a cracker.

4. Arrange 12 on a plate at a time. Microwave on Medium for 2 to 2½ minutes or until cheese is bubbly.

Tip: *Make ahead and freeze until firm; wrap and store in freezer. To serve, microwave 12 at a time on Medium for 3 minutes or until cheese is bubbly.*

Cheese Puffs

Topping with a bite; for 32 crackers

1 cup shredded sharp
   Cheddar cheese
1 tablespoon flour
1 teaspoon curry powder
1 teaspooon garlic salt
1 tablespoon dry sherry
   wine

2 egg whites

32 crackers

1. Mix together cheese, flour, and seasonings. Stir in wine.

2. Beat egg whites until stiff. Fold into first mixture.

3. Drop by level teaspoon onto cookie sheet. Freeze.

4. To serve, place 1 frozen cheese ball on each of 12 crisp crackers. Arrange crackers on 7-inch round paper plate. Microwave on High for 1¾ to 2 minutes. Repeat for remaining puffs.

Tip: *To store in the freezer until later, drop individual puffs onto a cookie sheet and freeze unwrapped. When puffs are solid, package them together in appropriate freezer wrap.*

Hot Roquefort Canapes

Tantalizing, a party winner

1 package (3 oz) cream
   cheese
¼ cup crumbled Roquefort
   or blue cheese
¼ cup finely chopped
   pecans
½ teaspoon Worcestershire
   sauce
Dash hot pepper sauce

Butter crackers

1. In small bowl, microwave cream cheese on High for 30 seconds. Blend in next four ingredients.

2. Spread mixture on crackers, using about 1 teaspoon for each cracker.

3. Place paper towel on plate. Arrange 12 canapes at a time on plate. Microwave on Medium for 1 to 2 minutes or until cheese spread begins to bubble. Serve warm.

Walnut Bacon Crisps

4 slices bacon, cut in thirds
12 walnut halves

1. Wrap short strips of bacon around large walnut halves; fasten with woodenpicks.

2. Place 12 in a circle on a paper plate lined with a double layer of paper towels. Cover with paper towel.

3. Microwave on High for 3½ to 4 minutes, or until bacon is browned and crispy. Rotate dish halfway through microwave time.

Tip: *Prepare ahead and freeze uncooked. To finish, microwave 12 crisps at a time on High for 6½ to 7½ minutes.*

Crab Balls

18 miniature crabcakes go fast at a party

1 can (6½ to 7½ oz)
    crabmeat
1 egg
½ cup salad dressing
⅓ cup dry bread crumbs
¼ cup finely chopped onion
1 teaspoon prepared
    horseradish
1 teaspoon lemon juice
½ teaspoon salt
Dash pepper

Rich round crackers,
    crushed

1. Drain and flake crabmeat. Combine remaining ingredients except cracker crumbs. Form mixture into 18 balls, 1 inch in diameter each.

2. Coat each ball with cracker crumbs. Place a single layer in a shallow dish. Freeze until firm. Package in heavy plastic bag and return to freezer.

3. Arrange frozen balls on glass plate. Microwave on High for 3 to 4 minutes, or until heated throughout.

Herbed Shrimp

A different way to prepare this party food

Pictured on page 18

½ cup (¼ lb) butter or margarine
½ teaspoon tarragon
⅛ teaspoon celery salt
Dash pepper
½ cup snipped parsley

1. In a 1½-quart glass casserole, place butter, tarragon, celery salt, pepper, and parsley.

2. Microwave on High for 1 to 2 minutes or until melted.

2 cups cooked shrimp

3. Stir in shrimp. Microwave on Medium, covered, for 1 to 2 minutes or until shrimp is heated, stirring once. Do not boil shrimp. Serve with woodenpicks.

Sweet-Sour Meatballs

20 to 24 crowd pleasers

1 can (10¾ oz) condensed tomato soup
3 tablespoons lemon juice
¼ cup packed brown sugar
¾ teaspoon seasoned salt

1. Combine soup, lemon juice, brown sugar, and salt in an 8x8x2-inch glass dish. Microwave on High for 7 minutes, stirring twice.

1 pound ground beef
1 onion, finely chopped
1 teaspoon salt

2. Combine ground beef, onion, and salt.

3. Roll ground beef into small meatballs. Place meatballs in sauce. Spoon some sauce over meatballs.

4. Microwave on Medium for 10 minutes. Turn halfway through microwave time.

1 can (13¼ oz) pineapple chunks, drained

5. Stir in pineapple. Microwave on High for 1 minute. Serve with woodenpicks.

Tips: *These meatballs are also good served as main dish. Accompany with cooked rice or whipped potatoes, as desired.*

See page 115 for a soy-vinegar version.

Foxy Franks

Quick and easy

Pictured on page 18

¾ cup prepared mustard
1 jar (10 oz) currant jelly

1 pound wieners, cut in
  1-inch pieces

1. Combine mustard and jelly in 1½-quart glass casserole. Cover.

2. Microwave on High, covered, for 2 minutes.

3. Stir until well blended. Add wieners. Microwave on Low for 8 minutes or until hot and bubbly. Serve with woodenpicks.

Tip: *For variety, substitute 2 packages cocktail sausages for wieners.*

Coquilles

Elegant, gourmet scallop-mushroom delight; serves 6 to 8

1 pound fresh or frozen
  scallops

1 pound fresh mushrooms,
  sliced
2 tablespoons chopped
  celery
1 tablespoon chopped green
  pepper
2 tablespoons butter or
  margarine
2 tablespoons lemon juice

⅔ cup dry white wine
¼ teaspoon savory
1 bay leaf
½ teaspoon salt
⅛ teaspoon pepper

3 tablespoons butter
3 tablespoons flour
1 cup light cream

½ cup toasted bread crumbs
Paprika
Pimento strips (optional)

1. Defrost frozen scallops. Cut large scallops into halves or fourths. Set aside.

2. Combine sliced mushrooms, celery, green pepper, 2 tablespoons butter, and lemon juice. Microwave on High, uncovered, for 4 minutes. Stir halfway through microwave time. Drain.

3. Combine wine, savory, bay leaf, salt, and pepper in a 1½-quart glass casserole. Add scallops. Microwave on High, uncovered, for 3 minutes. Drain. Reserve 1 cup of broth.

4. Place 3 tablespoons butter in a 2-quart dish. Microwave on High for 30 seconds or until butter is melted. Blend in flour to make a smooth paste. Gradually stir in broth and then light cream. Microwave on High, uncovered, for 5 to 6 minutes or until sauce thickens. Stir every 30 seconds.

5. Stir scallops and mushrooms into sauce. Microwave on High, uncovered, for 6 to 7 minutes, or until thoroughly heated.

6. Spoon into seashells or ramekins to serve. Garnish with sprinklings of bread crumbs and paprika. Add pimento strips if desired.

Tip: *Serve with rice for a company buffet.*

Oysters Casino

12 openface shells with oysters and a seasoned topping

2 dozen freshly opened oysters

3 slices bacon, cooked & crumbled
¼ cup seasoned bread crumbs
2 tablespoons minced onion
2 tablespoons minced green pepper
2 tablespoons minced parsley
2 tablespoons minced celery
1 tablespoon butter or margarine
1 teaspoon Worcestershire sauce
Dash hot pepper sauce

Paprika

1. Place 2 oysters in deep half of one shell. Repeat to fill 12 shell halves. Arrange filled shells on plastic tray or paper plate.

2. Combine remaining ingredients except paprika. Spoon over oysters.

3. Microwave on Medium for 6 minutes, rotating dish once.

4. Sprinkle with paprika. Serve hot.

Tip: *To substitute custard cups for oyster shells, arrange 6 cups at a time in a circle. Reduce microwave time to 3½ minutes to accommodate smaller oven load. Repeat for remaining custard cups.*

Escargot

Snails—4 servings to make early in the day and then refrigerate

½ cup butter or margarine
1 clove garlic, minced
1 tablespoon snipped parsley

Snail shells
1 can (7½ oz) snails (about 18)

1. In a 1-cup glass measure, combine butter, garlic and parsley. Microwave on High for 30 seconds or until butter is softened. Mix well.

2. Place about ¼ teaspoon butter mixture in each snail shell. Place snail in each shell. Fill to top with butter mixture. Refrigerate for several hours.

3. Just before serving, arrange 12 snails at a time in a glass escargot dish or in a glass pie plate. Cover with plastic film. Microwave on Low for 2½ to 3½ minutes or until butter begins to bubble.

Beverages

Hot beverages, whether as basic as a cup of instant coffee or as elegant as a party punch, can be prepared in your microwave oven. Variety is as great as the family's preferences. You can prepare coffee, tea, and hot chocolate quickly and easily to suit everyone's tastes—without messing up many pans. And for entertaining, choose a party punch, a pre-dinner cocktail, or a post-skiing warm-me-upper.

The list of containers also is long: mugs, everyday cups, juice jars without the lids, pitchers, even glass brandy snifters. Just be sure the container does not have metal trim or a metal signature on the underside. Throw-away styrofoam cups are also convenient, as well as paper cups for hot beverages.

For hot no-fuss nourishment, microwave a pint of milk in its waxed carton. Heat only until warm, not until steaming. Be sure the carton is not stapled together; the metal will arc in the microwave oven.

Watch milk closely. It scalds quickly once it reaches hot temperatures and can boil over if not watched carefully.

Since reheating beverages in your microwave oven is quick, disconnect the coffeepot after breakfast, and refrigerate the remaining coffee. Later in the day, reheat the coffee; it will taste less bitter than if it had been held at a serving temperature.

Instant Beverages

Coffee, tea, chocolate, or instant breakfast

Water

Instant mix (coffee, tea, chocolate drink, tea bag, instant breakfast)

1. Place water in mug or cup; microwave on High until steaming:

1 cup (6 oz)	1¼ to 2 minutes
2 cups (6 oz each)	2½ to 3 minutes

2. Add instant mix. Stir and serve. Or microwave on high for 30 seconds to reheat, if desired.

Tip: *Always remove tea bag before reheating beverages in the microwave oven. Arcing will occur if the metal staples (found on some tea bags) are exposed to microwave energy.*

Hot Mulled Cider (page 32)

Cocoa

3 to 4 servings for a cold day

2½ tablespoons cocoa
3 tablespoons sugar
¼ cup warm water

3 cups milk
Dash salt

1. Place cocoa, sugar, and water in a 1½-quart glass casserole or suitable pitcher. Microwave on High for 30 seconds.

2. Stir in milk and salt. Microwave on High for 5 to 5½ minutes or until steaming.

Mexican Hot Chocolate

With a hint of cinnamon; serves 4

2 squares (1 oz each) unsweetened chocolate
¼ cup sugar
¼ cup water
1 teaspoon ground cinnamon
Dash salt

1 quart milk
½ teaspoon vanilla

1. Place chocolate, sugar, water, cinnamon, and salt in a 2-quart glass casserole or suitable pitcher.

2. Microwave on High for 1 minute or until chocolate is melted, stirring once.

3. Add milk and vanilla. Microwave on High for 5 to 7 minutes until almost boiling, stirring once.

4. Beat until well-blended and foamy.

Cafe au Lait

Hot chocolate and hot coffee team up for 5 cups of winter warmth

1 square (1 oz) unsweetened chocolate

¼ cup sugar
⅛ teaspoon salt
1¼ cups water

¾ cup milk
¾ cup cream
2 cups freshly brewed coffee

1 teaspoon vanilla

1. Place chocolate in a 1½-quart glass casserole. Microwave on High for 1 minute or until melted.

2. Stir in sugar, salt, and water. Microwave on High for 2 minutes or until boiling.

3. Add milk, cream, and coffee. Stir; then microwave on High for 3 to 4 minutes.

4. Mix in vanilla. Serve.

Tip: *For an easy version, combine instant coffee with instant cocoa mix.*

Irish Coffee

Here's to your health

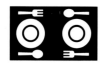

1 teaspoon sugar
1 cup strong coffee

1 jigger Irish whiskey
1 spoonful of whipped cream

1. Mix sugar and coffee in large cup or mug. Stir to dissolve.

2. Microwave on High for 1½ to 2 minutes or until hot.

3. Add Irish whiskey. Top with whipped cream and serve.

Russian Tea

Makes an instant mix; stores well

1 cup powdered orange flavor drink, unsweetened
1 cup sugar
½ cup instant tea mix, unsweetened
1 teaspoon ground cinnamon
1 teaspoon ground cloves

1. Mix ingredients well. Store in airtight container.

2. For an individual cup of tea, add 2 to 3 teaspoons of mix to 1 cup water in mug or coffee cup.

3. Microwave on High for 1¼ to 2 minutes or until hot.

Tomato Juice Cocktail

Makes one quart to serve hot

4 cups tomato juice
1 cup water
½ cup packed celery leaves
¼ cup diced onion
3 whole cloves
1 bay leaf
½ teaspoon salt
¼ teaspoon pepper

1. Combine ingredients in a 2-quart glass casserole.

2. Microwave on High for 15 minutes or until hot. Strain before serving.

Tip: *Add 1 teaspoon horseradish for zip.*

Hot Mulled Cider

Warms 2 or 3 people on a crisp day

Pictured on page 28

2 cups apple cider
3 cloves
1-inch piece of stick cinnamon
1 tablespoon brown sugar

1. Combine ingredients in a 1-quart glass measure.

2. Microwave on High for 3½ to 4 minutes or until hot. Stir halfway through microwave time.

3. Remove spices and serve.

Rosé Punch

Fruity, spicy, and hot; makes 17 party servings

2 tablespoons whole cloves
2 tablespoons whole allspice
2 tablespoons broken stick cinnamon
4 cups boiling water

3 to 4 tablespoons instant tea
1 can (6 oz) frozen tangerine or orange juice concentrate
1 can (6 oz) frozen Hawaiian Punch concentrate

2 bottles (25 oz each) rosé wine

1. Tie spices loosely in piece of cheese cloth. Place in a deep glass casserole with boiling water. Microwave on High for 5 minutes.

2. Remove spices. Add tea and juice concentrates. Microwave on High for 5 minutes longer. Stir every minute.

3. Stir in wine. Serve immediately.

Tips: *Garnish with lemon or orange slices.*

To reheat punch, microwave on High for 1 to 1½ minutes per cup.

Hot Rum Lemonade

Try it after skiing, by the fireside

¾ cup water
Juice of half lemon
1 teaspoon honey

1 jigger rum

1. Combine water, lemon juice, and honey in a 1-cup glass measure, or directly in a mug or cup.

2. Microwave on High for 1 to 1½ minutes or until steaming hot.

3. Add rum. Serve.

Breads

Many recipes in this chapter will help get your family started in the morning: Bran Muffins, Brown Sugar Coffeecake, and Spoon Bread, for instance. Others are the basis for company snacks; try finger sandwiches made with Apple-Cheese Nutbread or with Cranberry Nutbread. And for a dessert treat, serve Apricot Nutbread with whipped cream.

Just because browning of baked goods does not occur in the microwave oven is no reason why you shouldn't try some from-scratch breads.

- Select recipes with dark ingredients: whole wheat flour, bran, brown sugar, molasses, and spices.
- Add a topping: cinnamon-sugar, nuts, or confectioners' sugar.
- Serve with melted cheese or hot maple syrup.

You and your family will delight in microwave breads. This chapter contains many recipes using baking powder as the leavening agent. We've found that these breads and coffeecakes rise and bake quite nicely in the microwave oven.

Many recipes call for the batter to be poured around an empty custard cup, leaving an empty ring in the center of the baked bread. This food handling technique (see page 10) permits the batter to cook more evenly. Otherwise, the edges of the bread may finish cooking long before the center.

Microwave breads, coffeecakes, and muffins uncovered, allowing moisture to escape. If you cover the batter during microwave time, letting it steam, the finished bread will be soggy.

Yeast breads are better baked conventionally for hard, golden brown crusts. Moreover, the longer, slower conventional baking allows them to finish their light and airy rising process and to develop a tender, even texture.

In about two hours you can thaw and proof frozen bread dough in the microwave oven. (See page 43.) Then it's ready to be baked conventionally.

You may prefer to finish brown-and-serve rolls in the conventional oven, but microwave instructions are in the chart on page 35.

Reheating breads and rolls, whether bakery finished or your own from-scratch creations, can give a special touch to a formal dinner. It can also freshen up bread that's a few days old, making it taste less stale.

Breads and rolls reheat very quickly in the microwave oven because they are very porous. Watch time closely; if you overheat breads and rolls, they become dry and tough. Check the chart on the next page for specific times.

- Wrap the bread loosely in a paper napkin. The paper will absorb some of the moisture as it leaves the bread. Otherwise the moisture could be trapped between the bread and the dish, causing a soggy bottom.
- Or line a suitable basket with a cloth napkin, and heat all of the dinner rolls together.
- Reheat only until the outside of the bread/roll is warm. The inside (higher moisture content) will be warmer. Sugar fillings and frostings will be hot.
- **Do not overheat;** the bread will become dry, tough, or hard. Do not reheat a second time for the same reasons.

Warming Breads and Rolls

1. Place the food on a paper plate, paper towel, or napkin. The paper will absorb some of the moisture that otherwise could be trapped under the food, helping to prevent a soggy bottom.

2. Loosely cover with plastic film or waxed paper to retain moisture.

3. Microwave on High until the surface is warm; the inside (higher moisture content) will be warmer. Do not overheat; breads will toughen. Do not reheat a second time; breads will toughen.

Food	Servings	Microwave on High (allow more time if refrigerated or frozen)
Hamburger Buns Hot Dog Buns Heat and Serve Rolls	1	10 to 15 seconds
	2	15 to 20 seconds
	4	20 to 25 seconds
	6	25 to 30 seconds
	8	35 to 40 seconds
Muffins Biscuits	1	10 to 15 seconds
	2	20 to 30 seconds
	4	30 to 35 seconds
	6	40 to 45 seconds
Doughnuts Sweet Rolls Coffee Cake Wedge	1	10 to 15 seconds
	2	20 to 25 seconds
	4	35 to 40 seconds
	6	1 minute
Pancakes French Toast Waffles	1	20 to 25 seconds
	2	30 to 35 seconds
	4	1 to 1¼ minutes
French Bread	½ lb	1½ minutes

Apricot Nutbread (page 38)

Bran Muffins

24 to 28 breakfast delights

¾ cup water
2 cups all-bran cereal
½ cup butter or margarine

¾ cup packed brown sugar
2 eggs, beaten
1½ cups all-purpose flour
2 teaspoons baking powder
¼ teaspoon salt
1¼ cups buttermilk

½ cup chopped nuts
½ cup chopped dates

1. Pour water into a medium size bowl. Microwave on High for 2 minutes or until boiling. Add cereal and stir. Add butter. Let stand until butter is softened.

2. Mix in sugar and eggs. Blend in flour, baking powder, salt, and buttermilk. Stir just until moistened.

3. Fold in nuts and dates. Line custard cups with cupcake liners. Fill each cup half full.

4. Microwave 4 cups on Medium for 3 to 3½ minutes. Microwave 6 cups on Medium for 5 minutes. Remove from custard cups before cooling.

Tip: *Store extra batter in the refrigerator, covered, for 4 to 6 weeks. Use as needed, allowing more time to microwave chilled batter.*

Brown Sugar Coffeecake

Sprinkled with a cinnamon-nut topping

1 cup all-purpose flour
1 cup packed brown sugar
½ cup butter or margarine

1 egg, beaten
½ cup buttermilk
½ teaspoon soda
½ teaspoon vanilla

¼ cup chopped nuts
½ teaspoon cinnamon

1. In a medium size mixing bowl, blend flour, sugar, and margarine until crumbly. Reserve ½ cup for topping.

2. Blend egg, buttermilk, soda, and vanilla together. Stir into the flour mixture. Mix just until all is moistened but not smooth.

3. Place an empty small custard cup or juice glass, upright, in the center of an 8x8x2-inch dish. Pour batter into the dish around the cup.

4. Add nuts and cinnamon to reserved crumbs. Sprinkle over batter. Microwave on Medium, uncovered, for 8 minutes. Rotate dish halfway through microwave time.

5. Microwave on High for 2 to 3 minutes longer. Let stand on a wire rack to cool.

Tip: *To serve, cut cake and fill the custard cup with whipped butter or honey butter.*

Mincemeat Coffeecake

Serve with whipped cream or sauce

1½ cups moist mincemeat

2 cups packaged biscuit mix
½ cup packed brown sugar
1 egg, beaten
⅔ cup milk

1. Place an empty small custard cup or juice glass, upright, in the center of an 8x8x2-inch glass dish. Spread mincemeat evenly in the dish around the cup. Set aside.

2. Combine biscuit mix and brown sugar in a medium-size mixing bowl. Mix egg and milk together, and add to biscuit mix. Stir just until flour is moistened. Spread batter over mincemeat.

3. Microwave on Medium, uncovered, for 10 minutes. Rotate dish halfway through microwave time.

4. Microwave on High for 3 minutes longer, rotating dish once.

5. Let stand for 15 minutes; turn out onto a wire rack.

Tip: *To serve, place a custard cup filled with whipped cream or sauce in the center of the cake.*

Apple-Cheese Nutbread

Excellent for finger sandwiches

1 cup all-purpose flour
1 cup whole wheat flour
⅔ cup packed brown sugar
1 teaspoon baking powder
1 teaspoon baking soda
½ teaspoon salt
½ cup shredded Cheddar cheese
¼ cup chopped nuts

2 eggs, slightly beaten
1 cup sweetened applesauce
½ cup melted butter or margarine

1. Sift together flours, brown sugar, baking powder, baking soda and salt into a large bowl. Add cheese and nuts.

2. Combine eggs, applesauce, and melted butter. Add to dry ingredients; stir until just moistened.

3. Place an empty juice glass, upright, in the center of a 2-quart glass casserole. Pour batter around the glass.

4. Microwave on Medium, uncovered, for 8 minutes. Rotate dish twice.

5. Microwave on High for 4 minutes longer.

6. Allow to stand for 5 minutes. Turn out onto a wire rack to cool. Wrap in plastic film or foil to store.

Tip: *Excellent for finger sandwiches; spread with butter or cream cheese.*

Apricot Nutbread

Make the day before and allow flavors to mellow

Pictured on page 34

½ cup dried apricots
1 cup water

1½ cups all-purpose flour
½ cup whole wheat flour
½ cup sugar
1 tablespoon baking powder
¾ teaspoon salt
¼ teaspoon baking soda
1 cup chopped nuts

1 egg, beaten
½ cup honey
½ cup orange juice
¼ cup water
3 tablespoons melted butter
    or margarine

1. Place apricots and water in a small bowl. Soak for ½ hour. Drain, chop, and set aside.

2. Into a large bowl, sift together dry ingredients. Add nuts.

3. Thoroughly blend egg, honey, juice, water, and butter. Add to dry ingredients; stir until moistened. Fold in apricots.

4. Place an empty juice glass, upright, in the center of a 2-quart glass casserole. Pour batter into casserole around the glass. Microwave on Medium, uncovered, for 8 minutes. Rotate dish halfway through microwave time.

5. Microwave on High for 4 minutes longer.

6. Allow to stand 5 minutes. Turn out onto wire rack to cool. Wrap in plastic film.

Tips: *Flavor mellows and bread slices better if served the next day.*

Serve bread with whipped butter or cream cheese, or top with whipped cream as a dessert.

Cranberry Nutbread

Tasty, interesting with a hint of orange

1 cup fresh cranberries, chopped
¼ cup sugar

2½ cups all-purpose flour
½ cup whole wheat flour
4 teaspoons baking powder
1 teaspoon salt
½ cup chopped walnuts
Grated peel of 1 orange

1 egg, beaten
1½ cups milk
¼ cup melted butter or margarine
¼ cup honey

1. Mix cranberries and sugar in a small bowl; set aside.

2. Sift dry ingredients into a large bowl. Add nuts and orange peel.

3. Combine egg, milk, butter, and honey. Add to dry ingredients; stir just until moistened. Fold in sweetened cranberries.

4. Place an empty small custard cup, upright, in the center of an 8x8x2-inch glass dish. Pour batter into dish around the custard cup.

5. Microwave on Medium, uncovered, for 10 minutes. Rotate dish halfway through microwave time.

6. Microwave on High for 5 minutes longer.

7. Allow to stand for 5 minutes before turning out onto wire rack to cool. Wrap with plastic film or foil to store.

Tip: *Spread slices with cream cheese flavored with orange peel.*

Hawaiian Nutbread

Serve with remaining crushed pineapple

1½ cups all-purpose flour
½ cup whole wheat flour
1 tablespoon baking powder
½ cup packed brown sugar
1 teaspoon cinnamon
1 teaspoon salt
1 cup chopped nuts

2 eggs, beaten
1¼ cups crushed pineapple, undrained
½ cup melted butter or margarine

1. Sift together dry ingredients into a large bowl. Add nuts.

2. Blend eggs, pineapple and butter together. Add to dry ingredients; stir just enough to combine.

3. Place an empty custard cup, upright, in the center of an 8x8x2-inch glass dish. Pour batter into dish around the cup. Microwave on Medium, uncovered, for 8 minutes. Rotate dish halfway through microwave time.

4. Microwave on High for 5 minutes.

Tip: *Serve with lemon sauce; or drain remaining pineapple into the custard cup and place it in the center of the bread.*

Cheddar Cornbread

A new way to make an old favorite

1 cup yellow cornmeal
1 cup sifted all-purpose flour
¼ cup sugar
4 teaspoons baking powder
½ teaspoon salt

1 egg, beaten
1 cup milk
¼ cup soft shortening
½ cup shredded Cheddar cheese

1. In medium size bowl sift together cornmeal, flour, sugar, baking powder, and salt.

2. Mix in egg, milk, and shortening. Fold in cheese.

3. Place a small custard cup, upright, in the center of an 8x8x2-inch glass dish. Pour batter into the dish around the custard cup. Microwave on Medium, uncovered, for 5 minutes.

4. Rotate dish. Microwave on High for 3 to 4 minutes longer.

Tip: *Serve hot with butter, or drizzle melted cheese over the top.*

Irish Oatmeal Bread

Serve with honey butter or apple butter

2 cups all-purpose flour
1 cup whole wheat flour
½ cup packed brown sugar
1½ tablespoons baking powder
1 teaspoon salt
½ teaspoon cinnamon

1¼ cups milk
1¼ cups quick-cooking oats

1 egg, beaten
⅓ cup melted butter or margarine
¼ cup honey

1. In a large bowl, sift together flours, sugar, baking powder, salt, and cinnamon.

2. Pour milk into a 4-cup glass measure. Microwave on High, covered, for 2 minutes. Add oats, and mix well. Allow to stand, uncovered, for 2 minutes.

3. Add egg, butter, and honey to oats mixture. Mix well, and add to dry ingredients. Stir only until moistened.

4. Place a small empty juice glass, upright, in the center of a 2-quart glass casserole. Pour batter into the casserole around the glass.

5. Microwave on Medium, uncovered, for 8 minutes. Rotate dish halfway through microwave time.

6. Microwave on High for 4 minutes.

7. Allow to stand for 5 minutes; turn onto a wire rack to cool. Wrap in plastic film or foil to store.

Tip: *Spread toasted bread with honey butter or apple butter.*

Spoon Bread

Serve by spoonfuls; great with the breakfast ham for 6

1½ cups water
¾ cup yellow cornmeal

3 eggs, beaten
¾ cup milk
3 tablespoons melted butter or margarine
1½ teaspoons baking powder
½ teaspoon salt

1. Place water in a 1½-quart glass casserole. Microwave on High, covered, for 3 minutes or until boiling. Slowly add cornmeal. Mix with a wire whisk. Allow to stand, uncovered, for 2 minutes.

2. Combine remaining ingredients. Blend into cornmeal mixture.

3. Microwave on High, uncovered, for 3 minutes. Stir. Microwave on High for 2 minutes longer.

Tip: *Serve warm with butter or maple syrup.*

Seasoned French Bread

Three seasoned spreads follow

1 loaf (1 lb) baked French bread

Seasoned butter spread (recipes follow)

1. Cut loaf in half crosswise. Make diagonal cuts in each half at ¾-inch intervals, taking care not to cut through the bottom crust.

2. Spread seasoned butter spread on both sides of each slice. Place each half of bread on a paper plate.

3. Heat each half separately. Microwave on High for 1½ minutes or until butter is melted and bread is warm.

Dill Butter Spread

enough for ½ loaf

½ cup soft butter or margarine
½ teaspoon dill
½ teaspoon onion salt
¼ teaspoon marjoram
¼ teaspoon pepper

1. Combine all ingredients and mix well. Spread on ½ loaf. (See Seasoned French Bread recipe.)

Garlic Cheese Butter Spread

enough for ½ loaf

½ cup soft butter or margarine
3 tablespoons grated Parmesan cheese
½ teaspoon oregano
½ teaspoon marjoram
¼ teaspoon garlic salt
¼ teaspoon onion salt
¼ teaspoon pepper
¼ teaspoon paprika

1. Combine all ingredients and mix well. Spread on ½ loaf. (See Seasoned French Bread recipe.)

Celery Seed Butter Spread

enough for ½ loaf

½ cup soft butter or margarine
½ teaspoon celery seeds
¼ teaspoon salt
¼ teaspoon paprika
Dash cayenne

1. Combine all ingredients and mix well. Spread on ½ loaf. (See Seasoned French Bread recipe.)

Pancakes and Waffles

Pancakes, Waffles (conventionally precooked)

1. Stack precooked pancakes or waffles, separating each with a double thickness of waxed paper or other nonmetallic material.

2. Wrap the stack with a moistureproof, vaporproof freezer material, using the freezer-fold method (at least two folds for each seam). Freeze immediately.

3. Before serving, pierce the wrap to allow steam to escape. Then microwave on High, allowing approximately 1½ minutes to reheat 4 frozen pancakes.

Tips: *The next time you prepare pancakes, make a double batch; eat one now, and freeze the other for later.*

Package in quantities that you will be reheating at one time.

Use nonmetallic wrapping materials. The pancakes can then go straight from the freezer to the microwave oven.

To warm the pancake syrup, microwave on High for 1 to 2 minutes or until heated.

Frozen Bread Dough

Thaw and proof in the microwave oven; then bake conventionally

4 cups boiling water

1-pound loaf of frozen bread dough
Vegetable oil or shortening

1. Place a 4-cup glass measure, filled with boiling water, in the microwave oven. Leave water in the oven through step 5.

2. Grease an 8x4-inch glass loaf dish with an unsalted shortening or oil. Coat all sides of loaf generously with shortening or oil. Place frozen loaf in dish. Cover dish with waxed paper.

3. Microwave on High for 30 seconds. Then let dough stand for 20 minutes in the microwave oven. Keep the oven door closed during standing time to maintain the steambath. At end of standing time, rotate dish ¼ turn.

4. Repeat step 3 three more times.

5. Let dough stand for approximately 30 minutes longer, or until the dough is double in size.

6. Bake in conventional oven according to package directions.

Tip: *Thawing and proofing the dough in the microwave oven takes about two hours. Allow additional time to bake it in the conventional oven.*

The basis of a balanced meal can be as simple as a casserole or other main dish which combines food items from the four basic food groups. Serve these one-dish entrees for family dinners, party buffets, and plan-ahead meals.

Ingredients. Use the recipes in this chapter for ideas and techniques. Then create your own casserole or main dish. Start with your choice of meat, poultry, or fish; add vegetables, and rice or noodles. Then combine the ingredients together using eggs, milk, or cheese.

Cut meat and vegetables into pieces that are similar in size and shape; this allows the individual pieces to heat and cook evenly. Start to microwave those foods that take longest to cook; then add the other ingredients, including leftovers. Drain off excess fats and liquids as they accumulate. Add a cheese topping at the end of the microwave time; overcooked cheese becomes stringy, tough, or rubbery.

Microwave instructions. Cover most casseroles to retain the heat and to prevent spatters. Microwave most casseroles on High. However, use lower settings to tenderize some meats and to simmer egg, cream and cheese sauces.

Stir the food, or rotate the dish during microwave time to distribute the ingredients and to equalize the cooking. When the food is done, allow it to stand, covered, for a few minutes before serving.

Make-ahead tips. Prepare two family casseroles at a time—one to eat now and one to freeze for later. Or, up to one to three months before your next buffet party, prepare and freeze an elegant company casserole.

A glass-ceramic casserole dish that is suitable for microwave oven, freezer, and dining table is convenient to use. Or, you can line the glass casserole with aluminum foil and spoon the cooked food into it. Pull the ends of the foil together, and fold at least twice along each seamline (freezer-fold method).

Transfer the dish and wrapped casserole to the freezer.

- If the dish can withstand freezing temperatures, wait until the casserole is frozen before removing the dish.
- If the dish cannot withstand freezing temperatures, remove it once the food is cool enough to retain the shape of the dish.

To serve the casserole, remove the foil and place the food in the casserole dish. Thaw and reheat the casserole, covered, in the microwave oven. Stir during the thawing/reheating processes to equalize temperatures.

See the *Defrosting Foods* chapter for more details on thawing and reheating casseroles.

Easy Chicken Divan (page 52)

Beef, Noodles and Sour Cream Casserole

Serves a family of 5 or 6

2 cups uncooked noodles

1 pound ground beef
1 medium onion, chopped

1 can (8 oz) tomato sauce
1 package (3 oz) cream cheese
½ cup dairy sour cream
1 teaspoon sugar
1 teaspoon salt
¼ teaspoon pepper

½ cup grated Cheddar cheese

1. Cook noodles as directed on page 164. Drain and set aside.

2. Combine ground beef and onion in a 2-quart glass casserole. Microwave on High, covered, for 5 to 6 minutes or until meat has lost its pink color. Stir halfway through microwave time.

3. Drain off fat. Add remaining ingredients except Cheddar cheese. Microwave on High, covered, for 5 minutes, stirring halfway through microwave time.

4. Sprinkle Cheddar cheese on top. Microwave on High, covered, for 1 to 2 minutes or until cheese melts.

Beef 'n Tater

A quick and easy meat-and-potato dish to serve 6

1 pound ground beef

1 package (10 oz) frozen Tater Tots
2 teaspoons instant minced onion
1 can (10¾ oz) condensed cream of celery soup
1 can (10¾ oz) condensed cream of mushroom soup

1. Crumble ground beef into a 3-quart glass casserole. Microwave on High, covered, for 5 to 6 minutes. Stir halfway through microwave time. Drain off fat.

2. Top with Tater Tots and onion. Mix soups together. Pour over potatoes.

3. Microwave on High, covered, for 8 minutes, or until soup is bubbling. Rotate dish halfway through microwave time.

Hamburger-Rice Casserole

Hearty supper dish for family entertaining; serves 4 to 6

1 pound ground beef
½ cup chopped onion

1 can (10¾ oz) condensed
  cream of mushroom soup
1½ soup cans water
1 cup thinly sliced carrot
½ cup chopped celery
1 chicken bouillon cube
2 tablespoons soy sauce
½ teaspoon ground thyme

1 cup packaged precooked
  rice

1. Place ground beef and onion in a 3-quart glass casserole. Microwave on High, covered, for 5 to 6 minutes or until meat has lost its pink color.

2. Stir in remaining ingredients except rice. Microwave on High, covered, for 15 minutes, stirring twice.

3. Stir rice into meat mixture, being sure rice is moistened. Microwave on High, covered, for 5 minutes or until boiling, stirring once.

4. Let stand, covered, for 10 minutes before serving.

One-Dish Spaghetti

A no-fuss entree; serves 6

1 pound ground beef
1 cup chopped onion

4 ounces dry spaghetti,
  broken (1½ cups)
1 can (8 oz) tomato sauce
1 can (4 oz) sliced
  mushrooms, drained
3 cups tomato juice
2 teaspoons brown sugar
1 teaspoon salt
1 teaspoon Italian seasoning
¼ teaspoon pepper

Parmesan cheese (optional)

1. Place ground beef and onion in a 3-quart glass casserole. Microwave on High, covered, for 5 to 6 minutes or until meat has lost its pink color. Stir halfway through microwave time. Drain off fat.

2. Add remaining ingredients except cheese. Mix well, being sure all spaghetti is moistened.

3. Microwave on High, covered, for 10 minutes.

4. Microwave on Low for 15 minutes longer or until spaghetti is cooked. Serve with Parmesan cheese if desired.

Lasagna

Makes 6 to 8 servings to go with tossed salad and garlic bread

1 pound ground beef
1 large clove garlic, minced

1 envelope dry onion soup
   mix
1½ cups water
1 can (6 oz) tomato paste
1 can (8 oz) tomato sauce
1 teaspoon oregano
½ teaspoon salt
½ teaspoon sugar
¼ teaspoon pepper

½ pound lasagna noodles,
   cooked
1 carton (1 lb) ricotta or
   cottage cheese
½ pound Mozzarella cheese,
   grated
Parmesan cheese

1. Place ground beef and garlic in a 3-quart glass casserole. Microwave on High, covered, for 5 to 6 minutes, stirring once.

2. Drain off fat. Add onion soup mix, water, tomato paste, tomato sauce, oregano, salt, sugar, and pepper. Stir until well blended with ground beef.

3. Microwave on High, covered, for 10 minutes, stirring once.

4. In a 12x7½-inch glass dish, arrange by layers: ⅓ meat mixture, ½ noodles, ½ ricotta, and ½ Mozzarella cheese. Repeat layers, ending with meat sauce. Sprinkle with Parmesan cheese.

5. Cover dish with plastic film. Pierce film to allow steam to escape. Microwave on High for 11 to 13 minutes or until hot, rotating dish once.

Mexican Casserole

Olé; serves 6 to 8

1 pound ground beef
1 cup chopped onion

1 can (15 oz) chili without
   beans
1 can (15 oz) garbanzo beans,
   drained
1 can (16 oz) whole kernel
   corn, drained
½ cup cubed sharp Cheddar
   cheese
2 tablespoons parsley
½ teaspoon chili powder

1. Place ground beef and onion in a 3-quart glass casserole. Microwave on High, covered, for 5 to 6 minutes or until meat has lost its pink color.

2. Drain off fat. Stir in remaining ingredients.

3. Microwave on Medium, covered, for 10 minutes or until heated and cheese has melted.

Chinese Pea Pods and Beef Casserole

A one-dish meal for 4 to 6

1 package (6 or 7 oz) frozen Chinese pea pods

1 pound ground beef
½ cup sliced green onions

1 can (10¾ oz) condensed cream of mushroom soup
1 tablespoon soy sauce
⅛ teaspoon pepper

1 can (3 oz) chow mein noodles

1. Place frozen pea pods in a glass dish. Microwave on High for 1½ minutes or until partially thawed. Set aside.

2. Crumble meat into a 1½-quart glass casserole. Add onions and mix. Layer peas over meat mixture.

3. Blend soup, soy sauce, and pepper. Spoon over peas.

4. Microwave on Medium, covered, for 18 to 20 minutes or until meat mixture has lost its pink color. Rotate dish halfway through microwave time.

5. Let stand for 5 minutes before serving. Meanwhile, place noodles on a paper plate. Microwave on High for 1½ minutes, stirring halfway through heating time. Sprinkle over casserole before serving.

Oriental Beef and Vegetables

Spoon over rice to serve 4 or 5

1 small head cauliflower
1 pound beef tenderloin tip, sliced paper thin
1 small onion, thinly sliced
¼ cup soy sauce

1 package (6 oz) frozen pea pods

1 can (10½ oz) condensed beef broth
3 tablespoons cornstarch

Hot cooked rice

1. Cut cauliflower flowerettes into ¼-inch slices, and place in a 2-quart glass casserole. Add beef, onion, and soy sauce. Stir gently to coat.

2. Microwave on High, covered, for 10 to 12 minutes, stirring once.

3. Add frozen pea pods. Microwave on High, covered, for 3 to 4 minutes or until pea pods are thawed and cauliflower is tender-crisp. Set aside.

4. Combine broth and cornstarch in a 2-cup glass measure. Add juices drained from casserole. Microwave on High for 3½ to 4½ minutes or until mixture boils. Stir once during microwave time.

5. Stir broth into beef mixture. Serve over rice.

Dried Chipped Beef Casserole

Prepare it the night before; serves 6 to 8

2 cups uncooked elbow macaroni
½ pound longhorn cheese, cubed
¼ pound dried chipped beef, separated into pieces
2 cans (10¾ oz each) condensed cream of mushroom soup
2 cups milk
4 hard-cooked eggs, chopped
¼ cup chopped onion

1. Combine all ingredients in a 3-quart glass casserole. Cover and refrigerate for 12 to 15 hours or overnight.

2. Microwave on High, covered, for 20 minutes, or until bubbly and macaroni is cooked, stirring twice. Let stand for 5 minutes before serving.

Tips: *To avoid standing time in refrigerator, cook macaroni in boiling water until it begins to soften. Then complete the casserole, reducing milk to 1 cup. Cook immediately.*

For variety, use 1 cup of cooked diced chicken instead of dried beef. Just before serving, sprinkle seasoned stuffing crumbs over top.

Poor Man's Casserole

An economical meal; serves 4 to 6

1 package (6 oz) elbow macaroni

1 jar (8 oz) processed cheese spread

1 pound wieners, cut in ½-inch pieces
½ cup chopped green onion, including tops
1 tablespoon Dijon-style mustard

1. Prepare macaroni as directed on package, or on page 164. Drain.

2. Remove lid from cheese spread jar (and label if metallic). Microwave on Medium for 2 minutes or until melted.

3. Combine macaroni, cheese, and remaining ingredients in a 3-quart glass casserole. Microwave on Medium, covered, for 8 to 10 minutes or until hot.

Sweet-Sour Chop Suey

Made from yesterday's roast; 4 servings on top of rice or noodles

2 cups cubed, cooked pork or beef
1 can (16 oz) Chinese vegetables

1 package (1⅝ oz) chop suey sauce mix

Cooked rice

1. Place meat in a 2-quart glass casserole. Drain liquid from vegetables into casserole. Set vegetables aside.

2. Microwave meat on High, covered, for 3 minutes.

3. Stir in sauce mix and vegetables. Microwave on High, covered, for 5 minutes. Stir.

4. Microwave on Medium for 3 minutes. Serve over cooked rice.

Chinese Pork and Rice

A taste of the Far East to serve 4

2 tablespoons vegetable oil
⅔ cup uncooked rice

1½ cups boiling water
1 bouillon cube
2 teaspoons soy sauce
1 teaspoon salt

1 cup diced, cooked pork
1 medium green pepper, chopped
½ cup chopped onion
2 stalks celery, chopped

1. Mix oil and rice in a 2-quart glass casserole. Microwave on High, covered, for 3 minutes.

2. Add boiling water, bouillon cube, soy sauce, and salt. Microwave on High, covered, for 5 minutes.

3. Gently stir pork and vegetables into rice mixture. Microwave on High, covered, for 8 minutes or until vegetables are tender-crisp.

Tip: *To brown rice in the Frigidaire Browning Skillet accessory, first preheat skillet; microwave on High for 2 minutes. Add rice and oil; microwave on High for 3 minutes.*

Sweet and Sour Ham

4 delicious servings from leftover ham

2 tablespoons packed brown sugar
1½ tablespoons cornstarch
1 can (9 oz) pineapple tidbits

¾ cup water
1 tablespoon vinegar
2 teaspoons Dijon-style mustard
½ teaspoon Beau Monde seasoned salt
1 tablespoon chopped parsley

2 cups cubed, cooked ham
2 cups cooked rice

1. Combine sugar and cornstarch in a 4-cup glass measure. Drain juice from pineapple tidbits into sugar mixture. Set pineapple aside.

2. Stir water, vinegar, mustard, salt, and parsley into sugar mixture. Microwave on High for 2 to 3 minutes or until thickened.

3. Combine ham, rice, pineapple tidbits, and sauce in a 2-quart glass casserole. Microwave on Medium, covered, for 6 minutes or until hot.

Asparagus Ham Bundles

Easy entertaining for 4 to 6

8 slices (8-oz pkg) thin-sliced boiled ham
4 slices (6-oz pkg) Swiss cheese
1 can (15 oz) green asparagus spears, drained

1 can (11 oz) condensed Cheddar cheese soup
2 tablespoons water
¼ teaspoon celery salt

Sliced almonds

1. Separate ham slices and lay them on a flat, surface. Cut each cheese slice in half crosswise, and place atop each ham slice. Top each with 2 to 3 asparagus spears. Roll and place in a single layer, seam side down, in a 12x7½-inch glass baking dish.

2. Combine soup, water, and celery salt; spoon evenly over asparagus-ham rolls. Cover with plastic film.

3. Microwave on Medium for 8 to 10 minutes. Pierce a hole in the film for steam to escape. Sprinkle with almonds and serve.

Easy Chicken Divan

Soup makes the sauce; serves 6

Pictured on page 44

2 packages (10 oz each) frozen broccoli, cooked and drained
3 whole chicken breasts, cooked and sliced

1 can (10½ oz) condensed cream of chicken soup
½ cup salad dressing or mayonnaise
1 tablespoon lemon juice
½ teaspoon curry powder
1 package (4 oz) shredded Cheddar cheese

1. Arrange a layer of broccoli in a 12x7½-inch glass baking dish. Place sliced chicken over broccoli.

2. Combine next four ingredients; spread over chicken. Sprinkle with shredded cheese.

3. Microwave on Medium, covered, for 18 to 20 minutes. Rotate dish halfway through microwave time.

Tip: *To help use up the holiday bird, substitute 12 slices of chicken or turkey for the chicken breasts.*

Classic Chicken Divan

A from-scratch version to serve 6

2 packages (10 oz each) frozen broccoli

2 cups chicken broth
½ cup whipping cream

6 tablespoons cornstarch
6 tablespoons water

¼ cup grated Parmesan cheese
½ teaspoon salt
¼ teaspoon pepper
3 tablespoons cooking sherry

3 chicken breasts, cooked and thinly sliced
Paprika

1. Cook broccoli. Drain.

2. Combine chicken broth and cream in a 4-cup glass measure. Microwave on High, uncovered, for 4 minutes.

3. Blend cornstarch and water into a smooth paste. Gradually blend paste into broth mixture using a wire whisk. Microwave on High for 2½ minutes. Stir every minute.

4. Reserve 1 tablespoon of Parmesan cheese. Add remaining cheese, salt, pepper, and sherry to sauce. Stir well.

5. Place drained broccoli in a 12x7½-inch glass dish. Layer chicken slices over broccoli. Spread sauce over top. Sprinkle with remaining cheese and paprika. Cover dish with plastic film; pierce a hole for steam to escape. Microwave on High for 10 minutes.

6. Uncover, and microwave on Medium for 5 minutes or until heated through.

Easy Chicken Noodle Almondine

A good way to dress up a packaged noodle mix; serves 4

1 cup finely chopped celery
1 tablespoon butter or margarine

1 package (6 oz) noodles and almond mix
2 cups boiling water
1 cup diced cooked chicken
1 cup grated process cheese

1. Place celery and butter in a 1½-quart glass casserole. Microwave on High, covered, for 5 minutes or until celery is tender-crisp.

2. Add noodles and sauce mix, boiling water, chicken and cheese. Mix thoroughly. Microwave on High, covered, for 12 minutes, Stir twice.

3. Let stand, covered, for 10 minutes. Sprinkle with almonds.

Chicken Medley

Great for potluck supper, for easy entertaining; serves 6 to 8

2 cups cubed, cooked chicken
2 cups cooked rice
4 hard-cooked eggs, sliced
1½ cups chopped celery
1 small onion, chopped
1 cup mayonnaise
2 cans (10¾ oz) condensed cream of mushroom soup
2 tablespoons chopped pimento
2 tablespoons lemon juice
1 teaspoon salt

¼ cup slivered almonds

1. In a 3-quart glass casserole, combine all ingredients except almonds. Toss gently.

2. Microwave on High, covered, for 10 to 12 minutes or until hot, stirring twice.

3. Top with slivered almonds before serving. Garnish with snipped parsley, if desired.

Tip: *Double the recipe, and freeze one for later.*

After Holiday Casserole

This family-size dish doesn't taste like leftovers!

1 cup packaged precooked rice
2 tablespoons instant minced onion

½ package frozen green peas, thawed (approx 5 oz)
½ cup finely diced green pepper
6 slices cooked turkey

1 can (11 oz) condensed, Cheddar cheese soup
1 cup milk

1 cup finely crushed cheese crackers
3 tablespoons melted butter or margarine

1. Prepare rice according to directions on box, or see page 162, adding minced onion to boiling water.

2. Fluff rice with fork; spread in a 10x6-inch glass dish. Drain thawed peas. Sprinkle peas and green pepper over rice. Cover with turkey slices.

3. Mix soup with milk; pour over turkey. Cover dish with plastic film. Pierce a hole for steam to escape. Microwave on Medium for 16 to 18 minutes. Rotate dish halfway through microwave time.

4. Combine cracker crumbs and butter; sprinkle on top of casserole. Let stand, covered, for 5 minutes before serving.

Country Club Turkey

Try it for a luncheon;
serves 4

2 packages (10 oz each)
   frozen asparagus spears

1 can (10¾ oz) condensed
   cream of chicken soup
2 cups cubed, cooked turkey
½ cup sliced pitted ripe
   olives
½ cup diced pimento
½ teaspoon grated onion
⅛ teaspoon nutmeg

¼ cup shredded smokey
   cheese

1. Place asparagus in a 12x7½-inch glass dish. Cover with plastic film; pierce a hole for steam to escape. Microwave on High for 5 to 7 minutes or until partially cooked.

2. Drain, and arrange spears evenly in dish. Set aside.

3. Combine soup, turkey, olives, pimento, onion, and nutmeg. Spoon this mixture over asparagus.

4. Top with cheese. Microwave on Medium, uncovered, for 11 to 13 minutes, or until heated throughout.

Tuna Noodle Casserole

A basic family meal;
serves 5 or 6

1 package (8 oz) noodles,
   cooked and drained

1 can (6½ oz) tuna, drained
1 can (10¾ oz) condensed
   cream of mushroom soup
1 package (4 oz) shredded
   Cheddar cheese
¾ cup milk
1 egg, beaten
¼ cup crushed soda crackers

1. Cook noodles as directed on package or on page 164.

2. Combine noodles, tuna, soup, and cheese in a 2-quart glass casserole. Mix milk and egg; pour over casserole mixture. Top with crushed crackers.

3. Microwave on High, uncovered, for 9 to 10 minutes or until hot. Let stand a few minutes before serving.

Tip: *For variety, substitute spaghetti or shoestring potatoes for noodles. Add ¼ cup chopped pimento and ¼ cup chopped onion for color and flavor.*

Shrimp and Wild Rice Casserole

Elegant company casserole; serves 6 to 8

2 tablespoons butter or margarine
2 tablespoons flour
1 cup coffee cream
1 cup milk

¼ cup butter or margarine
½ cup thinly sliced onion
¼ cup thinly sliced green pepper
1 can (4 oz) sliced mushrooms, drained (about ½ cup)

1 tablespoon Worcestershire sauce
Few drops hot pepper sauce
½ teaspoon pepper
2 cups cooked packaged wild and white rice
1 pound cooked shrimp

1. Place 2 tablespoons butter in a 1-quart glass bowl. Microwave on High for 30 seconds or until melted. Stir in flour, cream, and milk. Microwave on High for 3 to 4 minutes or until consistency of thin cream sauce. Stir every minute. Set aside.

2. Combine ¼ cup butter, onion, green pepper, and mushrooms in a 2-quart glass casserole. Microwave on High, covered, for 2 to 3 minutes or until tender.

3. Add seasonings, rice, and shrimp. Fold in cream sauce. Microwave on Medium, covered, for 15 minutes. Rotate dish halfway through microwave time.

Tip: *Make this casserole up to 1 month ahead, and freeze. Do not heat shrimp casserole before freezing.*
To thaw casserole, microwave on Low, covered, for 15 minutes. Then microwave on Medium for 15 minutes or until hot.

Scalloped Ham and Oysters

Serves 8 at your next party buffet

1 cup soft bread crumbs
2 cups cracker crumbs
1 cup butter or margarine, melted
⅛ teaspoon cayenne
2 teaspoons Worcestershire sauce
¼ teaspoon pepper

2 cans (8 oz each) oysters, drained—or 1 pound fresh oysters, drained
2 cups cooked ham, cut in julienne strips
½ cup light cream

1. Mix crumbs, butter, and seasonings together.

2. In a 12x7½-inch glass dish, spread ⅓ of crumb mixture. Top with half of the oysters and half of the ham. Repeat layers, ending with crumbs on top. Pour cream over top.

3. Microwave on Medium, uncovered, for 15 minutes or until hot. Rotate dish halfway through microwave time.

Sea and Land Luncheon

4 to 6 servings of salmon and special vegetables prepared in a creamy sauce

1 package (9 oz) frozen Italian green beans
1 package (8 oz) frozen artichoke hearts
1 teaspoon salt
¼ cup water

1 can (1 lb) boned salmon chunks, drained (about 2 cups)

½ cup Hollandaise Sauce
⅓ cup dairy sour cream
½ teaspoon grated lemon peel
¼ teaspoon crushed tarragon

2 tablespoons toasted, slivered almonds

1. Combine frozen beans, artichoke hearts, salt, and water in a 2-quart glass casserole. Microwave on High, covered, for 10 to 12 minutes. Drain well.

2. Lightly mix salmon into vegetables.

3. Blend Hollandaise Sauce, sour cream, lemon peel, and tarragon. Spread over salmon. Microwave on Medium, uncovered, for 10 minutes or until sauce is bubbly.

4. Sprinkle with almonds.

Tip: *To make ½ cup Hollandaise Sauce, see page 178.*

Eggs and Cheese

Eggs

Eggs are a delicate food. You will have fun experimenting with egg recipes, developing your own techniques as you go. In general, most egg recipes are best microwaved on Medium. Microwave time varies with the size, quantity, and starting temperature of the eggs. Adjust microwave time accordingly.

If you overcook eggs in the microwave oven, they tend to become rubbery. Therefore, always stop the microwave oven while the egg dish is still slightly underdone. Generally allow a brief standing time, covered, for the food to finish cooking with stored-up heat.

Eggs with intact yolk and white. Do not microwave eggs in the shell; pressure will build up, causing the egg to explode. Use conventional methods to prepare soft-boiled and hard-cooked eggs.

For recipes such as Baked (fried) Eggs and Florentine Sunburst, carefully pierce the yolk membrane with the tines of a fork before microwave time. Steam will then be able to escape, minimizing the chance of eruption.

Cover the egg to steam it and to prevent spatters. Rotate the dish during microwave time.

Because the egg yolk is high in fat, it tends to cook quicker than the white. To compensate for this, microwave on Medium, covered, allowing the temperatures within the egg to equalize during microwave time. Stop the microwave oven while the egg white is still underdone. Let stand, covered, for cooking to continue.

Beaten egg mixtures. For Scrambled Eggs and other recipes calling for the yolk and white to be mixed together, microwave on Medium, covered to hold in the heat. Stir the food or rotate the dish during microwave time to equalize cooking.

Stop the microwave oven while the food is slightly underdone. Stir, cover, and let stand for the food to finish cooking.

Cheese

Cheese, another delicate food, can be used in many ways—throughout the food dish, as a sauce, as a garnish. Process cheeses are creamier and more tolerant of overcooking than are natural cheeses. But natural cheeses have a flavor bonus. Select cheese accordingly.

In general, microwave cheese dishes on Medium, and minimize the total microwave time. If overcooked, cheese tends to become stringy, tough, rubbery. Whenever possible, add cheese to the dish near the end of microwave time; continue to microwave only until the cheese is heated. Do not permit cheese to boil.

To soften cream cheese, remove the metallic wrapper and place the cheese in a suitable container. Microwave on Low for 1½ to 2 minutes for the 3-ounce size. Double the time for the larger size.

To soften cheese spreads, remove the lid from the glass container. If the container has a foil label or metallic printing on the label, remove the label also. Place the container in the oven, and microwave on Low for 2 to 3 minutes for the 8-ounce size.

Fluffy Omelet (page 62)

Baked Egg

*The popular fried egg,
microwave style*

**1 egg
Butter or margarine**

1. Break egg into a greased 5- or 6-ounce custard cup. Gently pierce yolk with tines of a fork. Top with dot of butter, if desired. Cover with plastic film.

2. Microwave on Low for 1½ minutes, rotating dish after 45 seconds. Let stand, covered, for 1 minute before serving.

Tip: *Microwave 2 eggs on Low for 2½ minutes, rotating dish after 1½ minutes.*

Poached Eggs

*High in protein,
low in calories*

1½ cups water

**2 teaspoons vinegar
4 eggs**

1. Pour water into a 1-quart glass casserole. To bring to a boil, microwave on High, covered, for 4 minutes.

2. Add vinegar to boiling water. Carefully break eggs into water. Cover with glass lid or plastic film.

3. Microwave on Medium for 2 to 3 minutes. Let stand 1 to 2 minutes, covered, until whites coagulate.

Tip: *To poach 1 egg, use ½ cup boiling water in a 10-ounce custard cup. Microwave on High for 30 seconds.*

Eggs Benedict

A classic dish for 4

**2 English muffins split,
    toasted, and buttered
4 slices ham, muffin size
4 poached eggs
Hollandaise Sauce
Paprika**

1. Arrange toasted muffins buttered side up in an 8x8x2-inch glass dish. Place ham slice on each muffin; top with poached egg. Spoon Hollandaise Sauce over eggs. Sprinkle with paprika, if desired.

2. Microwave on Medium for 2 to 2½ minutes or until heated through.

Tip: *See page 178 for Hollandaise Sauce.*

Scrambled Eggs

Make enough for one or for the family

1 egg
1 tablespoon milk
1 teaspoon butter or margarine

1. Combine desired number of eggs with milk in a small glass casserole or soup bowl; mix with fork until blended. Add butter or margarine. Cover with glass lid or plastic film.

2. Microwave on Medium until eggs are set yet moist, stirring once during microwave time.

1 egg	1 to 1½ minutes
2 eggs	2 to 2½ minutes
4 eggs	4½ to 5 minutes
6 eggs	6½ to 7½ minutes

Salt
Pepper

3. Season with salt and pepper. Stir with fork before serving.

Western Scrambled Eggs

Spoon over English muffins to serve 6 to 8

8 to 10 bacon slices

8 eggs
½ cup milk
½ cup salad dressing or mayonnaise
¼ cup chopped pimento
¼ cup chopped green pepper

1 medium tomato, cut into wedges
6 to 8 slices toast or toasted English muffins

1. Microwave bacon on High for 8 to 10 minutes. Cool, then crumble. Set aside.

2. Beat together eggs, milk, and salad dressing in a 2-quart glass casserole. Stir in pimento and green pepper.

3. Microwave on Medium, covered, for 12 to 15 minutes or until just about set, stirring twice during last half of microwave time.

4. Stir in tomato and crumbled bacon. Let stand a few minutes. Spoon over toast and serve.

Bacon and Eggs Casserole

Breakfast for overnight guests; serves 6

1 tablespoon butter or margarine
¼ cup chopped green pepper

4 eggs
½ can (10½ oz) condensed cream of chicken soup

6 bacon slices, cooked and crumbled
Salt
Pepper

1. Place butter in a 2-quart glass casserole with green pepper. To saute, microwave on High for 1 minute.

2. Stir eggs and soup together. Blend into sauteed mixture. Microwave on Medium for 6 to 8 minutes, stirring twice.

3. Season with salt and pepper to taste. Stir well. Crumble bacon on top. Let stand for 1 minute before serving.

Tip: *Mix remaining soup with ½ cup milk. Microwave on High for 1½ to 2 minutes. Use as a sauce for tomorrow's eggs.*

Fluffy Omelet

Rich, creamy, picture pretty for 2 or 3

Pictured on page 58

3 eggs, separated
⅓ cup mayonnaise
2 tablespoons water

2 tablespoons butter or margarine

½ cup shredded Cheddar cheese
1 tablespoon chopped stuffed olives

2 teaspoons chives or dill

1. Using electric mixer, beat egg whites until soft peaks form. Combine egg yolks, mayonnaise, and water; beat until smooth. Fold into egg whites.

2. Place butter in a 9-inch glass pie plate. Microwave on High for 15 seconds or until melted. Spread butter over bottom of pie plate.

3. Carefully pour egg mixture into pie plate. Microwave on Medium for 5½ minutes.

4. Combine cheese and olives. Spread over center of omelet. Microwave on Medium for 1 minute.

5. Fold omelet in half using a spatula. Place on a plate. Garnish with chives or dill, as desired.

Tip: *As a variation fill omelet with cooked asparagus spears and sour cream.*

Zesty Creamed Eggs

Hard-cooked eggs in a creamy sauce; serves 2 or 3

2 tablespoons butter or margarine
3 tablespoons flour
1 teaspoon prepared mustard
¼ teaspoon salt
Dash pepper
1 cup milk

1 teaspoon prepared horseradish
1 teaspoon lemon juice
4 hard-cooked eggs, sliced

Toast, cooked rice, or green vegetable

1. Melt butter in a 1-quart glass casserole; blend in flour, mustard, salt, and pepper. Gradually stir in milk.

2. Microwave on High for 3 to 4 minutes or until sauce is thickened; stir frequently.

3. Stir in horseradish and lemon juice. Fold in sliced eggs.

4. Microwave on High for 1 to 2 minutes or until heated.

5. Serve over toast, cooked rice, or a green vegetable.

Tip: *For quick sauce, combine a can of condensed cream of chicken soup with ½ cup milk; heat until bubbly; continue with steps 3, 4, 5.*

Welsh Rarebit

A classic! Melted cheese poured over toast to serve 6

2 eggs
1 cup beer
1 tablespoon butter or margarine
1 teaspoon dry mustard
1 teaspoon Worcestershire sauce
Dash cayenne

1 pound mild Cheddar cheese, shredded

6 slices toast
Sliced tomato

1. Beat eggs with rotary beater in a 1½-quart glass casserole. Stir in beer, butter, mustard, Worcestershire sauce, and cayenne. Microwave on High, uncovered, for 2 minutes or until warm.

2. Stir in cheese. Microwave on Medium for 6 to 7 minutes or until cheese is melted. Stir every 2 to 3 minutes. When cheese is melted, blend with rotary beater.

3. Arrange tomato slices on toast; top with cheese mixture.

Ham and Cheese Strata

6 openface sandwiches in a custard

6 slices firm white bread
1 can (4½ oz) deviled ham
6 slices process American cheese

1½ cups warm milk
1 tablespoon minced onion
1 tablespoon Worcestershire sauce
½ teaspoon salt
⅛ teaspoon pepper
Dash cayenne
3 eggs, beaten

1. Spread bread with deviled ham. Top with cheese slices. Arrange bread in a 2-quart glass casserole, layering if desired.

2. Mix milk with onions and seasonings. Slowly add to beaten eggs. Stir well. Pour over bread slices. Let stand for 10 minutes.

3. Microwave on Medium, covered, for 15 minutes, rotating dish once during microwave time.

4. Let stand, covered, for 5 minutes before serving.

Swiss Cheese Strata

A fondue-type dish that you can make ahead; serves 4

4 slices white bread
Soft butter or margarine

½ pound Swiss cheese, shredded

2 eggs
1 cup milk
½ teaspoon dry mustard
¼ teaspoon salt
¼ teaspoon paprika
Dash cayenne

1. Spread slices of bread with butter. Arrange slices in 8x8x2-inch glass dish.

2. Sprinkle cheese over bread.

3. Beat eggs with remaining ingredients. Pour over bread and cheese. Microwave on Medium, covered, for 10 to 12 minutes or until mixture is barely set.

Tip: *To make ahead, combine ingredients and refrigerate for several hours. Increase microwave time accordingly.*

Swiss Cheese Fondue

Makes 6 cups that you will be proud to serve

3 cups shredded Swiss cheese
1 cup finely diced Gruyere cheese
1½ tablespoons flour
¼ teaspoon nutmeg
¼ teaspoon pepper
1 clove garlic, pressed or finely chopped

2 cups dry white wine

3 tablespoons dry sherry
French bread, cut into 1-inch cubes

1. Toss cheeses, flour, nutmeg, pepper, and garlic together in a medium size bowl. Set aside.

2. Pour white wine into a 2-quart glass casserole. Microwave on High for 3 minutes, or until hot.

3. Stir in cheese mixture. Microwave on Medium for 4 minutes or until cheese is melted, stirring once.

4. Stir in sherry. Serve immediately with French bread.

Crustless Quiche Lorraine

A custard pie with bacon, cheese, and onion; brunch for 4

9 to 10 slices cooked and crumbled bacon
1 cup shredded Swiss cheese
¼ cup minced onion

4 eggs
1 can (13 oz) evaporated milk
¾ teaspoon salt
¼ teaspoon sugar
⅛ teaspoon cayenne

1. Sprinkle bacon, cheese, and onion into a 9-inch glass pie plate.

2. Beat eggs, milk, and seasonings with rotary beater until well blended. Pour over bacon mixture.

3. Microwave on Medium for 13 minutes, stirring twice. Let stand for 10 minutes before serving.

Florentine Sunburst

A make-ahead brunch for 6 to 8

2 packages (10 oz each) frozen chopped spinach

1 package (12 oz) frozen hash browns

2 tablespoons chopped onion
1 tablespoon lemon juice

1 can (11 oz) condensed Cheddar cheese soup
2 tablespoons water
1 tablespoon Worcestershire sauce

8 eggs

2 tablespoons butter or margarine
⅓ cup dry bread crumbs

1. Microwave spinach on High for 8 to 9 minutes or until thawed; drain.

2. Microwave potatoes on High for 4 to 5 minutes or until thawed.

3. Combine spinach, potatoes, onion, and lemon juice; spread evenly in a 12x7½-inch glass dish.

4. Mix soup, water, and Worcestershire sauce in a small bowl. Microwave on Medium for 3 minutes or until hot.

5. Stir with wire whisk until smooth. Spread sauce evenly over spinach mixture. Make 8 indentations in spinach mixture.

6. Break an egg into each indentation, and pierce the yolk.

7. To melt butter, microwave on High for 30 seconds. Stir in bread crumbs. Sprinkle crumbs over eggs.

8. Cover with waxed paper. Microwave on Medium for 16 to 18 minutes or until eggs are set. Rotate dish 3 to 4 times during microwave time. Let stand for a few minutes before serving.

Tips: *To make ahead, prepare through step 5 and refrigerate. To finish, microwave on Medium, covered, until hot; then add eggs and finish according to the recipe.*

For variation substitute Hollandaise Sauce (page 178) for Cheddar cheese soup.

Cakes and Frostings

For desserts, lunchboxes, and snacks, cakes are an alltime favorite. Now you can add a new dimension to cakes prepared from standard mixes and from scratch; microwave cakes have a light, moist texture over conventionally baked cakes.

Because browning of baked goods does not occur in the microwave oven, white cakes have really white top and sides. This can be an interesting contrast if you add colorful candied fruits to the batter, and then invert the baked cake before cooling it. Of course, if the cake is chocolate or has a topping (a cinnamon-nut mixture for instance), or if you plan to frost the cake, no one will notice the lack of browning.

Cakes

Cake dishes. Choose round, square, or rectangular glass baking dishes. Generally, cakes microwave more evenly in round dishes than in rectangular ones.

Don't grease or flour the cake dish unless specified in the recipe; a grease/flour liner forms a tough layer on the bottom and sides of a microwave cake. Place a sheet of waxed paper on the bottom of the baking dish if you plan to invert the cake onto a plate before serving. Otherwise, pour the batter directly into a clean cake dish.

Since microwave cakes raise higher than conventional cakes, fill the cake dish only ½ full. Make cupcakes with excess batter.

Microwave instructions. Generally microwave one layer at a time, uncovered, unless otherwise specified. Start the cake on a lower setting, allowing it to raise. Then switch to High to finish the cake. Rotate the dish during microwave time, if specified in the recipe, to distribute the foodload within the pattern of microwaves.

Do not overcook the cake, or it will dehydrate and become tough. Test cake for doneness with a woodenpick. When the pick comes out clean, the cake is done. Don't be misled by moist spots on the top of the cake; these will evaporate during the cooldown time.

Cooling. Let cake layers stand for five minutes to set; then invert the cake onto a wire cake rack to cool. If the cake is to be served from the baking dish, cool on a wire cake rack.

Cupcakes. Whether you are making a few cupcakes from excess cake batter, or three dozen cupcakes from an entire mix, microwave cupcakes are simple to make. Many of the tips for cakes still apply, but a few are different.

Place paper cupcake liners in glass custard cups. Add batter until ⅓ full. Arrange cupcakes in the oven to form a circle. Don't place a cupcake in the center of the circle; leave it empty. (See *Food Handling Techniques*, page 11.)

Microwave cupcakes on Medium throughout microwave time, unless otherwise specified. Remove cooked cupcakes from the custard cups immediately, and place them on a wire rack to cool. Otherwise, condensation will form in the bottom of the custard cup, causing soggy cupcakes.

Frostings

While the cake is cooling, prepare the frosting. Use a glass mixing bowl that can hold about double the amount of frosting to guard against boilovers.

Microwave high-sugar mixtures on Medium. Microwave other mixtures on High. Stir or beat the frosting as specified in the recipe to equalize the cooking.

After the mixture has cooled, frost the cooled cake or cupcakes. Refrigerate excess frosting for later use; then simply microwave on High for about five seconds per cup, or until softened.

Oatmeal Coconut Cake (page 71) with Caramel Topping (page 74)

Microwave Cakes from Prepared Mixes

Cake mix
Eggs
Water

1. Prepare batter as directed on package.

2. Use glass dish specified in the chart, even if different from size specified on package.

3. Fill cake dish ½ full; fill cupcake liners ⅓ full. Microwave cakes rise higher than conventional cakes.

4. Microwave, uncovered, as specified in the chart.

5. Rotate ½ turn about halfway through microwave time.

6. Let cakes stand for 5 minutes to set; then turn out onto cooling rack.

Cake Mix	Yield	Glass Dish Size	Microwave Instructions
Standard cake mix (17 to 18½ oz)	Two layers*	8- or 9-inch round	Each layer separately: Medium for 3 min; then High for 3 to 4 min
		8x8x2-inch square	Each layer separately: Medium for 4 min; then High for 4 to 5 min
	One layer*	12x7-inch oblong	Medium for 5 min; then High for 5 to 6 min
	Two doz cupcakes	Custard cups, with paper cupcake liners	2 cupcakes: Medium for 2 to 2½ min 4 cupcakes: Medium for 3 to 3½ min 6 cupcakes: Medium for 5 min
Snackin' Cake® Mix (14½ oz)	One layer	8x8x2-inch square or 8-inch round	Low for 8 min; then High for 4 min
Gingerbread mix or Nutbread mix (14½ to 15 oz)	One layer	8x8x2-inch square	Medium for 12 min
Pound cake mix (16 to 17 oz)	Two loaves	8½x4½x2½ inch loaf dish	Both loaves together: Medium for 5 min; then High for 5 to 6 min (One loaf may be done before the other)

*Make cupcakes from excess batter, if any.

Banana Cake

Watch this 2-layer cake go fast

½ cup butter or margarine
1½ cups sugar

3 eggs, separated
1 cup mashed bananas

1 teaspoon baking soda
½ cup dairy sour cream
2 cups all-purpose flour

1 teaspoon vanilla

Creamy Whipped Frosting

1. Cream butter and sugar.

2. Beat egg yolks and stir into sugar mixture. Add bananas.

3. Combine baking soda with sour cream. Add flour and sour cream alternately to creamed mixture, beating just until well blended.

4. Beat egg whites until stiff, and fold in with vanilla. Pour batter into two 8-inch round glass cake dishes which have been lined with waxed paper.

5. Microwave one layer at a time. Microwave on Medium for 5 minutes; rotate dish. Microwave on High for 3 minutes longer or until woodenpick inserted near center comes out clean.

6. Bake second layer. Cool.

7. Frost with Creamy Whipped Frosting, page 75.

Carrot Cake

A tribute to the South

½ cup butter or margarine
¾ cup packed brown sugar
2 eggs

2 cups grated carrot (2 large)
¾ cup unsifted all-purpose flour
½ teaspoon soda
½ teaspoon baking powder
½ teaspoon salt
½ teaspoon cinnamon
½ teaspoon nutmeg
1 cup crushed wheat cereal squares

Lemon Sauce, or Cream Cheese Frosting

1. Place butter in a glass mixing bowl. Microwave on High for about ½ minute or until softened. Blend in brown sugar; beat in eggs.

2. Stir in remaining ingredients, mixing until combined. Spread in an 8x8x2-inch glass baking dish.

3. Microwave on Medium, uncovered, for 15 minutes. Rotate dish ½ turn. Microwave on High for 2 minutes longer.

4. Serve warm topped with Lemon Sauce, page 180. Or cool and frost with Cream Cheese Frosting, page 75.

Coconut-Crunch Torte

Top with butter-brickle ice cream; serves 6 to 8

1 cup graham cracker crumbs
½ cup flaked coconut
¼ cup chopped walnuts

4 egg whites
¼ teaspoon salt
1 teaspoon vanilla
1 cup sugar

1 pint butter-brickle ice cream

1. Combine graham cracker crumbs, coconut, and nuts.

2. Beat egg whites with salt and vanilla until foamy. Gradually add sugar, and continue beating until egg whites form stiff peaks.

3. Fold graham cracker mixture into egg-white mixture. Spread into a 9-inch pie plate or a 10x6x1½-inch baking dish. Microwave on Medium for 10 minutes.

4. Cool. Cut in wedges and top with scoops of ice cream.

Cheese Cake Supreme

Make it the day before the party, and chill overnight

⅓ cup butter or margarine
1¼ cups graham cracker crumbs
1 teaspoon cinnamon

1½ packages (8 oz each) cream cheese
¾ cup sugar
2 eggs
1 teaspoon vanilla
1 teaspoon grated lemon peel

1 cup dairy sour cream
2 tablespoons sugar
1 teaspoon lemon juice
½ teaspoon vanilla

Melba Sauce (optional)

1. Place butter in an 8-inch round glass cake dish. Microwave on High for 30 seconds. Add crumbs and cinnamon, blending thoroughly. Press mixture over the bottom and ⅔ the way up the sides of the dish; set aside.

2. Place cream cheese in a 4-cup glass measure. Microwave on Low for 4 to 5 minutes or until softened. Gradually beat in sugar, eggs, and flavorings. Pour into crust.

3. Microwave on Medium, uncovered, for 10 minutes.

4. Combine sour cream, sugar, lemon juice, and vanilla. Pour over cheese cake. Microwave on Medium for 1 to 2 minutes. Chill at least 8 hours or overnight before serving.

5. Cut in wedges. Serve topped with canned cherry pie filling or Melba Sauce (page 181).

Oatmeal Coconut Cake

Delicious, worth the effort

Pictured on page 66

1 cup oats (quick or old fashioned) 1½ cups water	1. Combine oats and water in a glass mixing bowl.
	2. Microwave on High, uncovered, for 3 to 4 minutes or until mixture boils, stirring once; set aside.
½ cup butter or margarine	3. In a large glass mixing bowl, microwave butter on High for about ½ minute or until softened.
1 cup sugar 1 cup packed brown sugar 2 eggs 1½ cups unsifted all-purpose flour 1 teaspoon soda 1 teaspoon cinnamon ½ teaspoon salt ½ teaspoon powdered cloves 1 teaspoon vanilla	4. Blend sugars with butter until well mixed. Beat in eggs. Add remaining ingredients and oat mixture; stir until just combined.
	5. Pour into a 12x7½-inch glass baking dish, greased on the bottom.
	6. Microwave on Medium, uncovered, for 15 minutes, rotating dish once.
	7. Microwave on High for 5 minutes longer or until a woodenpick inserted near the center comes out clean.
Caramel Topping	8. Spoon Caramel Topping (page 74) over cake, spreading to cover. Cool.

Butter Brickle Peach Cake

Good tasting cake mix made even better; 12 to 16 slices

1 can (1 lb, 13 oz) sliced peaches	1. Empty peaches and syrup into a 12x7½-inch glass dish.
1 package butter brickle cake mix ½ cup butter or margarine, softened	2. Blend dry cake mix with butter. Sprinkle over peaches.
	3. Microwave on Medium for 15 minutes, rotating dish after first 10 minutes.
	4. Microwave on High for 10 to 11 minutes longer.

Fudge Pudding Cake

8 servings to eat while warm

1 cup all-purpose flour
½ cup sugar
3 tablespoons cocoa
1 teaspoon baking powder
½ teaspoon salt
½ cup milk
2 tablespoons butter or margarine, melted
1 teaspoon vanilla
½ cup chopped nuts

1. Measure first 8 ingredients into a medium-size mixing bowl. Beat until well blended. Stir in nuts.

1⅔ cups boiling water
½ cup sugar
5 tablespoons cocoa
¼ teaspoon salt

Confectioners' sugar

2. Combine boiling water with remaining sugar, cocoa, and salt in an 8x8x2-inch glass dish. Drop batter by rounded tablespoons into boiling mixture.

3. Microwave on Medium for 6 minutes. Rotate dish ½ turn. Microwave on High for 6 minutes. Sprinkle with confectioners' sugar. While still warm, spoon out to serve.

Tip: *Serve with a sauce or whipped cream, if desired.*

Orange Crumb Cake

12 to 16 squares that freeze well

2 cups all-purpose flour
1 cup sugar
½ cup butter or margarine

1. Mix flour, sugar, and butter together until mixture is crumbly like cornmeal.

1 teaspoon cinnamon

2. Combine 1 cup of crumb mixture with cinnamon; reserve for topping.

2 teaspoons baking powder

3. Stir baking powder into remainder of crumb mixture and blend.

2 eggs
1 cup orange juice

4. Beat eggs with orange juice; mix lightly into crumb mixture.

5. Pour cake batter in a 12x7½-inch glass baking dish; spread evenly into corners. Sprinkle batter with cinnamon topping.

6. Microwave on Medium for 7 minutes. Rotate dish ½ turn, and microwave on Medium for 4 minutes longer.

Tip: *Cut into squares and freeze. Serve later for a quick brunch treat.*

Pineapple Upside-down Cake

Made with canned fruit and a cake mix

3 tablespoons butter or margarine

½ cup packed dark brown sugar

1 can (8 oz) sliced pineapple

1 package (9 oz) one-layer yellow cake mix
Eggs (see cake package)

1. Place butter in an 8x8x2-inch glass cake dish. Microwave on High for 45 seconds or until melted.

2. Blend brown sugar with butter; spread evenly in bottom of dish.

3. Drain pineapple juice into measuring cup and set aside. Arrange pineapple slices over brown sugar mixture.

4. Prepare cake mix as directed on package, substituting pineapple juice for water. Pour cake batter into dish, spreading batter evenly over entire surface.

5. Microwave on Medium for 7 minutes, rotating dish once.

6. Microwave on High for 3 to 5 minutes longer or until woodenpick inserted near center comes out clean.

7. Let cake cool for 1 minute. Loosen edge of cake, and invert onto serving plate. Serve warm or cold.

Surprise Cupcakes

36 chocolaty and cheesey treats

1 package (8 oz) cream cheese
⅓ cup sugar
1 egg
Dash salt
1 package (6 oz) semisweet chocolate pieces

1 package (18½ oz) chocolate cake mix
Eggs, water (see cake package)

1. To soften cream cheese, microwave on Low for 2 minutes. Cream together sugar and cheese. Mix in egg and salt; beat until smooth. Fold in chocolate pieces. Set aside.

2. Mix cake mix with eggs and water according to package directions.

3. Line 6 custard cups with paper cupcake liners. Drop rounded tablespoon of batter into each. Drop rounded teaspoon of cream cheese mixture into center of cake batter. Cover with another rounded tablespoon of chocolate batter.

4. Arrange 6 cupcakes in a circle in the oven. Microwave on High for 3 to 4 minutes. Remove cupcakes from custard cups to cooling rack immediately.

5. Repeat procedure for remaining cake batter.

Tip: *Frost cupcakes with favorite icing, if desired.*

Caramel Topping

Similar to German Chocolate cake topping; for a 12x7½-inch cake

Pictured on page 66

¾ cup packed brown sugar
6 tablespoons butter or margarine
2 tablespoons milk

1 cup flaked coconut
½ cup chopped nuts

1. Combine sugar, butter, and milk in a 4-cup glass measure.

2. Microwave on High, uncovered, for 3 to 4 minutes or until bubbly and thickened, stirring several times.

3. Stir in coconut and nuts.

4. Spread on warm or cooled cake.

Chocolate Icing Deluxe

Enough for 3 dozen cupcakes or a 2-layer cake

1 large egg
2 cups confectioners' sugar

2 squares unsweetened chocolate

⅓ cup butter or margarine, softened
1 teaspoon vanilla
¼ teaspoon salt

1. Beat egg with mixer until fluffy. Continue to beat while adding sugar gradually.

2. To melt chocolate, place wrapped squares on a paper plate or waxed paper. Microwave on High for 1½ to 2 minutes.

3. Stir chocolate, butter, and salt into egg and sugar mixture. Beat until smooth and creamy. Stir in vanilla.

Peanut Butter Frosting

Makes enough frosting for a 12x7½-inch cake

1 cup packed brown sugar
⅔ cup chunk-style peanut butter
3 tablespoons milk

Peanuts

1. Combine all ingredients except peanuts in a 1-quart glass bowl.

2. Microwave on High, uncovered, for 2 to 3 minutes or until mixture boils.

3. Let cool slightly before spreading on cake. Garnish with peanuts, if desired.

Tip: *Delicious over ice cream or as a dip for apples on sticks.*

Cream Cheese Frosting

Frosts one 8-inch cake layer

1 tablespoon butter or margarine
1 package (3 oz) cream cheese

1½ cups confectioners' sugar
½ teaspoon vanilla
Few drops milk

1. Place butter and cream cheese in a glass bowl. Microwave on Low for 2 minutes to soften.

2. Beat in sugar and vanilla. Add milk, if needed, to make spreading consistency.

Creamy Whipped Frosting

Frosts two 8- or 9-inch layers; see Tip for Banana Cake Torte

1 package (15¼ oz) creamy white frosting mix

1½ cups whipping cream

½ cup chopped nuts

1. Empty frosting mix into mixer bowl; refrigerate dry mix and beaters while cake cools.

2. Add cream to frosting mix; beat with electric mixer until fluffy and smooth.

3. Fold in nuts.

Tip: *For scrumptious Banana Cake Torte, substitute 1 package Banana Frosting mix in above recipe. Split 2 layers of Banana Cake (page 69) horizontally, making 4 layers. Spread Creamy Whipped Frosting between layers and over top of Banana Cake. Garnish with sliced bananas. Refrigerate.*

Fluffy Marshmallow Frosting

Enough fluff for a 12x7½-inch cake

2 egg whites
¼ teaspoon salt
¼ cup sugar

¾ cup light corn syrup

1 teaspoon vanilla

1. Beat egg whites and salt at high speed until frothy. Gradually add sugar, beating until soft peaks form.

2. Pour syrup into a 2-cup glass measure. Microwave on High, uncovered, for 1½ to 2 minutes or until syrup boils.

3. Pour syrup in thin stream over egg whites while beating at high speed. Continue beating until frosting is of spreading consistency. Beat in vanilla.

Cookies and Candies

For lunchbox treats, afterschool snacks, or through-out-the-day munching, cookies and candies are a traditional standard. Small, bite-size, and easy-to-pack, these finger snacks can be grabbed in a hurry.

Cookies

Selection. Some cookies, such as most bar cookies, react quite favorably to microwave cooking. Others, such as many drop cookies, bake unevenly or do not set. Store-purchased refrigerator cookies (ready to slice and bake) are unsatisfactory when baked in the microwave oven.

Since cookies do not brown in a microwave oven, select recipes that are made with brown sugar, chocolate, or other dark ingredients. Or add a cinnamon-sugar topping, a glaze, or a frosting to improve the appearance of light-batter cookies.

If the recipe makes a large quantity of cookies, you will probably save time and effort if you bake them conventionally.

Preparation. If you are unsure of a recipe that you are preparing, test a few cookies in the microwave oven. Then finish the batch, as desired, in the microwave oven or in the conventional oven.

Don't grease or flour the dish unless specified in the microwave recipe; a grease/flour liner forms a tough layer on the cookies.

Leave enough space between the cookies to allow them to spread.

Microwave uncovered, unless otherwise specified.

Be careful not to overbake cookies in the microwave oven; they will become hard and dry. Since you can't judge doneness by browning, test bar cookies with a woodenpick as you would for cakes. Touch drop cookies lightly with your finger; it shouldn't leave an imprint. Don't be misled by moist spots on the top of the cookies; these will evaporate during the cooling process.

Candies

Constant stirring is not needed; nor is scorching a problem. Since the candy does not rest directly on a hot surface unit, the conventional candy problems do not apply to microwave candy. Of course, you have to stir occasionally to distribute the heat.

Select a utensil that withstands the high temperatures that boiling sugar mixtures reach. Also, the utensil should be large enough to hold double the actual amount of mixture; the extra space will allow for boiling and will help prevent boilovers.

Microwave uncovered, unless otherwise specified.

> Boiling sugar mixtures reach high temperatures. Follow carefully the cautionary instructions on page 12.

Do not use a conventional candy thermometer in an operating microwave oven. Use the out-of-the-oven technique, page 13. Or perform the conventional candy tests for the soft-ball and hard-ball stages.

Left: Marble Fudge (page 81); Date-Nut Torte (page 79)
Right: Dream Bars (page 80)

Applesauce Squares

Spices and raisins/walnuts add interest; makes 2 dozen

½ cup butter or margarine, softened
1 cup packed brown sugar
1 egg
½ cup sweetened applesauce
2 teaspoons grated lemon peel

1½ cups all-purpose flour
1 teaspoon cinnamon
¼ teaspoon ground cloves
½ teaspoon soda
¾ cup raisins or walnuts

Confectioners' sugar (optional)

1. In a large bowl, cream butter and sugar. Beat in egg, applesauce, and lemon peel.

2. Blend flour, spices, and soda into creamed mixture. Stir in raisins or walnuts. Spread batter evenly in an ungreased 10x6-inch glass dish.

3. Microwave on Medium, uncovered, for 5 minutes. Rotate dish. Microwave on High for 5 minutes.

4. Cool. Sprinkle with confectioners' sugar, if desired. Cut into squares.

Brownies

Makes 24 lunchbox treats

⅔ cup butter or margarine
1 cup sugar

2 eggs
2 tablespoons water
1 teaspoon vanilla

1 cup sifted all-purpose flour
½ teaspoon baking powder
½ teaspoon salt
½ cup cocoa

½ cup chopped walnuts

1. Place butter in a 12x7½-inch glass dish. Microwave on High for 1½ minutes or until melted. Stir in sugar. Set aside to cool.

2. Combine eggs, water, and vanilla. Blend well. Stir into butter mixture.

3. Sift together flour, baking powder, salt, and cocoa into butter mixture. Mix well.

4. Fold in nuts. Microwave on High, uncovered, for 1 minute.

5. Stir batter. Microwave on High for 2 minutes longer.

6. Rotate dish and microwave on High for 4 minutes. Cool before serving.

Date-Nut Torte

9 light squares to serve with whipped cream

Pictured on page 76

¼ cup all-purpose flour
½ teaspoon baking powder
¼ teaspoon salt
1½ cups chopped, pitted dates
1½ cups chopped nuts

2 eggs, separated
¾ cup sugar
½ teaspoon vanilla

Whipped cream (optional)

1. Sift together flour, baking powder, and salt. Mix well with dates and nuts.

2. Beat egg yolks until very thick. Add sugar gradually while continuing to beat until very thick and fluffy. Fold in date-nut mixture and vanilla.

3. Beat egg whites until stiff but not dry. Fold into creamed mixture. Turn into a well-greased 8x8x2-inch glass dish.

4. Microwave on Medium, uncovered, for 5 minutes. Rotate dish. Microwave on Medium for another 5 minutes.

5. Rotate dish, and microwave on High for 3 minutes longer.

6. Cool and cut into squares. Top with whipped cream to serve.

Fruity Nut Squares

Choose the fruit and nuts you prefer

1 cup chopped walnuts or pecans
1 cup diced fruit mix—or chopped prunes, dates or other moist dried fruits
1 cup packed brown sugar
¾ cup all-purpose flour
1½ teaspoons baking powder
¼ teaspoon salt

3 eggs
2 tablespoons water
1 teaspoon vanilla

Cinnamon
Sugar

1. Thoroughly mix first 6 ingredients.

2. Beat eggs with water and vanilla. Stir in fruit-nut mixture, blending thoroughly. Spread in an 8x8x2-inch glass dish sprayed with vegetable coating. Cover loosely with plastic film.

3. Microwave on Medium for 7 minutes. Rotate dish. Microwave on High for 3 to 4 minutes.

4. Let stand for 10 minutes. Turn out on cooling rack. Sprinkle with cinnamon and sugar. When cool, cut into squares.

Dream Bars

*36 graham-
chocolate-coconut
cookies*

Pictured on page 76

**22 graham crackers, crushed
(about 1 cup crumbs)
1 package (6 oz) semisweet
chocolate pieces
1 can (3½ oz) flaked coconut
1 can (15 oz) sweetened
condensed milk**

1. Combine all ingredients. Spread in an
8x8x2-inch glass dish.

2. Microwave on Medium, uncovered, for 5
minutes. Rotate dish. Microwave on High for 4
to 5 minutes.

3. Cool. Cut into bars.

Some-Mores

Favorite with youngsters

**1 large marshmallow
1 square milk chocolate
2 graham cracker squares**

1. Place marshmallow and candy square between
graham crackers. Place on paper plate, or wrap
between paper napkin or towel.

2. Microwave on High for 30 to 45 seconds.

Crunchy Fudge Sandwiches

*25 squares; watch
them go fast*

**1 package (6 oz) butterscotch
pieces
½ cup peanut butter

4 cups crisp rice cereal**

1. Place butterscotch pieces and peanut butter in a
glass bowl. Microwave on High for 2 minutes or
until melted.

2. Add rice cereal; stir until well-coated. Press half
of cereal mixture into a buttered 8x8x2-inch
glass dish. Chill while preparing fudge mixture.
Set remaining cereal mixture aside.

**1 package (6 oz) semisweet
chocolate pieces
½ cup sifted confectioners'
sugar
2 tablespoons soft butter or
margarine
1 tablespoon water**

3. Combine chocolate pieces, sugar, butter, and
water in a glass dish. Microwave on High for 2
minutes to melt chocolate.

4. Spread fudge mixture over chilled cereal.
Spread remaining cereal over top. Chill.

5. Remove from refrigerator about 10 minutes
before cutting into squares.

Marble Fudge

36 squares, five flavors in each

Pictured on page 76

1 package (12 oz) semisweet
   chocolate pieces
1 package (12 oz)
   butterscotch pieces
1 cup peanut butter

1 package (10½ oz)
   miniature marshmallows
1 cup salted peanuts

1. Combine chocolate, butterscotch, and peanut butter in a large glass mixing bowl.

2. Microwave on Medium for about 5 minutes. Stir until melted.

3. Fold in marshmallows and peanuts. Spread in a buttered 13x9-inch pan.

4. Refrigerate for several hours or until set. Cut into squares.

Satin Fudge

Makes 8 to 9 dozen squares; some to eat now; some to freeze for later

3 cups sugar
½ cup butter or margarine
1 can (6 oz) evaporated milk
   (⅔ cup)

1 package (12 oz) semisweet
   chocolate pieces
1 jar (7½ oz) marshmallow
   creme
1 cup chopped nuts
1 teaspoon vanilla

1. Combine sugar, butter, and evaporated milk in a 3-quart glass casserole or bowl.

2. Microwave on High, uncovered, for 5½ to 6½ minutes or until mixture comes to a boil, stirring once or twice.

3. Microwave on High, uncovered, for 3 minutes longer, stirring occasionally. If necessary, occasionally stop cooking to prevent mixture from boiling over.

4. Stir in chocolate pieces until melted. Blend in remaining ingredients. Pour into a buttered 13x9-inch pan. Refrigerate for several hours or until set; cut into squares.

Tip: *This fudge freezes well; just wrap tightly and freeze for up to 3 months.*

To remove remaining marshmallow creme from sides of glass jar, microwave on High for ¼ to ½ minute or until warm. Use rubber scraper to remove creme.

Fruits

Full of flavor, plump, and juicy—microwave fruits are great for dessert. Start with fresh, frozen, canned, or dried fruits; and create a dessert. But be sure to prepare enough; your family will want seconds.

In general microwave fruits on High. Scorching tends not to be a problem. The actual time required depends on the size, shape, and temperature of the fruit, as well as on its sugar content. Judge microwave time accordingly.

Since fruit dishes reheat beautifully, prepare the dessert in advance and refrigerate. Before serving, simply microwave the dessert for a brief time.

For fruits that are to hold their shape, microwave them in an uncovered glass baking dish. If the serving platter for fresh fruits is suitable for microwave use, you may prefer to arrange the fruits on the platter; microwave the fruit just before serving.

To get more fresh-squeezed juice, microwave the lemon or orange on High for about 30 seconds, and then squeeze.

To peel the skin off of fruits such as peaches, microwave the fruit on High for a few minutes; let stand for several minutes; and then peel off the skin.

To plump dried fruits, place fruit in a glass bowl, and cover with waxed paper. Microwave on High for 3 to 5 minutes or until moist. Use in cakes or as desired.

To soften raisins, place them in a glass bowl, and add a small amount of water or fruit juice. Microwave on High, uncovered, for 3 minutes. Let stand for 3 minutes, and then drain.

Frozen Fruits

From the freezer to the table in minutes

1 package (10 to 12 oz) frozen fruits

1. Open original package and turn fruit into a 1-quart glass casserole. Cover.

   If fruits are packed in a plastic bag, pierce a few holes in the plastic for steam to escape. Place in a glass casserole, but do not cover.

2. Microwave on Low until individual pieces can be separated with a fork. Do not thaw completely.

Strawberries	3 to 4 minutes
Sliced Peaches	2 to 3 minutes
Raspberries	2 to 3 minutes
Pineapple Chunks	2 to 3 minutes
Mixed Fruit	2 to 3 minutes

3. Serve while still slightly frosty.

Tip: *For home frozen fruit, increase microwave time by 1 to 2 minutes, or longer if needed.*

Swedish Fruit Soup (page 89)

Apple Crisp

Tender apples with a crunchy topping; 6 servings

5 cups sliced pared apples

1 cup all-purpose flour
1 cup packed brown sugar
¾ cup quick-cooking oats
1 teaspoon cinnamon
½ teaspoon salt

½ cup butter or margarine

Ice cream

1. Place apple slices in a 12x7½-inch glass dish.
2. Combine flour, brown sugar, oats, cinnamon, and salt.
3. Cut in butter until mixture is crumbly. Sprinkle evenly over sliced apples.
4. Microwave on High, uncovered, for 15 minutes or until apples are tender. Rotate dish halfway through microwave time.
5. Serve warm with ice cream.

Applesauce

An Autumn favorite that you can prepare year'round

4 to 5 tart apples, peeled and sliced (4 cups)
½ cup water

¼ to ½ cup sugar
½ teaspoon cinnamon

1. Place apples and water in a 1½-quart glass casserole. Microwave on High, covered, for 6 to 8 minutes, or until apples are tender.
2. Put cooked apples through a sieve, or whirl in blender, if desired.
3. Stir in sugar and cinnamon. Sweeten to taste. Cool.

Baked Apples

Basic recipe; add your favorite filling

4 medium-size apples

¼ cup packed brown sugar
Butter or margarine

1. Core apples, and slice thin circle of peel from top of each apple. Arrange apples in a 9-inch round glass dish.
2. Fill each apple with 1 tablespoon of brown sugar. Dot with butter.
3. Microwave on High, uncovered, for 4 to 5 minutes or until apples are tender. Rotate dish once. Exact time will depend on size and type of apples. Let apples stand for a few minutes before serving.

Tip: *Fill apples with mincemeat, whole cranberry sauce, or raisins and nuts. Increase microwave time by 1 or 2 minutes.*

Caramel Apples

7 or 8 carnival and Halloween treats

1 pound (2½ cups) caramels
1 tablespoon water

1. Place caramels and water in a glass bowl. Microwave on Medium, covered, for 2 minutes.

2. Stir; then microwave on Medium for 1 to 2 minutes longer or until melted.

Wooden sticks
7 or 8 medium apples

3. Insert sticks into apples. Dip apples into melted caramel mixture, twirling until apples are coated. Place on buttered waxed paper.

Tip: *For 1 apple, melt 8 or 9 caramels with 1 teaspoon water.*

Stewed Dried Apricots

An easy way to prepare dried fruits

1 package (12 oz) dried apricots
1½ cups water
3 tablespoons sugar

1. Place fruit, water, and sugar in a 1½-quart glass casserole.

2. Microwave on High, covered, for 10 to 12 minutes.

3. Let stand, covered, for 30 minutes. Refrigerate covered.

Tip: *Use this method to prepare dried prunes, apricots, or mixed fruit.*

Crunchy Cherry Dessert

6 servings of cherry filling between two layers of crunch

1½ cups sifted all-purpose flour
1 cup packed brown sugar
¾ cup quick-cooking oats
½ teaspoon soda
½ teaspoon salt

1. Mix flour, brown sugar, oats, soda, and salt in a large bowl.

½ cup softened butter or margarine

2. Cut in butter, and blend until particles are small and uniform. Pat half of crumb mixture into an 8x8x2-inch glass baking dish.

1 can (1 lb, 5 oz) prepared cherry pie filling

3. Cover crumb layer evenly with pie filling. Sprinkle remaining crumb mixture over filling.

4. Microwave on High, uncovered, for about 15 minutes. Rotate dish every 5 minutes. Serve warm or cold.

Cranberry Sauce

2 cups to serve with the turkey

1 pound cranberries

2 cups sugar
½ cup water

1. Wash cranberries; place in a 3-quart glass casserole.

2. Add sugar and water.

3. Microwave on High, covered, for 8 to 10 minutes or until mixture boils and berries pop.

4. Let stand, covered, for 10 to 15 minutes. Serve warm or cold.

Tip: *For a tasty variation, substitute orange juice for water.*

Baked Grapefruit

For breakfast or light dessert

1 grapefruit

Brown sugar
Butter

1. Cut grapefruit in half, and cut around each section with a sharp knife. Remove seeds.

2. Sprinkle brown sugar over top. Dot with butter.

3. Place grapefruit on a paper or china plate. Microwave on High, uncovered, for 2½ minutes. Serve hot.

Pear Streusel a la Mode

Gingersnaps add flavor bonus; 6 delicious servings

1 can (1 lb) pear halves, well-drained

12 gingersnaps, finely crushed
¼ cup sugar
¼ cup soft butter or margarine

Vanilla ice cream

1. Place pears in a 9-inch round glass dish.

2. Combine gingersnap crumbs and sugar in a small bowl. Blend well. Cut in butter until mixture is crumbly. Sprinkle over pears.

3. Microwave on High, uncovered, for about 4 minutes. Rotate dish halfway through microwave time.

4. Serve warm, topped with vanilla ice cream.

Raisin-Carrot Pudding

Makes 8 squares of a New England favorite

½ cup butter or margarine
½ cup packed brown sugar
1 egg
1 cup currants
1 cup firmly packed grated raw carrots
½ cup seedless raisins
2 teaspoons chopped candied ginger

1. Cream margarine and brown sugar. Beat in egg until well-blended. Stir in currants, carrots, raisins, and ginger.

1¼ cups sifted cake flour
1 teaspoon baking powder
½ teaspoon soda
½ teaspoon cinnamon
½ teaspoon nutmeg

2. Sift together flour, baking powder, soda, cinnamon, and nutmeg. Stir into creamed mixture until well-blended.

3. Turn into a greased 8x8x2-inch glass dish. Microwave on High, uncovered, for 15 minutes, rotating dish every 5 minutes.

Sauce (optional)

4. Cut pudding into squares while warm. Serve with hard sauce or Lemon Sauce (page 180) if desired.

Raspberry Salad/ Dessert

Pretty holiday or party salad for 8 or 9

1 can (6 oz) frozen lemonade concentrate
1 package (10 oz) frozen red raspberries

1. Thaw lemonade and raspberries. (See page 83.) Set aside.

2 cups water

2. Measure water into a 2-quart glass casserole. Microwave on High for 5 minutes or until water is almost boiling.

1 package (6 oz) raspberry-flavored gelatin

3. Mix raspberry-flavored gelatin into water, stirring until dissolved. Add lemonade and raspberries.

1 pint vanilla ice cream

4. Add ice cream by spoonfuls, stirring to melt.

5. Pour into an 8x8x2-inch dish or a 2-quart mold. Refrigerate, covered, until set. Cut into squares and serve.

Fresh Rhubarb Sauce

A tasty sauce to perk up a meal

2 cups rhubarb, in ½-inch pieces
2 tablespoons water
Dash salt

½ cup sugar

1. Place rhubarb and water into a 2-quart glass casserole. Add salt.

2. Microwave on High, covered, for 4 minutes.

3. Add sugar; microwave on High for 1 minute longer. Keep rhubarb covered while cooling.

Rhubarb Crisp

An easy dessert at harvest time; 8 servings

4 cups rhubarb, in ½-inch pieces
½ cup sugar
2 tablespoons lemon juice
1 teaspoon grated lemon peel

1 cup packed brown sugar
1 cup all-purpose flour
½ cup soft butter or margarine

1. Combine rhubarb, sugar, lemon juice, and lemon peel. Spread in an 8x8x2-inch glass dish.

2. Mix together brown sugar, flour, and butter until crumbly. Sprinkle over rhubarb. Microwave on Medium, uncovered, for 10 minutes.

3. Rotate dish. Microwave on High for 4 minutes or until rhubarb is tender.

Tip: *Serve warm or cold. Top with whipped cream or vanilla ice cream.*

Curried Fruit Compote

Serve warm as meat accompaniment for 8, or as a dessert

1 can (1 lb, 4 oz) chunk pineapple
1 can (1 lb) pear halves
1 can (1 lb) peach or apricot halves
5 maraschino cherries

¼ cup butter or margarine
½ cup packed brown sugar
1 tablespoon curry powder

1. Drain fruits, and arrange in a 1½-quart glass baking dish. Set aside.

2. Microwave butter on High for 30 to 45 seconds or until melted. Stir in brown sugar and curry powder. Pour over fruit.

3. Microwave on Medium, uncovered, for 8 to 10 minutes or until heated through, rotating dish once.

Spiced Fruit Compote

A perky fruit trio

2 medium-size apples, peeled, cored, and cut in eighths
1 can (1 lb) pear halves, cut in half lengthwise

½ cup whole cranberry sauce
⅛ teaspoon cinnamon
$1/16$ teaspoon cloves
$1/16$ teaspoon allspice

1. Layer apples and pears in a 1½-quart glass casserole. Reserve 1 tablespoon pear syrup.

2. Combine whole cranberry sauce with spices and 1 tablespoon pear syrup. Spoon over fruits.

3. Microwave on Medium, uncovered, for 12 to 15 minutes or until apples are tender. Serve warm or chilled.

Tip: *For a variation, substitute 1 can (1 lb) pineapple chunks or apricot halves for the pears.*

Swedish Fruit Soup

It's a dessert or a breakfast dish

Pictured on page 82 and on back cover

1 package (12 oz) mixed dried fruit
1 package (12 oz) dried apricots
½ cup raisins
½ lemon, thinly sliced
2 quarts water

1 cup sugar
2 tablespoons quick-cooking tapioca
½ teaspoon salt
3 cinnamon sticks

1. Combine mixed fruits, apricots, raisins, lemon slices, and water in a 3-quart glass casserole.

2. Stir in sugar, tapioca, salt, and cinnamon sticks.

3. Microwave on High, covered, for about 15 minutes or until boiling.

4. Microwave on Medium for 25 minutes longer, or until fruits are tender. Serve hot or cold.

Pies have traditionally been part of our heritage. Remember when good cooks were judged by the flakiness of their pie crusts? And what could be more American than apple pie!

With your microwave oven, you can add another dimension to this heritage. Try some of the recipes in this chapter to get the feel of microwave pies. Then adapt your family-treasured recipes, and start your own collection of family favorites.

Crumb crusts. Since crackers and cookies are browned conventionally, they make excellent ingredients to use in microwave crusts. Start with melted butter; then mix in desired cracker crumbs or cookie crumbs. Add sugar to unsweetened crackers.

For a handy mold, use an 8-inch pie plate to press the crumbs into a 9-inch glass pie plate. Microwave on Medium for a few minutes to set the crust, rotating the dish once during microwave time.

Cool the crust before adding the prepared filling. This will help prevent the crust from becoming soggy.

Pastry shells. Whether you make pie crust from scratch, or use store purchased sticks, mixes, or frozen shells, microwave pastries are flaky and tender.

Since browning does not occur in the microwave oven, you may prefer to bake all two-crust pies conventionally. For a browning effect of one-crust pies, try one of the following:

• Add a few drops of yellow food coloring to the liquid before you add it to the dry ingredients.
• Brush the unbaked shell with vanilla.
• Brush the unbaked shell with beaten egg white or with beaten egg yolk.

Line a 9-inch glass pie plate with dough. Then either prick the bottom and sides with a fork, or cover the dough with a paper towel and a second pie plate. Microwave on Medium, rotating the dish halfway through microwave time.

Cool the shell first; then add the prepared filling. This will help prevent the pastry from becoming soggy.

Fillings are as numerous as your imagination lets them be. Generally add the prepared filling to a baked, cooled shell.

Microwave the filling as you would the individual ingredient. For instance, microwave egg-based fillings (custards, pumpkin, etc) on Medium; gelatin-based fillings on High until the gelatin is melted. Stir the filling, or rotate the dish during microwave time. This helps to distribute the heat, as well as prevent curdling, separation, or lumping.

Meringue topping shrinks and becomes tough in the microwave oven. For best results use a conventional baking method. Or, you can fold the meringue into the hot filling.

Reheated pieces of pie taste as if they were freshly baked. Microwave on High, uncovered, until hot. One piece heats in 15 seconds; two pieces in 25 seconds; four pieces in 1 minute. Tip: Since four pieces at a time do not heat evenly, you may prefer to reheat them two at a time.

Ginger Cheese Pie (page 95), garnished with strawberries

Frozen Pie Shell

1 frozen pie shell

1. Allow pie shell to thaw. Then transfer it to a glass pie plate.
2. Press into pie plate. Prick bottom and sides with a fork. Microwave on Medium for 5 to 6 minutes. Cool before filling.

Pie Crust Mix

1 package pie crust mix

1. Prepare as directed on the package.
2. Place dough in a 9-inch glass pie plate. Flute edge; prick bottom and sides of crust.
3. Microwave on Medium for 7 to 9 minutes. Rotate dish halfway through microwave time. Cool before filling.

Pastry Shell

9-inch shell for a 1-crust pie

1 cup all-purpose flour
½ cup shortening
½ teaspoon salt
4 to 5 tablespoons cold milk

1. Sift flour and salt together. Cut in shortening with a pastry blender. Sprinkle 1 tablespoon milk over flour mixture. Gently toss with fork. Repeat until all is moistened.
2. Flatten on a lightly floured board. Roll from center to edge until dough is ⅛ inch thick. Allow to rest.
3. Place dough in a 9-inch glass pie plate. Trim and flute edge. Cover shell with a paper towel. Top with an 8-inch glass pie plate to keep dough flat and to prevent shrinkage.
4. Microwave on Medium for 7 to 9 minutes. Rotate dish halfway through microwave time. Cool before filling.

Tips: *If desired, simply prick the sides and bottom of the crust generously with a fork. Then bake; no need to cover with paper towel and glass pie plate.*

To improve color, mix 1 or 2 drops of yellow food coloring into milk before adding it to the dry ingredients.

Cookie or Cracker Crumb Crust

A precooked shell for a 9-inch pie

Butter or margarine

Crumbs
Sugar

1. Place butter in a 9-inch glass pie plate. Microwave on High for 30 seconds or until melted.

2. Mix in cookie or cracker crumbs, and sugar if required. Press crumb mixture firmly against bottom and sides of pie plate.

3. Microwave on Medium, uncovered, for 2 to 3 minutes, rotating dish after 2 minutes.

4. Cool on wire rack. Fill as desired.

Tip: *To press crumbs into place in a 9-inch glass pie plate, use an 8-inch pie plate.*

Cookies or Crackers	Crumbs	Butter or Margarine	Sugar
Graham Crackers, approx 18 to 20 squares	1¼ cups	⅓ cup	¼ cup
Gingersnaps, approx 30	1⅓ cups	⅓ cup	—
Coconut Cookies	2 cups	¼ cup	—
Creme-filled Chocolate Sandwich Cookies, approx 22	1⅔ cups	¼ cup	—
Vanilla Wafers, approx 36	1½ cups	¼ cup	—

1-2-3 Apple Pie

A one-crust pie with a creamy topping

1 can (1 lb 5 oz) apple pie filling
1 baked 9-inch pastry shell

¾ cup milk
1 cup dairy sour cream
1 package (3¾ or 3⅝ oz) instant vanilla pudding mix

2 tablespoons sliced almonds

1. Turn pie filling into baked pastry shell.

2. In medium bowl, combine milk with sour cream. Mix well. Stir in pudding mix; beat according to package directions.

3. Pour pudding mixture over pie filling. Chill.

4. Spread almonds on paper plate. To toast, microwave on High for about 2 minutes. Stir halfway through microwave time.

5. Sprinkle toasted almonds over pie before serving.

Banana Cream Pie

Everyone will want seconds

1 package (3⅛ oz) vanilla pudding and pie filling mix
1¾ cups milk

1 large banana, sliced
Few drops lemon juice
1 baked 9-inch pastry shell or crumb crust

1½ cups miniature marshmallows
½ cup heavy cream, whipped

1. Empty pudding mix into a 1-quart glass casserole. Gradually stir in milk.

2. Microwave on High for 2 minutes. Stir.

3. Microwave on High for 3 to 4 minutes longer or until pudding is thickened. Stir every minute.

4. Cover with waxed paper; refrigerate.

5. Moisten banana slices with lemon juice to prevent darkening. Place banana slices evenly on bottom of pie shell.

6. To cooled pudding mixture, mix in marshmallows and whipped cream. Pour into banana-lined pie shell. Chill for several hours.

Chocolate Pie Filling

Creamy, smooth, and oh so good; fills a 9-inch shell

1 baked 9-inch pastry shell or crumb crust

1 package (6 oz) semisweet chocolate pieces
2 tablespoons sugar
3 tablespoons milk

3 separated eggs, room-temperature

1. Prepare pastry shell.

2. Combine chocolate pieces, sugar, and milk in a 1½-quart glass bowl. Microwave on Medium for 3 minutes. Stir after 2 minutes.

3. Beat egg yolks into chocolate mixture, one at a time. In another bowl, beat egg whites until moderately stiff peaks are formed.

4. Fold egg whites into chocolate. Pour filling into prepared crust. Chill until firm.

Tip: *Serve with dollops of whipped topping.*

Ginger Cheese Pie

A tasty variation of the always-good cheesecake

Pictured on pages 90 and 176

¼ cup butter or margarine
12 graham cracker squares, crushed (⅔ cup crumbs)
2 tablespoons flour
2 tablespoons sugar

1 package (8 oz) cream cheese
⅓ cup sugar
2 eggs
1 teaspoon powdered ginger (optional)

1 cup dairy sour cream
3 tablespoons sugar
½ teaspoon vanilla

2 tablespoons chopped candied ginger (optional)

1. Place butter in an 8-inch glass pie plate. Microwave on High for 30 seconds or until melted. Mix in crumbs, flour and 2 tablespoons sugar. Press crumb mixture firmly against bottom and sides of pie plate.

2. Place cream cheese in a glass bowl. Microwave on Low for 4 minutes or until softened. Beat in ⅓ cup sugar, eggs, and ginger; blend until smooth. Pour into pie crust.

3. Microwave on Medium for 8 minutes or until set, rotating dish once.

4. Mix sour cream, 3 tablespoons sugar, and vanilla. Spread over pie filling. Microwave on Medium for 2 minutes.

5. Refrigerate for several hours before serving. Garnish with candied ginger.

Grasshopper Pie

Cremes and marshmallows in a chocolate shell

22 large marshmallows
½ cup milk

1. Place marshmallows and milk in a large glass bowl. Microwave on High for 3 to 5 minutes or until marshmallows are melted. Stir halfway through microwave time. Cool to room temperature.

2 tablespoons green creme de menthe
1 tablespoon creme de cocoa
½ pint heavy cream, whipped

2. Stir in creme de menthe and creme de cocoa. Fold in whipped cream.

Crumb Crust from Creme-filled Chocolate Sandwich Cookies

3. Pour mixture into pie shell (page 93) and chill.

Semisweet chocolate shavings
Maraschino cherries

4. Garnish with semisweet chocolate shavings and maraschino cherries; serve.

Tip: *Make ahead through step 3. Allow pie top to become firm to prevent it from sticking to the wrapping material. Then wrap and freeze. Thaw in refrigerator overnight.*

Orange Mallow Pie

Make this early in the day, and chill well

32 large or 3 cups miniature marshmallows
1 tablespoon grated orange peel
¾ cup orange juice
2 tablespoons lemon juice

1. Combine marshmallows, orange peel, and juices in a 1½-quart glass casserole. Microwave on Medium for 3 to 4 minutes or until marshmallows begin to soften. Stir. Chill until partially set.

1½ cups chilled whipping cream, or 1 package whipped topping

2. In a chilled bowl, whip cream until stiff. Fold in marshmallow mixture.

Baked 9-inch pastry shell or crumb crust

3. Pour into pie shell. Chill until set, about 4 hours.

Tip: *Garnish with chopped toasted almonds or grated orange peel, if desired.*

For a good flavor combination, use this filling with Gingersnap Crumb Crust, page 93.

Southern Pecan Pie

A rich, sweet dessert

¼ cup butter or margarine, softened
½ cup packed brown sugar
1 cup light corn syrup
½ teaspoon vanilla

3 eggs

1½ cups pecan halves
9-inch baked pastry shell

1. Cream butter and brown sugar until fluffy. Stir in corn syrup and vanilla. Beat well.

2. Add eggs one at a time, beating well after each addition.

3. Spread pecans evenly in pastry shell. Pour egg mixture over pecans.

4. Microwave on Low, uncovered, for 10 minutes. Rotate dish.

5. Microwave on Low for 10 minutes longer or until knife inserted into pie about 2" from the edge comes out clean.

6. Cool on wire rack.

Pumpkin Pie

Thanksgiving dinner wouldn't be complete without this traditional dessert

2 eggs
1 can (1 lb) pumpkin
¾ cup sugar
½ teaspoon salt
1 teaspoon cinnamon
½ teaspoon ginger
¼ teaspoon cloves
1 cup evaporated milk

1 baked 9-inch pastry shell

Whipped topping

1. In a mixing bowl beat eggs slightly; blend in remaining ingredients except pastry shell.

2. Pour into baked pastry shell. Cover with plastic film. Pierce a hole for steam to escape.

3. Microwave on Medium for 5 minutes or until edges begin to set. Stir filling carefully.

4. Microwave on High, uncovered, for 5 minutes or until center begins to thicken. Rotate dish after 3 minutes, if needed.

5. Let stand for 10 minutes. Knife inserted near center should come out clean.

6. Cool on wire rack. Serve with whipped topping.

Never before have puddings and custards been so smooth, so creamy than since the advent of microwave cooking!

On a conventional surface unit, concentrated heat is applied to the bottom of the pan. You have to constantly stir the mixture to keep it smooth and to guard against scorching.

Not so with microwave puddings and custards. The mixture generates heat throughout itself—top, bottom, and all sides—instead of being subjected to an intense bottom heat source. Of course, you have to stir frequently to guard against separating/curdling. But constant stirring is not needed, nor is scorching a problem.

Preparation. Generally, these mixtures fall into three groups: puddings and pie filling mixes, soft custards, and baked custards. Prepare the mixture as you normally would. Follow instructions on the package or in your favorite recipe. No special preparation techniques are needed. Microwave instructions differ, however; see this page.

Choose a glass container that can hold double the actual amount of mixture; the extra space will help prevent boilovers. Consider using a container with a pouring spout (such as a 4-cup measure) so you can more easily pour the cooked mixture into individual serving dishes to cool.

Or choose individual glass custard cups. Fill only half full. See Baked custards, on this page, for more microwave tips.

Pudding and pie filling mixes. Microwave on High, uncovered, stirring frequently. Allow the mixture to come to a boil. These mixes contain a stabilizer, increasing the likelihood of smooth and creamy results. Pour into individual serving dishes before standing time, if desired.

Soft custards. Microwave on Medium (because of their high egg content), uncovered, stirring frequently. Keep the mixture well below the boiling point, and don't overcook. Otherwise the mixture will separate, curdle, and become lumpy.

Baked custards. Pour the mixture into individual custard cups, filling only half full. Arrange the cups in a circular pattern. Don't place a cup in the center of the circle. (See page 11.)

Microwave on Low, uncovered, until set. Since you do not stir this type of custard, the Low setting helps keep the mixture from curdling.

Switch the position of cups during microwave time to expose each to a different pattern of microwaves. Don't stir the mixture.

Remove the custard, one cup at a time, as required. Individual cups of custard cook at different rates.

General microwave instructions. Regardless of the mixture, stop the microwave oven frequently. Stir the mixture, or rearrange the individual cups of baked custard. Then restart the oven. If you use a metal stirring spoon, be sure to remove it before you restart the oven.

If the mixture is heating up too rapidly or is beginning to boil over, stop the microwave oven. Let stand briefly before continuing according to the recipe.

Do not overcook the mixture. Remove while slightly underdone. Let stand; cooking will continue during this standing time.

Tapioca Pudding (page 102)

Quick Egg Custard

Makes six ½-cup servings

2 cups milk
1 package (3 oz) egg custard
   mix

Nutmeg

1. Mix milk and custard mix in a 4-cup glass measure. Microwave on Medium for 5 minutes. Stir.

2. Microwave on Medium for 5 minutes longer or until mixture boils. Mixture will be thin.

3. Pour into dessert dishes and sprinkle with nutmeg. Refrigerate.

Baked Custard

Makes five from-scratch servings

1¾ cups milk

3 eggs
¼ cup sugar
¼ teaspoon salt
½ teaspoon vanilla

Nutmeg

1. Measure milk into a 1-quart glass measure. Microwave on High for 3 to 4 minutes or until almost boiling.

2. Meanwhile, place remaining ingredients except nutmeg in a medium bowl; beat with rotary beater.

3. Slowly add hot milk to egg mixture stirring constantly. Pour mixture into five 6-ounce custard cups, filling about ¾ full. Sprinkle with nutmeg, if desired.

4. Arrange cups in circle in the microwave oven. Microwave on Low, uncovered, for 12 to 15 minutes or until knife inserted near center comes out clean.

5. Let stand for 5 minutes before serving; or chill and serve.

Tip: *Custards may cook at slightly different rates. Check during the last three minutes of microwave time, and remove individual custards as they finish cooking.*

Easy Pudding

Choose whichever flavor you want; serves 4

1 package (3½ oz) pudding
   and pie filling mix
2 cups milk

1. Turn package of pudding into a 1-quart glass casserole. Stir in enough milk to dissolve pudding. Stir in remaining milk.

2. Microwave on High for 2 minutes. Stir.

3. Microwave on High for 3 to 4 minutes longer or until pudding is thickened. Stir every minute.

Coconut Custard

Rich, tasty; serves 6

3 whole eggs
3 egg yolks
½ cup sugar
¼ teaspoon salt

1. Beat eggs, egg yolks, sugar, and salt together; set aside.

2 cups coffee cream

2. Measure cream into a 1½-quart glass casserole. Microwave on High, uncovered, for 2 to 3 minutes or until scalded.

3. Gradually add part of hot cream to egg mixture. Stir well. Blend egg mixture into hot cream.

4. Microwave on High, uncovered, for 6 minutes or until thickened. Beat with wire whisk every minute.

1½ teaspoons vanilla
¾ teaspoon almond extract
¾ cup flaked coconut

5. Stir in flavorings and coconut. Pour into six dessert dishes. Chill.

Mocha Pot De Creme

Chocolate-coffee flavor with whipped cream richness; serves 6

1 package (3½ oz) chocolate pudding and pie filling mix
¼ cup sugar
2 teaspoons instant coffee crystals
1½ cups milk

1. Combine pudding mix, sugar, and coffee in a 1-quart glass casserole. Stir in milk gradually until smooth.

2. Microwave on High, uncovered, for 4 to 5 minutes, stirring at 1-minute intervals.

2 egg yolks

3. Beat egg yolks slightly. Add a small amount of hot mixture; stir well. Pour egg mixture into hot mixture, stirring thoroughly.

1 teaspoon vanilla

4. Microwave on High for 1 minute. Stir in vanilla. Allow to cool.

½ cup heavy cream, whipped

5. When custard is cool, fold in whipped cream. Spoon into 6 dessert dishes. Refrigerate until chilled.

Whipped cream (optional)
Shaved chocolate (optional)

6. To serve, garnish with whipped cream and shaved chocolate, if desired.

Vanilla Cream Pudding

Smooth, creamy; makes 4 or 5 servings

2 cups milk

1. Measure milk in a 1½-quart glass casserole. Microwave on High for 2½ minutes or until almost boiling.

⅓ cup sugar
¼ cup cornstarch
½ teaspoon salt

2. Meanwhile, mix sugar, cornstarch, and salt. Blend into hot milk, using a wire whisk.

3. Microwave on High, uncovered, for 2 minutes, stirring twice.

3 egg yolks

4. In a separate bowl, beat egg yolks; gradually mix in a small amount of hot pudding, stirring constantly. Pour egg mixture into hot pudding, stirring constantly.

5. Microwave on High for 30 seconds.

2 tablespoons butter or margarine
½ teaspoon vanilla

6. Beat well for smooth consistency. Mix in butter and vanilla. Blend well. Pour into 4 or 5 dessert dishes.

Tapioca Pudding

A light, airy dessert for 6

Pictured on page 98

3 tablespoons quick-cooking tapioca
3 tablespoons sugar
⅛ teaspoon salt
2 cups milk
1 egg, separated

1. Mix tapioca, 3 tablespoons sugar, salt, milk, and egg yolk in a 1½-quart glass casserole. Let stand for 5 minutes.

2. Microwave on High, uncovered, for 3 minutes. Stir, then microwave on High for 2½ to 3 minutes or until mixture comes to a full boil.

½ teaspoon vanilla

3. Stir in vanilla. Set aside while preparing egg white.

2 tablespoons sugar

4. Beat egg white until foamy. Gradually beat in 2 tablespoons sugar, beating until soft peaks form. Gradually fold in hot mixture. Serve warm or chilled.

Easy Rice Pudding

Let it stand during the meal; then spoon it into 4 to 6 dessert bowls

3 cups milk
1 package (3¼ oz) vanilla pudding and pie filling mix
1 cup packaged precooked rice
½ cup raisins
¼ teaspoon salt

1. Mix all ingredients together in a 2-quart glass casserole.

2. Microwave on High, covered, for 8 to 9 minutes, stirring twice. Let stand for 10 to 20 minutes or until set.

Tip: *Sprinkle with cinnamon before serving.*

Butterscotch Bread Pudding

Short-cut method, serves 4

1 package (4 oz) butterscotch pudding and pie filling mix
2 cups milk
⅓ cup raisins
1⅓ cups soft white bread cubes, without crust

1. Combine all ingredients in a 1-quart glass casserole, mixing well.

2. Microwave on High, uncovered, for 6 to 7 minutes or until mixture begins to boil and thicken. Stir every minute during the last 3 to 4 minutes of microwave time. Serve warm or cooled.

Tip: *Serve with dollops of whipped cream.*

Old-Fashioned Bread Pudding

6 stick-to-the-ribs servings, made from scratch

4 cups soft bread cubes (day-old bread)
½ cup seedless raisins

1¾ cups milk
1 tablespoon margarine

3 large eggs, slightly beaten
½ cup sugar

1 teaspoon cinnamon or nutmeg
¼ teaspoon salt
½ teaspoon vanilla

1. Place bread cubes in a 10x6-inch glass dish. Sprinkle with raisins. Set aside.

2. Place milk and margarine in a 4-cup glass measure. Microwave on High for 3½ minutes or until almost boiling.

3. Meanwhile, beat eggs slightly in a medium bowl. Add sugar, beating until well mixed.

4. Stir cinnamon and salt into egg mixture. Slowly stir in hot milk. Add vanilla; stir.

5. Pour over bread cubes and raisins, stirring to moisten well. Microwave on Low for 15 minutes, rotating dish every 5 minutes.

Meats

General

As you browse through this chapter, you'll find many recipes for your favorite meats. Some are basic roasts; others are elegant entrees. You'll find recipes for family meals, as well as for company brunches and buffets.

This chapter is divided into three sections:

● Beef, including veal
● Lamb
● Pork, including bacon, ham, and sausage

Each section begins with the basics—instructions and a chart to help you prepare that particular meat (beef roasts, meat loaf, and patties, for instance). Use these basic instructions as you adapt your favorite recipes to microwave methods.

A few generalized tips follow. These will apply to all meats as you prepare them in the microwave oven.

Utensils. Select an appropriate glass dish, as specified in the recipe. Cover it to help prevent spatters. Some specialized utensils are:

● Nonmetallic roasting rack: For meats that develop drippings, use a nonmetallic roasting rack to elevate the meat above the glass dish. Meat juice and fat will then drain away from the meat during microwave time, permitting you to baste them off.

If you do not have a nonmetallic roasting rack, use an inverted saucer. However, the saucer must be able to withstand the weight and heat of the food without breaking. It must also be suitable for microwave use.

● Skewers: Use wooden skewers. Metal ones will cause arcing.
● Browning Skillet accessory is available from your Frigidaire Dealer at extra charge. Follow instructions supplied with it.

Salt and other seasonings. Do not salt meat before microwave time. Salt draws the natural moisture out of the meat, resulting in dry meat. After the meat is cooked, salt it to taste.

You may add other seasonings, as desired, before microwave time.

Browning. Browning will occur with larger roasts that require over 15 minutes of microwave time. The meat fats reach high temperatures, allowing browning to occur. If the roast has a thin area, use the Shielding technique (see page 12) to prevent overcooking of this area before the thicker areas are done.

Browning does not occur with smaller cuts of meat. To achieve a browned exterior, you may wish to:

● Use a dark ingredient on the meat's surface: a gravy mix, dry onion soup paste, Kitchen Bouquet, Worcestershire sauce, soy sauce, teriyaki sauce, etc.
● Use a jelly glaze.
● Use the Browning Skillet accessory.
● Use the conventional range or grill to sear the meat. Then finish cooking it in the microwave oven.

Steaks. To sear steaks, use the Browning Skillet accessory, or use a conventional method (broiler, grill, etc). See recipe on page 108 for more specifics.

Roasts. Choose compact roasts, weighing three pounds or more. A boned, rolled, and tied beef roast is an excellent example of a compact shape. Generally such roasts cook more evenly than do the irregularly shaped ones. Choose lamb and pork roasts accordingly.

Baste off juice and excess moisture during microwave time, using a spoon or baster. Reserve the liquid drippings for gravy, if desired.

To serve rare, medium, and well done portions of beef at the same meal, remove the roast at minimum doneness; carve off servings. Return the rest of the roast, or an individual serving, to the microwave oven for more cooking, as required.

Rolled Rib Roast (page 106); Canned Carrots (page 198); Frozen Brussels Sprouts (page 197)

Pot roasts, braised beef. These dishes are generally made from less tender cuts of meat. To help tenderize the meat, follow these tips.

Cut the meat lengthwise into pieces that you can easily turn and rearrange during microwave time. Place the meat in a glass baking dish. Add a sauce and let marinate, covered, for several hours or overnight in the refrigerator, if desired.

Microwave on Low, covered with plastic film. Before you remove the film, pierce it and wait for steam to escape. Then turn the meat, rearrange it, and continue with the recipe.

Microwave instructions. Microwave more tender cuts of meat on Medium. For less tender cuts, you may wish to marinate them for several hours or overnight; then microwave on Low.

For larger roasts, microwave on High for 5 or 10 minutes to start the cooking. Then switch to Medium and continue to microwave as specified. See the basic instructions and charts in this chapter for more details.

Turn the meat during microwave time, as specified in the individual recipes and charts.

Meat thermometer. Never use a conventional meat thermometer in an operating microwave oven. See page 13 for the out-of-the-oven technique.

To use a thermometer specifically designed for microwave use, follow manufacturer's instructions. A Frigidaire Microwave Thermometer is available from your Frigidaire Dealer, at extra charge.

Standing time. Remove meat while it is slightly underdone. Let stand as specified in the recipe and charts; cooking will continue during this standing time. Internal temperature of roasts may rise as much as 10° to 15°F.

If the meat does not finish cooking as completely as you prefer during the standing time, remove the conventional meat thermometer. Then return the meat to the microwave oven for as long as needed. Pork should always be served well done.

Beef and Veal

Roast Beef, Roast Veal

Pictured on page 104

1. Place the roast on a nonmetallic roasting rack in a glass baking dish, fat side down.
2. Microwave as specified in the chart. In general, for most roasts over four pounds (see chart) microwave on High for 10 minutes to start. Then switch to Medium and microwave according to weight. Turn fat side up halfway through total microwave time.

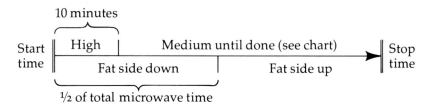

(Instructions and chart are continued on the next page.)

3. During microwave time, baste off any excess juice as it accumulates so it doesn't slow the cooking process. Set aside for gravy, if desired.

4. During the last quarter of microwave time, check internal temperature. Remove the roast when the temperature specified in the chart is reached.

   ● Do not use a conventional meat thermometer in an operating microwave oven. See page 13 for out-of-the-oven technique.

   ● Follow manufacturer's instructions if you use a thermometer specifically designed for microwave use.

5. Cover the roast loosely with foil, dull side out. Let stand as specified in the chart. Temperatures will continue to rise during this standing time.

6. Season to taste before serving.

Beef/Veal	Degree of Doneness	Total Microwave Time	Microwave Instructions	Internal Temp at Stop Time	Standing Time, covered (Temp continues to rise)
Standing Rib, 6 to 9 lb	Rare Medium Well	10 min + 7 to 8 min/lb 10 min + 8 to 9 min/lb 10 min + 9 to 11 min/lb	High for 10 min; then Medium for specified min/lb	130° F 140° F 155° F	10 to 20 min
Rolled Rib, 4 to 6 lb	Rare Medium Well	10 min + 8 to 9 min/lb 10 min + 9 to 10 min/lb 10 min + 10 to 12 min/lb	Start with fat side down; turn fat side up halfway through total microwave time	130° F 140° F 155° F	10 to 20 min
Sirloin Tip, 4 to 6 lb	Rare Medium Well	10 min + 10 to 12 min/lb 10 min + 12 to 14 min/lb 10 min + 14 to 16 min/lb		130° F 140° F 155° F	10 to 20 min
Rump Roast, 4 to 6 lb	Well	10 min + 14 to 16 min/lb	High for 10 min; then Medium for 1st half of min/lb; then Low for remaining time	155° F	10 to 20 min
Veal Roast, 2 to 4 lb	Medium	13 to 15 min/lb	Medium	170° F	10 to 20 min

Ground Beef

1. For individual patties, microwave on High, covered, until done. See Hamburgers, page 172. Use the Frigidaire Browning Skillet accessory if desired.
2. For meat loaf, microwave on Medium, uncovered, until done.

Beef/Veal	Degree of Doneness	Total Microwave Time	Microwave Instructions	Internal Temp at Stop Time	Standing Time, covered (Temp continues to rise)
Meat Loaf, 1 to 2 lb	Medium	14 to 16 min/lb	Medium	140° F	5 to 10 min
Patties, 1 lb	Medium	5 to 7 min/lb	High	—	2 to 5 min

T-bone or Sirloin Steaks

Team up the microwave oven with conventional broiler, outside grill, or Browning Skillet

T-bone steaks, or Sirloin steaks

These steaks cook so quickly in the microwave oven that little or no browning occurs. For best results, follow one of these suggestions:

A. Cook steaks ahead of time on outside grill, or broil in conventional oven (use metal pan) to desired doneness. Refrigerate. When ready to serve, place in a glass dish and microwave on High until hot.

B. Or, arrange steak on a nonmetallic roasting rack in a shallow glass dish. Microwave on High for 2 or 3 minutes. Finish cooking under broil unit in conventional oven (use metal pan) or on outside grill. Steak will brown and finish cooking quickly.

C. Or, use Frigidaire Browning Skillet accessory. Preheat on High. Add steak. Microwave on High for 2 or 3 minutes, turning halfway through microwave time.

Tip: *To add color and flavor, marinate steak for several hours in teriyaki sauce, or brush with soy sauce.*

Swiss Steak

6 simmering-good servings

1 can (1 lb) tomatoes

2 pounds round steak, ½ inch thick

1 envelope dry onion soup mix

1 green pepper, sliced

1 tablespoon flour

1. Drain tomatoes, reserving ½ cup juice.

2. Cut steak into serving pieces, and place in a 2-quart glass casserole. Sprinkle with soup mix. Add green pepper and drained tomatoes.

3. Mix reserved tomato juice and flour in a 1-cup glass measure. Microwave on High for 1½ minutes or until hot and thickened. Pour over steak.

4. Microwave on Low, covered, for 50 to 55 minutes.

Sukiyaki

An oriental dinner for 4

1½ pounds round or sirloin steak

1 tablespoon shortening

1 can (5 oz) bamboo shoots, drained

1 can (4 oz) water chestnuts, drained

1 can (16 oz) bean sprouts, drained

1 can (3 or 4 oz) mushrooms, or ½ pound fresh mushrooms, sliced

1 medium onion, thinly sliced

3 stalks celery, sliced diagonally

3 tablespoons sugar

⅓ cup soy sauce

½ cup beef bouillon

1. Slice steak very thinly, diagonally across the grain.

2. Place shortening in a 3-quart glass casserole. Microwave on High for 30 seconds or until melted. Add beef strips. Microwave on High for 5 minutes or until meat has lost its pink color. Stir once.

3. Arrange browned meat strips in center of dish. Add vegetables around meat.

4. Combine sugar, soy sauce, and bouillon. Pour over meat and vegetables.

5. Microwave on Medium for 8 to 10 minutes. Do not overcook. Vegetables should be quite crisp.

Shish Kabobs

Use wooden skewers

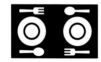

16 cubes (¾ in) sirloin steak
16 squares green pepper
12 fresh or canned mushroom caps
8 small whole onions, canned or frozen

Steak or barbecue sauce

1. Thread meat and vegetables alternately on four wooden skewers, starting and ending with steak cubes. Lay four kabobs diagonally across a 12x7½-inch glass dish.

2. Brush with sauce on all sides. Microwave on High, uncovered, for 5 minutes.

3. Roll kabobs halfway over; rotate dish. Microwave on High for 5 to 7 minutes.

Tips: *For easier threading, pierce foods first with a metal skewer; then slide onto a wooden skewer.*

Serve 2 shish kabobs over a bed of rice per person.

Double the recipe for 4 servings.

Pot Roast with Vegetables

Old-fashioned good; serves 6 to 8

1 tablespoon butter or margarine

3 pounds pot roast
1½ teaspoons salt
2 large onions, sliced

1 can (16 oz) stewed tomatoes
1 tablespoon sugar
2 tablespoons minced green pepper
3 to 4 medium carrots, peeled and sliced ½ inch thick
5 to 6 small red potatoes, scraped
2 stalks celery, cut on slant, 1-inch pieces
Salt
Pepper

1. Place butter in a 3-quart glass casserole. Microwave on High for 30 seconds or until melted.

2. Add boned pot roast. Season with salt, and cover with sliced onions. Microwave on High, covered, for 10 minutes. Rotate dish halfway through microwave time.

3. Add remaining ingredients. Microwave on Low, covered, for 60 to 80 minutes, or until meat and vegetables are tender. Season to taste with salt and pepper.

Burgundy Pot Roast

Slow cooking allows flavors to develop; serves 6

3 pounds beef chuck roast
¼ cup prepared horseradish

¾ cup Burgundy wine
½ package dry onion soup

2 bay leaves
6 whole allspice
Beau Monde seasoning salt
Mei Yen seasoning salt
Salt
Pepper

1. Brown pot roast in Browning Skillet accessory or in skillet on range. Transfer to a 3-quart glass casserole. Spread the entire exterior surface of the roast with horseradish. Set aside.

2. Combine Burgundy and dry onion soup mix in a 2-cup glass measure. Microwave on High for 1¼ minutes.

3. Pour Burgundy mixture over roast without washing off the horseradish. Add bay leaves, allspice, salts, and pepper. Microwave on Low, covered, for 90 minutes or until meat is tender.

Braised Beef with Mushroom Gravy

This method tenderizes the meat

3 pounds beef chuck (arm pot roast)

1 package Brown Gravy mix

1 beef-flavored bouillon cube
¼ cup boiling water
1 can (4 oz) sliced mushrooms

1. Cut beef into serving-size pieces. Place in 12x7½-inch glass baking dish. Microwave on High for 10 minutes.

2. Turn beef pieces over. Sprinkle gravy mix on all pieces.

3. Dissolve bouillon cube in water. Pour broth over meat. Spread mushrooms on top of meat. Cover with plastic film. Microwave on Low for 30 minutes.

4. Turn pieces over and recover. Microwave on Low, covered, for 30 minutes longer or until fork tender.

Company Stroganoff

4 to 6 servings that you will be proud to serve

1½ teaspoons salt
¼ teaspoon pepper
2 medium onions, sliced and separated into rings
2 tablespoons butter or margarine

1 pound beef tenderloin, sliced ¼ inch thick
1 can (10½ oz) condensed cream of chicken soup
1 can (4 oz) sliced mushrooms with liquid

½ pint dairy sour cream
Buttered noodles

1. Combine salt, pepper, onions, and butter in a 2-quart glass casserole. Microwave on Medium, covered, for 6 or 7 minutes or until onions are tender.

2. Add meat, soup, and mushrooms. Stir together. Microwave on Medium, covered, for 10 to 12 minutes or until heated through.

3. Stir in sour cream, and serve over buttered noodles.

Tip: *Make ahead through step 2, stopping when meat is slightly underdone. Freeze. To finish, thaw overnight in the refrigerator. Microwave on High, covered, until reheated and meat is done. Then continue with step 3.*

Meatball Stroganoff

This easy version serves 4

1 pound ground beef

1 tablespoon butter or margarine

1 package stroganoff sauce mix
1⅓ cups milk

¾ cup packaged precooked rice

1. Shape ground beef into twenty meatballs. Set aside.

2. Place butter in an 8x8x2-inch glass dish. Microwave on High for 30 seconds or until melted.

3. Add meatballs. Microwave on High for 7 minutes or until meat loses its pink color. Stir once during microwave time.

4. Sprinkle sauce mix over meatballs and drippings. Gradually stir in milk, blending thoroughly. Microwave on Medium for 6 minutes or until bubbly.

5. Add rice and mix well. Cover with plastic film; let stand for 5 minutes.

Ground Beef Stroganoff

A family dish for 4

1 pound ground beef
½ cup finely chopped onion

1 can (4 oz) mushrooms,
   drained
2 tablespoons flour
1 teaspoon salt
½ teaspoon paprika
1 can (10½ oz) condensed
   cream of chicken soup

½ pint dairy sour cream

Cooked noodles or rice

1. Place ground beef and onion in a 2-quart glass casserole. Microwave on High for 6 minutes. Stir halfway through microwave time.

2. Add mushrooms, flour, salt, and paprika. Blend in soup.

3. Microwave on Medium for 7 minutes.

4. Add sour cream. Microwave on Medium for 4 minutes or until heated through.

5. Serve over cooked noodles or rice.

Family Meat Loaf

Serves 4 to 6

Mix up an extra loaf and freeze it uncooked

1 pound lean ground beef
1 egg, beaten
6 saltines, crushed
1 small onion, minced
1 tablespoon minced parsley
1 teaspoon garlic powder
¾ teaspoon salt
¼ teaspoon pepper
¼ cup chopped green
   pepper
¼ cup chopped celery
½ cup tomato juice

¼ cup catsup

1. Toss together all ingredients except catsup; mix lightly but thoroughly. Spoon into an 8x4-inch glass loaf dish; do not pack.

2. Microwave on Medium, uncovered, for 12 minutes.

3. Spread catsup over top of meat loaf. Rotate dish a half-turn. Microwave on Medium for 12 minutes longer.

4. Let stand for 5 minutes before slicing.

Jiffy Meat Loaf

Use onion soup mix for seasoning; serves 6

1 pound ground beef
⅔ cup (6 oz can) evaporated milk
1 package (1¼ oz) dry onion soup mix

1. Combine ingredients in a medium-size bowl.

2. Spoon into a 9x5-inch glass loaf pan. Do not pack.

3. Microwave on Medium, uncovered, for 12 minutes.

4. Rotate dish. Microwave on Medium for 12 minutes longer.

Swedish Meatballs

Serve with woodenpicks at your next party buffet; makes 2 dozen

⅔ cup milk
½ cup dry bread crumbs

½ pound ground round steak
½ pound ground lean pork
1 egg, beaten
1 teaspoon salt
¼ teaspooon pepper
1 tablespoon steak sauce
1 tablespoon instant minced onion

1. Pour milk over bread crumbs. Let stand for 15 minutes.

2. Lightly mix in meats, egg, and seasonings. Shap into 24 balls.

3. Arrange 12 meatballs in a 1½-quart glass dish. Microwave on High, uncovered, for 3 minutes. Turn meatballs over, and microwave on High for 3 minutes longer. Remove meatballs from dish and set aside. Repeat with 12 more meatballs.

2 tablespoons butter or margarine
¼ cup flour
1 cup water
2 teaspoons instant bouillon

4. Remove meatballs from dish; add 2 tablespoons butter to dish. Microwave on High for 30 seconds or until melted. Sprinkle in flour, and mix until a smooth paste. Gradually blend in water and bouillon. Microwave on High for 3 minutes. Stir every 30 seconds with a wire whisk.

5. Place meatballs in gravy. Microwave on High, covered, for 3 minutes.

Tip: *For more browning, brown meatballs in 2 tablespoons shortening in Frigidaire Browning Skillet accessory. Omit step 3.*

Sweet and Sour Meatballs

Makes 20; see page 25 for a tomato soup version

1 egg, slightly beaten
1 pound ground beef
¼ cup fine dry bread crumbs
2 tablespoons chopped onion
1 teaspoon salt
Dash of pepper
½ cup water

1. In medium bowl beat egg; add ground beef, bread crumbs, onion, salt, pepper, and ½ cup water. Mix until well blended. Shape into 20 meatballs, about 1½ inches in diameter.

2 tablespoons cooking oil

2. Place oil and 10 meatballs in a 3-quart glass casserole. Microwave on High, uncovered, for 3 minutes. Turn meatballs; microwave on High for 3 minutes longer. Remove meatballs and set aside. Repeat with remaining meatballs. Remove and set aside.

1 cup sliced celery
2 green peppers, cut into strips

3. Place celery and green pepper in casserole. Microwave on High, uncovered, for 5 minutes or until soft, stirring once. Set aside.

1½ cups water
⅓ cup vinegar
⅓ cup brown sugar
2 tablespoons soy sauce
2 tablespoons cornstarch
2 tablespoons cold water

4. Combine 1½ cups water, vinegar, brown sugar, and soy sauce in a 1-quart glass casserole. Mix cornstarch and cold water. Stir into sauce mixture. Microwave on High for 5 minutes, or until thickened, stirring every minute.

4 pineapple slices, cut into quarters

5. Return meatballs to casserole with celery and green pepper. Add pineapple and sauce mixture. Mix until all is covered with sauce. Microwave on High, covered, for 4 minutes, or until heated through.

Salisbury Steak

6 patties in a golden mushroom sauce

1½ pounds ground beef
1 can (10½ oz) condensed golden mushroom soup
½ cup dry bread crumbs
1 egg, slightly beaten
¼ cup chopped onion
Dash of pepper
⅓ cup milk

1. Combine ground beef, ¼ cup soup, bread crumbs, egg, onion, pepper, and milk. Shape into 6 patties; place in a 2-quart glass dish.

2. Microwave on High for 10 minutes. Turn patties and drain fat halfway through microwave time.

⅓ cup water

3. Blend remaining soup with water. Pour over meat. Cover dish with plastic film; pierce a hole for steam to escape. Microwave on High for 4 minutes longer.

Stuffed Cabbage Rolls

12 to 16 rolls for a hearty family meal

12 to 16 cabbage leaves
½ teaspoon salt
2 cups boiling water

1 pound ground beef
1½ cups soft bread crumbs
½ cup finely chopped onion
2 eggs, beaten
1½ teaspoons salt
¼ teaspoon pepper

1 can (10¾ oz) condensed
    tomato soup

1. Place cabbage leaves and salt in a 3-quart glass casserole. Pour boiling water over leaves. Microwave on High, covered, for 5 minutes. Let stand, covered, while preparing meat mixture.

2. Combine ground beef, bread crumbs, onion, eggs, salt, and pepper. Drain cabbage leaves. Place about ¼ cup of meat mixture on each leaf. Roll and secure with a woodenpick.

3. Place rolls in a 12x7½-inch glass dish; top with tomato soup. Cover dish with plastic film.

4. Microwave on High for 15 minutes. Pierce plastic film to release steam before removing film from dish.

Stuffed Peppers

A good way to use up leftover roast beef; makes 4

4 medium green peppers

1 cup finely diced, cooked
    roast beef
1 cup cooked rice
1 can (7½ oz) tomato sauce
¼ cup finely chopped celery
1 tablespoon minced onion
½ teaspoon seasoned salt
Dash pepper

1. Wash peppers. Slice off tops; remove seeds and membrane. Arrange peppers in a 2-quart glass casserole. Set aside.

2. Combine remaining ingredients; spoon into peppers.

3. Microwave on Medium, covered, for 12 to 15 minutes or until peppers are done and filling is heated through.

Tip: *Prepare peppers ahead through step 2. Wrap and freeze. To finish, microwave on Low until defrosted; then continue with step 3.*

Creamed Dried Beef

Doesn't require as much stirring as with conventional methods; serves 2

3 tablespoons butter or margarine

3 tablespoons flour

1½ cups milk

1 package (4 oz) dried beef Pepper

Toast

1. Place butter in a 1-quart glass casserole. Microwave on High for 30 to 45 seconds or until melted.

2. Stir in flour. Blend to smooth paste. Microwave on High for 1 minute.

3. Gradually stir in milk. Microwave on High for 4 minutes, stirring every minute.

4. Tear dried beef into pieces, and stir into sauce. Season with pepper. Microwave on High for 1 minute.

5. Serve over toast.

Veal Scallopini

4 servings can marinate overnight in refrigerator

1 pound thinly sliced veal
¼ cup vegetable oil
1 clove garlic

¾ cup sliced onion
1 can (6 oz) mushrooms, drained

2 tablespoons flour
½ teaspoon salt
⅛ teaspoon pepper

1 can (8 oz) tomato sauce
½ cup water

1. Place veal, vegetable oil, and garlic in a 3-quart glass casserole. Microwave on High, covered, for 2 to 3 minutes, or until meat has lost its pink color. Turn meat halfway through microwave time. Remove garlic and veal from oil. Set veal aside.

2. Stir onions and mushrooms into oil. Microwave on High, covered, for 3 minutes.

3. Stir in flour, salt, and pepper until well blended. Microwave on High, covered, for 2 minutes.

4. Gradually stir in tomato sauce and water. Microwave on Medium, covered, for 8 minutes. Stir halfway through microwave time.

5. Return veal to casserole. Microwave on Medium, covered, for 9 minutes or until veal is tender.

Tips: *Brown veal in Frigidaire Browning Skillet accessory, if desired.*

For more tender veal, prepare as above, and let marinate overnight in refrigerator. To reheat, microwave on High.

Lamb

Roast Lamb

1. Place the roast on a nonmetallic roasting rack in a glass baking dish, fat side down.

2. Microwave as specified in the chart. In general, for roasts over 4 pounds, microwave on High for 5 to 10 minutes to start. Then switch to Medium and microwave according to weight. Turn roast over several times during the total microwave time.

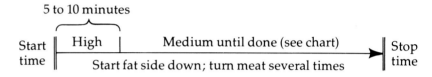

3. During microwave time, baste off any excess juice as it accumulates so it doesn't slow the cooking process. Set aside for gravy, if desired.

4. During the last quarter of microwave time, check internal temperature. Remove roast when the temperature specified in the chart is reached.

   • Do not use a conventional meat thermometer in an operating microwave oven. See page 13 for out-of-the-oven technique.

   • Follow manufacturer's instructions if you use a thermometer specifically designed for microwave use.

5. Cover the roast loosely with foil, dull side out. Let stand as specified in the chart. Temperatures will continue to rise during this standing time.

6. Season to taste before serving.

(Chart is continued on next page.)

Lamb Chops and Patties

1. Arrange pieces in a glass dish. Place larger, meaty areas around the outer edges of the dish; narrower, bony areas toward the center.
2. Cover dish with plastic film.
3. Microwave on Medium, covered, as specified in the chart or until fork tender.
4. Let stand, covered, for temperatures to equalize. Before removing the film, pierce a hole in it for steam to escape.

Tip: *Brown chops and patties in the Frigidaire Browning Skillet accessory, if desired.*

Lamb	Degree of Doneness	Total Microwave Time	Microwave Instructions	Internal Temp at Stop Time	Standing Time, covered (Temp continues to rise)
Leg, 5 to 7 lb	Medium	10 min + 9 to 11 min/lb	High for 5 to 10 min; then Medium for specified min/lb	155° F	10 to 15 min
	Well	10 min + 10 to 12 min/lb	Start with fat side down; turn fat side up halfway through total microwave time	160° F	10 to 15 min
Shoulder Roast, Rolled, 3 to 5 lb	Well	10 min + 9 to 11 min/lb		160° F	5 to 10 min
Loin Chops, 1½ to 2½ lb	Well	9 to 11 min/lb	Medium	—	2 to 5 min
Ground Patties, 1 to 2 lb	Well	8 to 10 min/lb	Medium	—	2 to 5 min

Roast Leg of Lamb

A springtime holiday treat, served with a tasty sauce

**6-pound leg of lamb
Clove of garlic**

1. Place a nonmetallic roasting rack in a 12x7½-inch glass dish. Rub lamb with clove of garlic. Place lamb, fat side down, on rack. Microwave on High, uncovered, for 5 minutes.

2. Switch to Medium; continue to microwave, uncovered, for 30 minutes.

Mint Sauce, or Orange Marmalade Sauce (recipes follow)

3. Turn lamb fat side up. Baste with sauce. Rotate dish. Microwave on Medium for 25 minutes or until internal temperature registers 155° to 160° F, basting once more with sauce.

4. Cover with foil; let stand for 10 minutes. Cooking will continue during standing time.

Tips: *See page 13 for how to use a conventional meat thermometer.*

Cooking time will vary with the size leg of lamb and bone structure. If required, slice lamb after standing time and microwave on Medium to finish cooking to desired doneness.

Mint Sauce

**⅔ cup mint jelly
2 tablespoons flour
2 teaspoons grated lemon peel
1 teaspoon parsley flakes
1 teaspoon salt
½ teaspoon pepper**

Sauces to accompany Leg of Lamb

1. Combine all ingredients for either sauce in a small bowl. Mix well. Use to baste lamb.

2. If you desire to serve extra sauce at the table, microwave on High for 1 to 2 minutes or until bubbly and thickened.

Orange Marmalade Sauce

**½ cup orange marmalade
2 tablespoons flour
1 teaspoon grated lemon peel
1 teaspoon powdered ginger
1 teaspoon parsley flakes
1 teaspoon salt
½ teaspoon pepper**

Lamb Kabobs (page 123); over a Bed of Rice (page 162)

Glazed Lamb Shoulder

Serve with an orange-almond-mint sauce

4 pounds rolled lamb shoulder roast

1 can (6 oz) frozen orange juice concentrate, thawed
¼ cup lemon juice
¼ cup butter or margarine
1 tablespoon flour
½ teaspoon salt

1. Place roast, fat side down, on a nonmetallic roasting rack in a 12x7½-inch glass dish.

2. In a 1-quart glass casserole combine orange juice concentrate, lemon juice, butter, flour, and salt. Microwave on High, uncovered, for 3 minutes or until boiling.

3. Brush roast with orange sauce. Microwave on Medium for 24 minutes. Halfway through microwave time brush meat with sauce again; rotate dish.

4. Turn roast fat side up and brush with sauce. Microwave on Medium for 24 minutes longer, or until thermometer registers 155° to 160° F. Halfway through microwave time brush with sauce again; rotate dish.

5. Remove roast to serving platter. Cover with foil, and let stand for 10 minutes. Cooking will continue during standing time.

½ cup finely chopped celery
½ cup slivered blanched almonds
1 tablespoon mint flakes, or ¼ cup chopped fresh mint

6. Add celery, almonds, and mint flakes to remaining sauce. Microwave on High for 2 to 3 minutes or until hot. Serve over sliced lamb.

Tip: *See page 13 for how to use a conventional meat thermometer.*

Lamb Kabobs

Thread marinated foods onto wooden skewers; serves 4 to 6

Pictured on page 120

½ cup wine vinegar
½ teaspoon cinnamon
½ teaspoon powdered clove

1 onion, chopped
1 clove garlic, minced
1 cup oil
2 pounds leg of lamb or shoulder, uncooked, cut into 1½-inch cubes

1 pint cherry tomatoes, cut in halves
2 green peppers, cut in 1¼-inch squares
1 bag (20 oz) frozen small whole onions, thawed
1 pound fresh mushrooms, washed and stems removed

½ cup bottled barbecue sauce
2 tablespoons brown sugar

Cooked rice

1. Combine vinegar, cinnamon, and cloves. Microwave on High for 1½ minutes. Cool.

2. Combine onion, garlic, and oil in a 2-quart glass casserole. Add vinegar mixture. Stir in meat pieces. Cover; let stand at room temperature for 2 hours or overnight in the refrigerator.

3. Alternate tomatoes, green pepper, onions, mushrooms and meat on 10-inch wooden skewers. Prepare 8 to 12 kabobs.

4. Place 4 kabobs diagonally across a 12x7½-inch glass dish. Brush on mixture of barbecue sauce and sugar. Microwave on High, uncovered, for 3 minutes. Drain excess juice, and turn kabobs. Microwave on Medium for 10 minutes. Repeat this for each set of 4 kabobs.

5. Serve with cooked rice, allowing 2 kabobs per person.

Tips: *For easier threading, pierce foods first with a metal skewer; then slide onto a wooden skewer.*

Cook kabobs ahead of time; cover and refrigerate. Reheat just before serving.

For variety, substitute bottled garlic salad dressing for marinade.

Cheese-Capped Lamb Chops

3 servings, topped with melted cheese

6 lamb chops, ½ inch thick

1. Arrange lamb chops in a 12x7½-inch glass dish; cover dish with plastic film. Microwave on High for 4 minutes.

2. Pierce a hole in the film for steam to escape. Remove the film. Microwave on Medium, uncovered, for 4 minutes.

3. Drain fat. Turn chops, and rotate dish. Microwave on Medium, uncovered, for 4 minutes longer.

½ cup grated Swiss cheese, or crumbled blue cheese
2 green onions, chopped, including tops
¼ teaspoon salt

4. Combine cheese, onion, and salt. Spread over top of each chop. Microwave on High, uncovered, for 30 seconds to melt cheese.

Lamb Patties

Makes 4 jelly-topped patties

1 pound ground lamb
2 tablespoons bacon onion seasoning
1 tablespoon chopped parsley

1. Combine ground lamb, seasoning, and parsley. Shape into 4 patties about 1 inch thick. Place patties on a nonmetallic roasting rack in a 12x7½-inch glass dish. Cover dish with plastic film.

2. Microwave on Medium, covered, for 10 minutes. Rotate dish halfway through microwave time.

¼ cup currant jelly
⅛ teaspoon grated orange peel

3. Combine jelly and orange peel. Pierce a hole in the film for steam to escape. Spread jelly mixture over patties just before serving.

Ragout Lamb

Quick; 4 very tasty servings from yesterday's roast

2 tablespoons butter or margarine
¼ cup chopped onion
¼ cup thinly sliced celery
¼ cup chopped green pepper

1. Place butter, onion, celery, and green pepper in a 1½-quart glass casserole. Microwave on High, covered, for 2 minutes.

1 can (10½ oz) chicken gravy
2 cups cubed cooked lamb
⅔ cup pared, diced apple
½ teaspoon allspice
¼ teaspoon Beau Monde seasoned salt

2. Add remaining ingredients except toast. Stir until well blended. Microwave on Medium, covered, for 8 to 10 minutes or until heated through.

4 slices of toast

3. Serve over toast.

Tip: *Substitute curry for allspice, if desired.*

Lamb Imperial

Casserole made with rice, peas, and yesterday's roast; serves 4 to 6

1 cup water
1 chicken bouillon cube
1 tablespoon butter or margarine
½ teaspoon salt
½ teaspoon sweet basil
½ teaspoon grated orange peel
2 tablespoons orange juice

1 cup packaged precooked rice

1 medium onion, finely chopped
1 small green pepper, chopped
2 tablespoons butter or margarine
2 cups cubed cooked lamb

1 package (10 oz) frozen peas, thawed

1. Combine water, bouillon, butter, salt, basil, orange peel and juice in a 1½-quart glass casserole. Microwave on High, covered, for 2 minutes.

2. Stir in rice. Cover and let stand.

3. Combine onion, green pepper, and butter in a 4-cup glass measure. Microwave on High for 3 minutes. Stir in cubed lamb.

4. In a 2-quart glass casserole arrange by layers: ½ rice mixture, ½ peas, ½ lamb mixture. Repeat layers, ending with lamb mixture. Microwave on Medium, covered, for 8 minutes.

Lamb Loaf

Tasty family dish; serves 6 to 8

1½ pounds ground lamb
1½ cups soft bread crumbs
½ cup milk
1 egg
¾ cup cooked rice
2 tablespoons chopped pimento
¼ cup chopped onion
1 tablespoon chopped parsley
1½ teaspoons Beau Monde seasoned salt
⅛ teaspoon pepper
1 cup cooked peas

1 tablespoon soy sauce

1. Combine all ingredients except peas and soy sauce in a large bowl. Mix well. Add peas and mix lightly. Spread into an 8x8x2-inch glass dish. Do not pack tightly. Cover dish with plastic film.

2. Microwave on Medium, covered, for 10 minutes.

3. Pierce a hole in the film for steam to escape; remove the film. Drain fat. Brush soy sauce over top of meat. Rotate dish.

4. Microwave on Medium, covered, for 11 to 13 minutes longer.

Pork

Roast Pork, Baked Ham

1. Place the roast on a nonmetallic roasting rack in a glass baking dish, fat side down.

2. Microwave as specified in the chart. In general, microwave hams on Medium until heated. If necessary, shield small areas on top of ham during last half of microwave time. (See Shielding, page 12.)

   For pork roasts over 4 pounds, microwave on High for 10 minutes to start. Then switch to Medium, and microwave according to weight. Turn fat side up halfway through total microwave time; rotate dish.

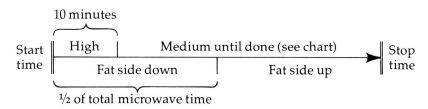

3. During microwave time, baste off any excess juice as it accumulates so it doesn't slow the cooking process. Set aside for gravy, if desired.

4. During the last quarter of microwave time, check internal temperature. Remove the roast when the temperature specified in the chart is reached.

   • Do not use a conventional meat thermometer in an operating microwave oven. See page 13 for out-of-the-oven technique.

   • Follow manufacturer's instructions if you use a thermometer specifically designed for microwave use.

5. Cover the roast loosely with foil, dull side out. Let stand as specified in the chart. Temperatures will continue to rise during this standing time. Meat is done when the juice and meat are no longer pink. Pork roasts should be well done at the end of standing time. If not, return to the microwave oven, as needed.

   (Chart is continued on next page.)

Pork/Ham	Degree of Doneness	Total Microwave Time	Microwave Instructions	Internal Temp at Stop Time	Standing Time, covered (Temp continues to rise)
Pork Loin, Center Rib, 4 to 5 lb	Well	10 min + 12 to 14 min/lb	High for 10 min; then Medium for specified min/lb	170° F	10 to 20 min
Pork Loin, Boneless, 4 to 5 lb	Well	10 min + 12 to 14 min/lb	Start with fat side down; turn fat side up halfway through total microwave time	170° F	10 to 20 min
Ham, fully cooked, 4 to 6 lb	Heated	10 to 12 min/lb	Medium	130° F	10 to 20 min
Ham, Canned 3 to 5 lb	Heated	8 to 9 min/lb	Medium	130° F	10 to 20 min
Ham Steaks, fully cooked, 1 to 2½ lb	Heated	8 to 10 min/lb	Medium	—	5 to 10 min

Sausage Links, Patties

1. Prick or score sausage links, allowing for steam to escape.
2. Arrange in an appropriate utensil (see chart), and cover.
3. Microwave as specified in the chart.

Sausage	Utensil	Microwave Instructions	Special Instructions
Bratwurst or similar sausage, 2 links (4 oz)	1-quart glass casserole, covered	High for 4 minutes	Turn sausage twice
Brown & Serve Sausage, 1 package (8 oz)	9-inch glass pie dish, lined with paper towels	High for 5 minutes	Turn sausage once
Sausage Links 12 links (12-oz pkg)	12x7½-inch glass dish with nonmetallic roasting rack	High for 7 to 8 minutes	After 5 min, drain fat and rotate dish. Finish cooking
Sausage Patties 11 to 12 patties (1 lb)	Cover with plastic film. Pierce hole for steam to escape before removing the film	High for 8 to 10 minutes	Let stand, covered, for 3 min

Bacon, Canadian Bacon

1. Line an appropriate utensil (see chart) with paper towels.
2. Spread bacon across paper towels, and cover with paper towel. (If Canadian bacon, score edge of each slice with a sharp knife.) Repeat layers of bacon and paper towels, if specified in the chart.
3. Microwave as specified in the chart.

Food	Utensil	Microwave Instructions
Bacon 2 slices	Glass pie plate or paper plate	High for 2 to 2½ min
4 slices	Glass pie plate or paper plate	High for 4 to 4½ min
6 slices	Glass pie plate or paper plate	High for 5 to 6 min
8 slices	12x7½-inch glass dish, 4 slices of bacon per layer	High for 8 to 9 min
Canadian Bacon 4 slices	Glass pie plate or paper plate	Medium for 2 to 3 min
6 slices	12x7½-inch glass dish, 3 slices of bacon per layer	Medium for 4 to 5 min; rotate dish once
8 slices	12x7½-inch glass dish, 4 slices of bacon per layer	Medium for 6 min; rotate dish once

Baked Canadian Bacon

Serves 10 to 12 hungry overnight guests

2 pounds sliced Canadian bacon (about 54 slices, ⅛ inch thick)

½ cup packed brown sugar
½ cup unsweetened pineapple juice
½ teaspoon dry mustard

1. Arrange bacon slices in a stack or loaf; secure with string. Place in a 10x6-inch glass dish.

2. Combine brown sugar, pineapple juice, and mustard. Pour over bacon. Cover dish with plastic film. Microwave on High for 6 minutes.

3. Rotate dish; microwave on Medium for 10 minutes longer. Pierce a hole in the plastic film for steam to escape; remove film.

Tip: *You may also use this method to prepare thicker slices of bacon.*

Pork Loin Center Rib Roast

Makes 6 to 8 servings

5-pound pork loin center rib roast

1. Place roast, fat side down, on a nonmetallic roasting rack in a glass baking dish. Cover meat with paper towels to avoid spattering.

2. Microwave on High for 10 minutes; then switch to Medium and microwave for 20 minutes longer.

3. Turn fat side up; microwave on Medium for 30 minutes, rotating dish halfway through microwave time.

4. Test for doneness with meat thermometer. (See page 13.) Thermometer should register 170° F. Cover loosely with foil.

5. Let stand for 10 minutes before serving.

Pork Chops with Herb Dressing

Easier than stuffed pork chops, but just as good; serves 5

4 cubs herb seasoned croutons
1 small onion, chopped
⅓ cup chopped celery
¼ cup chopped green pepper
¼ cup chopped pimento
¼ teaspoon salt
½ cup water

1. In a 12x7½-inch glass dish combine croutons, onion, celery, green pepper, pimento, salt, and water. Spread in an even layer.

5 pork chops, ½ inch thick each
1 can (10¾ oz) condensed cream of chicken soup

2. Place chops on dressing; top with soup. Cover dish with plastic film.

3. Microwave on High for 12 minutes. Switch to Medium and microwave for 5 minutes longer or until meat is done. Pierce a hole in the plastic film for steam to escape; remove film.

Barbecued Country Ribs

Garnish with orange slices, and serve 6

Pictured on facing page and on front cover

3 pounds country-style pork ribs

1 can (8 oz) tomato sauce
1 tablespoon minced onion
1 clove garlic, minced
2 tablespoons brown sugar
1 tablespoon Worcestershire sauce
1 tablespoon lemon juice
1 teaspoon prepared mustard
1/4 teaspoon salt

1. Cut meat into individual ribs. Place in a 12x7½-inch glass dish. Cover dish with waxed paper. Microwave on Medium for 20 minutes or until meat is no longer pink. Drain fat.

2. Combine remaining ingredients. Brush over ribs, using all of the sauce.

3. Microwave on Medium, covered, for 8 minutes or until ribs are done. Garnish with orange slices, if desired.

Half Ham with Bone

A spring treat for the family get-together

½ fully cooked ham, bone in (about 6½ lb)

1. Place ham, cut side down, on a nonmetallic roasting rack in a 12x7½-inch glass baking dish. Microwave on Medium for 25 minutes.

2. Turn ham fat side down, and rotate dish one half turn. Microwave on Medium for 25 minutes longer.

3. Turn ham, fat side up, and microwave on Medium for another 25 minutes.

4. Test for doneness with meat thermometer. (See page 13.) Thermometer should register 130° F. Cover loosely with foil. Let stand for 10 minutes before serving.

Glazed Canned Ham

Clove-orange glaze on a 5-pound ham

5-pound precooked canned ham

Whole cloves
½ cup packed brown sugar
1/3 cup orange marmalade
2 teaspoons dry mustard

1. Remove ham from can; place on a nonmetallic roasting rack in a 12x7½-inch glass dish. Microwave on Medium for 10 minutes.

2. Drain fat. Score top of ham with a sharp knife. Place whole cloves in scored surface. Combine brown sugar, marmalade, and dry mustard. Spread mixture over top of ham.

3. Microwave on Medium for 30 minutes. Rotate dish one half turn halfway through microwave time. Test for doneness with meat thermometer. (See page 13.) Thermometer should register 130° F. Cover ham loosely with foil. Let stand for 10 minutes before serving.

Barbecued Country Ribs (this page)

Sliced Ham with Raisin Sauce

4 to 6 servings; pass the cider-cinnamon sauce to perk up the appetite

2 center-cut ham slices (1 lb each, cut 1 inch thick)
1 large onion, sliced
1 cup sweet cider or apple juice
3 tablespoons brown sugar

1. Place ham slices on a nonmetallic roasting rack in a 12x7½-inch glass dish. Arrange onion slices over ham. Combine cider and brown sugar; pour over top of ham. Cover dish with plastic film.

2. Microwave on High for 6 to 8 minutes. Rotate dish. Switch to Medium, and microwave for 10 minutes longer. Before removing plastic film, pierce a hole for steam to escape.

½ cup ham drippings
½ cup corn syrup
½ cup seedless raisins

3. Combine ham drippings, corn syrup, and raisins in a 4-cup glass measure. Microwave on High for 45 seconds.

2 tablespoons cornstarch
2 tablespoons water
¼ teaspoon cinnamon
⅛ teaspoon nutmeg

4. Combine cornstarch, water, and spices. Stir into raisin mixture. Microwave on High for 2 minutes, stirring halfway through microwave time. Serve with ham.

Ham Tetrazzini

Spaghetti, mushrooms, and cubed ham in a creamy sauce; serves 6 to 8

1 package (7 oz) spaghetti

1 can (4 oz) sliced mushrooms

½ cup chopped onion
½ cup chopped celery
6 tablespoons butter or margarine

6 tablespoons flour
¼ teaspoon pepper

1. Break spaghetti into thirds; cook and drain.

2. Drain mushrooms. Reserve liquid. Add enough water to measure 2 cups. Set aside.

3. Place onion, celery, and butter in a 3-quart glass casserole. Microwave on High for 4 minutes or until vegetables are soft. Stir halfway through microwave time.

4. Add flour, pepper, and reserved liquid. Stir until smooth. Microwave on High for 5 minutes, stirring every minute with a wire whisk.

1 cup light cream
2 teaspoons instant chicken bouillon
3 cups cubed cooked ham
3 tablespoons dry sherry
¼ cup Parmesan cheese

5. Blend in cream and chicken bouillon. Lightly stir in mushrooms, ham, spaghetti, and sherry. Sprinkle with Parmesan cheese.

6. Microwave on High, covered, for 18 to 20 minutes, or until center of casserole is hot and slightly bubbly. Rotate dish every 5 minutes.

Ham Loaves

Individual loaves to serve 8

2 pounds ground smoked
  ham
½ pound ground pork
1 cup soft bread crumbs
½ cup milk
1 egg, beaten
3 tablespoons chopped
  onion
1 tablespoon chopped
  parsley
2 tablespoons catsup
2 tablespoons prepared
  mustard
½ teaspoon salt
¼ teaspoon pepper

1. Combine ham and pork in a large bowl. Add bread crumbs, milk, egg, onion, parsley, catsup, mustard, salt, and pepper. Mix until well blended.

2. Shape ham loaf mixture into eight individual loaves; place in a 12x7½-inch glass dish. Cover dish with plastic film.

3. Microwave on High, covered, for 20 minutes.

½ cup packed brown sugar
3 tablespoons vinegar
1 teaspoon dry mustard

4. Pierce a hole in the film for steam to escape. Drain fat. Combine brown sugar, vinegar and mustard. Pour sauce over loaves. Microwave on High, covered, for 10 minutes.

5. Let stand for 5 minutes before serving.

Ham-Vegetable Medley

Made from yesterday's ham roast; serves 8

¼ cup butter or margarine
¼ cup chopped onion

1. Place butter in a 3-quart glass casserole. Microwave on High for 1 minute or until melted. Add onion. Microwave on High for 2 minutes until onions are transparent.

¼ cup flour
¾ teaspoon salt
⅛ teaspoon pepper
2 cups milk

2. Blend in flour, salt, and pepper. Gradually stir in milk. Microwave on High for 5½ to 6 minutes or until thickened. Stir well every 2 minutes.

6 medium potatoes, cooked
  and diced
1 package (10 oz) green peas,
  cooked
2 cups diced, cooked ham

3. Add diced potatoes, peas, and ham. Microwave on High, covered, for 3 minutes, stirring once.

3 slices process American
  cheese

4. Cut cheese slices in half; arrange on top of casserole. Microwave on High, covered, for 2 minutes.

Poultry

Juicy and tender. Delicious, too. That's how best to describe poultry that has been prepared in a microwave oven. A few tips follow to help you achieve success everytime.

See the *Defrosting Foods* chapter for how to thaw poultry in your microwave oven.

Browning. Natural browning will occur when you roast large whole birds. The fat reaches high enough temperatures to cause browning during the microwave time. Use the Shielding technique (see page 12) to prevent overcooking of wing tips and leg bones before the meatier breast and thighs are done.

Browning does not occur with most pieces and smaller birds because of short microwave times. To improve the color of the cooked poultry, you may wish to:

- Use a dark ingredient on the poultry's surface: a gravy mix, soy sauce, paprika, jam, etc.
- Bake in a cream sauce, condensed soup, or a colorful fruit sauce.
- Use the Browning Skillet accessory.
- Use the conventional range or grill to brown the poultry. Then finish cooking it in the microwave oven.

Whole poultry. Select a bird that is no heavier than 12 to 15 pounds (8 to 12 pounds is better). Although a larger bird can be roasted in the microwave oven, its size and weight makes it difficult to handle when it is hot. It requires frequent turning for even cooking results. Drippings, if not basted off, can overflow the baking dish; spatters may be excessive.

Complete instructions for roasting whole poultry follow on the next page. Read these instructions carefully before you begin. You may also wish to review applicable sections of the *Food Handling Techniques* chapter.

Pieces. Wash pieces and prepare according to the recipe. Arrange them so that thicker pieces/parts are toward the outside of the dish. This food handling technique (see page 11) permits more even cooking of the pieces. Cover as specified in the recipe to prevent spattering and to hold in the heat.

Giblets. You may prefer to cook them conventionally for more satisfactory results. Here are a few microwave tips if you prepare the giblets with the rest of the bird.

Since the gizzard and heart tend to get tough, arrange them in the center of the cooking utensil with meatier poultry pieces around them. Consider adding a sauce to help tenderize these pieces.

Since the liver tends to explode, pierce it several times with the tines of a fork. To minimize the popping, place the liver under a wing or other nonmeaty piece.

Cornish Hens (page 141)

Whole Poultry

1. Remove wire clip holding legs together; discard. Prepare bird.

   Add seasonings to the body cavity, if desired. Stuff, if desired. If stuffed, microwave for the longer minutes per pound that is specified in the chart.

   Wrap wings and legs of large birds with string, holding them close to the body. Brush exterior with an unsalted vegetable oil or Kitchen Bouquet, if desired, to improve the color of the cooked bird. Do not salt the exterior nor use a salted butter; salt will draw out the natural moisture, drying out the meat.

2. Place bird on a nonmetallic roasting rack in a glass baking dish, breast side down. Exception: for Cornish hens, place bird breast side up.

3. Microwave as specified in the chart. In general, for most birds microwave on High for the first half of total microwave time; then microwave on Medium for the second half. Turn bird every quarter of total microwave time.

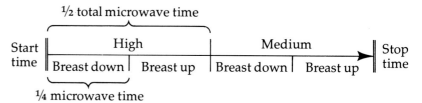

4. During the second quarter of microwave time, cover wing tips and ends of legs with small pieces of aluminum foil. See Shielding on page 12 for complete details.

   Baste off any excess juice as it accumulates so it doesn't slow the cooking process. Set aside for gravy, if desired.

5. During the last quarter of microwave time, check breast and thigh internal temperature. Test inside part of thigh in both legs. Remove bird when the temperature specified in the chart is reached.

   ● Do not use a conventional meat thermometer in an operating microwave oven. See page 13 for the out-of-the-oven technique.
   ● Follow manufacturer's instructions if you use a thermometer specifically designed for microwave use.

   If you do not have a thermometer, remove bird when:

   ● The legs move freely in their joints.
   ● The bird is not pink when you slash it between the leg and body.

   Do not rely on pop-up indicators in poultry. If you wait until the indicator pops up, the bird will be overdone since temperatures continue to rise during the standing time.

6. Cover bird tightly with foil, dull side out. Let stand as specified in the chart. Temperatures will continue to rise during this standing time; pop-up indicators may pop up.

7. Season to taste before serving.

(Chart is continued on next page.)

Poultry Pieces

1. Arrange pieces in a glass dish, skin side down. Place larger pieces around the outer edges of the dish, smaller pieces toward the center. (See page 11.)
2. Cover dish with plastic film; pierce a hole in the film for steam to escape. Do not cover breaded pieces; see recipe on page 143.
3. Microwave on High, covered, turning pieces as specified in the chart.
4. Let stand, covered; cooking will continue.

Tip: *Brown pieces in the Frigidaire Browning Skillet accessory, if desired.*

Poultry	Total Microwave Time	Microwave Instructions	Internal Temp at Stop time	Standing Time, covered (Temp continues to rise)
Chicken Pieces, 1 to 3½ lb	8 to 10 min/lb	High, covered. Start with skin side down; turn halfway through total microwave time	—	5 to 10 min if 3 lb or more 2 to 5 min if under 3 lb
Whole, 3 to 5 lb	8 to 10 min/lb	High for 1st half of time; then Medium for 2nd half Start with breast side down; turn bird every quarter of microwave time, ending with breast side up	180°F	5 to 10 min
Turkey Whole, 10 to 14 lb	9 to 11 min/lb		175°F	10 to 15 min
6 to 9 lb	7 to 8 min/lb			
Breast, bone in, 5 to 7 lb	8 to 10 min/lb		175°F	5 to 10 min
Duckling, 3 to 5 lb	8 to 10 min/lb		180°F	5 to 10 min
Capon, 6 to 8 lb	8 to 9 min/lb		180°F	10 to 15 min
Cornish Hens (2), 1¼ lb each	8 to 10 min/lb	High, covered. Breast side up the entire time. Rotate dish	180°F	5 to 10 min

Roast Whole Turkey

For a family holiday

12-pound frozen turkey, thawed

Salt
Stuffing, if desired

Vegetable oil

1. Thaw turkey according to instructions on page 220.

2. Wash completely thawed turkey; set aside giblets. Sprinkle salt inside cavity. Stuff cavity and neck opening, if desired. Secure opening with woodenpicks. Using twine, tie drumsticks together and wings to body.

3. Place bird, breast side down, on nonmetallic roasting rack in 12x7½-inch glass baking dish. Brush with vegetable oil.

4. Microwave on High for 30 minutes, rotating dish once.

5. Turn breast side up and continue cooking on High for 30 minutes, rotating dish once more.

6. Turn breast side down. Some areas may cook more rapidly than others; cover these with small pieces of foil to slow down cooking. (See Shielding, page 12.)

7. Microwave on Medium for 30 minutes.

8. Turn breast side up and continue cooking on Medium for 30 minutes.

9. Remove turkey from oven and test for doneness with a meat thermometer. (See page 13.) Thermometer should register 175° F when inserted in thickest part of the thigh. Let stand, covered with foil, for 10 to 15 minutes before serving. Temperature will increase during this time.

Roast Capon

With a tasty mushroom stuffing

½ cup butter or margarine
1 can (4 oz) mushrooms, drained
2 stalks celery, chopped
½ cup chopped onion

8 slices day-old bread, cubed
1 teaspoon salt
1 teaspoon poultry seasoning
1 teaspoon Worcestershire sauce

6- to 8-pound capon
Salt

2 tablespoons vegetable oil
1 teaspoon leaf tarragon
½ teaspoon paprika
1 teaspoon soy sauce

1. Combine butter, mushrooms, celery, and onion in a large glass bowl. Microwave on High for 7 minutes or until vegetables are barely tender, stirring once.

2. Stir in bread, salt, poultry seasoning, and Worcestershire sauce.

3. Sprinkle cavity of capon lightly with salt. Spoon stuffing mixture into cavity. Truss opening with thread.

4. Combine remaining ingredients. Brush over capon.

5. Place capon, breast side down, on a nonmetallic roasting rack in a 12x7½-inch glass dish. Microwave on High, uncovered, for 18 minutes.

6. Turn breast side up, and microwave on High for 18 minutes.

7. Turn breast side down, and microwave on Medium for 18 minutes.

8. Then turn breast side up, and microwave on Medium for 18 minutes longer.

9. Remove from oven and test for doneness with a meat thermometer. (See page 13.) Thermometer should register 180° F when inserted in thickest part of thigh or breast. Let stand, covered with foil, for 10 minutes before serving. Temperature will rise during this standing time.

Roast Duck

With orange and plum preserves

4- to 5-pound duckling
Pepper
1 orange, quartered

1. Remove giblets; rinse duck and pat dry. Prick skin in several places with a fork. Sprinkle cavity and skin with pepper. Place orange wedges in cavity. Secure wings and neck skin with woodenpicks; tie legs with string.

2. Place duck, breast side down, on a nonmetallic roasting rack in a 12x7½-inch glass dish. Microwave on High, uncovered, for 10 minutes.

3. Turn breast side up. Microwave on High for 10 minutes longer. Drain off juices, and reserve.

½ cup plum preserves
1 tablespoon soy sauce

4. Meanwhile, mix together preserves and soy sauce. Reserve ¼ cup. Turn duck breast side down; brush with preserves mixture. Microwave on Medium, uncovered, for 10 minutes.

5. Drain off juices and reserve. Turn duck breast side up; add remaining glaze. Microwave on Medium for 10 minutes.

6. Drain juices again. Remove and test for doneness with a meat thermometer. (See page 13.) Thermometer should register 180° F when inserted in thickest part of thigh or breast. Let stand, covered with foil, for 10 minutes before serving. Temperature will rise during this standing time.

¼ cup water
1 tablespoon cornstarch
1 tablespoon water

7. Meanwhile, skim fat from reserved juices. Pour juices into a 2-cup glass measure. Add ¼ cup water. Microwave on High for 1½ minutes. Blend cornstarch and water; add with reserved preserves to juices. Blend well. Microwave on High for 1 minute. Stir every 30 seconds. Serve sauce with sliced duck.

Roast Turkey Breast

Add your own garnishes, and serve to a hungry group

8- to 9-pound turkey breast

2 tablespoons vegetable oil

1. Place breast, skin side down, on a nonmetallic roasting rack in a 12x7½-inch glass dish.

2. Microwave on High, uncovered, for 20 minutes.

3. Turn skin side up. Brush with vegetable oil. Cover loosely with plastic film. Microwave on High for 15 minutes.

4. Turn breast side down; microwave on Medium for 20 minutes.

5. Then turn breast side up and microwave for 20 minutes longer or until meat is done.

6. Test for doneness with a meat thermometer. (See page 13.) Thermometer should register 175° F when inserted into breast. Cover with foil, and let stand for 10 minutes before serving. Temperature will increase during this standing time.

Tip: *Allow 8 minutes per pound for smaller turkey breasts. Microwave on High for the first half of the time and on Medium for the second half of the time.*

Cornish Hens

Add candlelight and soft music

Picture on page 134

2 Rock Cornish hens (1 lb each)

¼ cup pineapple preserves
2 tablespoons catsup
2 tablespoons soy sauce
Dash garlic salt
Dash onion salt

1. Tie legs and wings to body with string. Place hens, breast side up and legs toward center, on a nonmetallic roasting rack in a 12x7½-inch dish.

2. Make glaze by combining remaining ingredients in a small bowl. Baste hens with preserves mixture, and cover loosely with plastic film.

3. Microwave on High for 9 minutes.

4. Remove cover, and baste hens with remaining glaze. Recover with plastic film, and rotate dish one half turn.

5. Microwave on High for 9 minutes longer; uncover after first 5 minutes.

6. Test for doneness with a meat thermometer. (See page 13.) Thermometer should register 180°F when inserted in thickest part of thigh. Allow to stand for 5 minutes before serving.

Chicken Fantastic

Cooks in a sweet sauce; makes 4 to 6 servings

3 chicken breasts, split

1 jar (8 oz) Russian salad dressing
1 jar (12 oz) apricot preserves
1 package dry onion soup mix

1. Arrange chicken breasts in a 12x7½-inch glass dish.

2. Combine dressing, preserves, and soup mix in a medium size bowl. Spoon sauce over chicken. Cover dish with waxed paper.

3. Microwave on Medium, covered, for 17 to 20 minutes, or until chicken is done. Rotate dish halfway through microwave time.

Chicken Parisienne

Ideal for company buffet; makes 4 to 6 servings

3 chicken breasts, split
12 thin slices smoked sliced beef (1½ oz)

1 can (10¾ oz) condensed cream of mushroom soup
1 can (3 oz) mushrooms, drained
1 cup dairy sour cream
⅓ cup sherry
Paprika

Cooked rice

1. Skin and bone chicken, keeping each half intact. Arrange 2 slices of smoked beef on each chicken half; roll each lengthwise and fasten with a woodenpick. Arrange chicken rolls in a 12x7½-inch glass baking dish.

2. Combine soup, mushrooms, sour cream, and sherry. Spoon over chicken; sprinkle with paprika. Cover with plastic film; pierce a hole for steam to escape.

3. Microwave on Medium for 40 minutes, rotating dish twice.

4. Serve over rice.

Mandarin Chicken

Chicken a la Orange to serve 4

⅓ cup chopped onion
⅓ cup sliced celery
¼ teaspoon allspice
2 tablespoons butter or margarine

1½ cups diced, cooked chicken
1 can (10½ oz) chicken gravy
1 can (11 oz) mandarin oranges, drained

Cooked rice

1. Combine onion, celery, allspice, and butter in a 2-quart glass casserole. Microwave on High, uncovered, for 3 minutes. Stir halfway through microwave time.

2. Stir in chicken, gravy, and oranges. Microwave on Medium, uncovered, for 6 minutes, stirring once.

3. Serve over cooked rice.

Tip: *Curry can be used as a substitute for allspice. Mix with hot rice, if desired.*

Oven-fried Chicken

Serves 4

2- to 2½-pound chicken, cut up

1 package seasoned coating mix
1 teaspoon salt
¼ teaspoon pepper

1. Wash chicken and drain.

2. Combine remaining ingredients in a bag. Coat chicken according to directions on package. Arrange pieces in a 12x7½-inch glass dish with large pieces at corners and near the edge of the dish, with small ones in the center. (See page 11.) Cover dish with waxed paper.

3. Microwave on High for 18 to 21 minutes or until chicken is done, rotating dish halfway through microwave time.

Turkey-Ham Royale

With mushrooms and water chestnuts in a cream sauce; serves 6

1½ tablespoons butter or margarine
½ cup dry bread crumbs

2 tablespoons butter or margarine
½ cup chopped onion
3 tablespoons flour
½ teaspoon salt
⅛ teaspoon pepper
1 can (4 oz) sliced mushrooms, undrained
1 cup light cream
2 tablespoons dry sherry

1. Place 1½ tablespoons butter in a small glass bowl. Microwave on High for 30 seconds or until melted. Mix with bread crumbs. Set aside.

2. In a 2-quart glass casserole, place 2 tablespoons butter and onions; microwave on High for 2 minutes. Blend in flour, salt, and pepper. Stir in mushrooms, cream and sherry.

3. Microwave on High, uncovered, for 1 minute. Stir well. Microwave on High, uncovered, for 3 minutes longer, stirring once.

2 cups cubed, cooked turkey
1 cup cubed, cooked ham
1 can (5 oz) water chestnuts, drained and sliced

4. Gently stir in turkey, ham, and water chestnuts. Microwave on Medium, covered, for 12 minutes, stirring once.

½ cup shredded process Swiss cheese
Paprika

5. Top with cheese and wreath of buttered crumbs. Sprinkle with paprika. Microwave on High, uncovered, for 1 minute.

Tropical Gumbo

Like curry with condiments; great for a crowd from 8 to 10

4 cups diced cooked chicken or turkey
2 quarts chicken broth or bouillon

1 jar (18 oz) creamy peanut butter

2 eggs, hard-cooked and quartered
Cooked rice

1 cup salted peanuts
1 cup roasted pecans
1 cup grated carrots
1 cup raisins
1 cup fresh or toasted coconut
1 cup chutney
1 can (20 oz) pineapple chunks, drained
1 can (11 oz) mandarin oranges, drained
1 green pepper, slivered
2 tomatoes, diced
2 bananas, sliced
1 avocado, sliced

1. In a 4-quart glass mixing bowl combine chicken and broth. Cover with plastic film; pierce a hole for steam to escape. Microwave on High for 25 minutes, or until boiling.

2. Blend 1½ cups of hot broth with peanut butter to make a smooth paste. Add paste to broth, blending well. Microwave on High, covered, for 15 to 18 minutes. Stir well every 2 minutes.

3. Just prior to serving, add eggs. Serve over rice; top with a sprinkling of remaining ingredients.

Tip: *Serve the chicken mixture and rice in a large bowl. Arrange smaller bowls of fruits, vegetables, and nuts around it. Let each person prepare his own serving.*

Water Chestnut Dressing

4 to 5 servings to accompany the bird

3 cups dry bread cubes
⅓ cup light cream

⅓ cup chopped onion
⅓ cup chopped celery
2 tablespoons chopped parsley
⅓ cup butter or margarine

1 can (8 oz) water chestnuts, drained and chopped
1 teaspoon Beau Monde seasoned salt
¼ teaspoon poultry seasonings
⅛ teaspoon pepper

1. Combine bread cubes and cream in an 8x8x2-inch glass dish. Set aside.

2. Combine onion, celery, parsley, and butter in a 1-quart casserole. Microwave on High, uncovered, for 3 minutes or until tender.

3. Add onion-celery mixture, water chestnuts, and seasoning to bread cubes. Mix well.

4. Cover dish with plastic film; pierce a hole for steam to escape. Microwave on High for 6 minutes.

Nutty Dressing

4 to 6 servings of crunchy herb dressing or stuffing

4 cups dry bread cubes
⅔ cup chopped walnuts
½ cup chopped ripe olives
½ cup chopped celery
6 slices cooked bacon, crumbled
1½ teaspoons Beau Monde seasoning salt
½ teaspoon thyme
½ teaspoon sage
½ teaspoon marjoram

½ cup milk
½ cup butter or margarine

1. Combine first nine ingredients in an 8x8x2-inch glass dish.

2. Place milk and butter in a 2-cup glass measure. Microwave on High for 2 minutes until butter is melted. Pour over dressing.

3. Cover with plastic film. Microwave on High for 5 to 6 minutes. Pierce film to release steam before removing from dish.

Fish and Seafood

Whether your catch is from the natural waters or from your grocer's fresh and frozen cases, it's time to let your microwave oven shine. The microwave cooking process takes already-great fish and seafood dishes and makes them better yet—more flaky, more tender, and more delicate than with conventional cooking.

Ranging all the way from Fish 'n Chips to Lobster Tails, the recipes in this chapter are outstanding. You will find freshwater fish stuffed, baked in a variety of sauces, and poached; seafood delicacies baked in lemon butter, combined with other ingredients for Newburgs, creoles, kabobs, and salads. Serve these tasty dishes to your family and guests for compliments year 'round.

Prepare fish. Some fish are interchangeable in many of these recipes. You can substitute flounder for cod, for instance.

See the *Defrosting Foods* chapter to thaw fish in your microwave oven.

Prepare fish according to the recipe. Arrange fish so that thicker pieces are toward the outside of the dish. This food handling technique (see page 11) permits more even cooking of the pieces.

Microwave instructions. Since fish and seafood cook quite rapidly in the microwave oven, watch microwave time closely. Remember that cooking continues during the standing time. If overcooked, fish becomes dry, strong, and tough.

Cover most dishes to steam the fish and to seal in the natural juices. However, do not cover if the fish has a cracker- or bread-coating or other topping that should become crisp.

Microwave as specified in the recipe, turning the pieces or rotating the dish during microwave time. Then allow a standing time, covered, for the fish to continue cooking.

Fish is done when you can flake the center or thickest part with a fork.

Make-ahead tips. Cooked fish does not reheat well; it tends to overcook. If you prepare the dish early in the day, refrigerate it while it is still underdone. The fish will finish cooking during the reheating and standing times.

Sauterne Baked Sole (page 151); Fresh Carrots (page 195) with Vinaigrette Sauce (page 199).

Fish and Seafood

1. Arrange fish in a glass baking dish. Place thicker pieces around the outer edges of the dish, thinner pieces toward the center. (See page 11.) Add seasonings or sauces as desired.
2. Cover the dish with plastic film; pierce a hole in the film for steam to escape.
3. Microwave as specified in the chart, covered.
4. Let stand, covered; cooking will continue. Fish is done when it can be flaked with a fork. Serve immediately.

Fish/Seafood	Weight	Microwave Instructions	Standing Time, covered (Cooking continues)
Fillets	1 lb	High for 6 to 7 min/lb	2 to 3 min
Whole Fish	1½ to 2 lb	High for 6 to 7 min/lb	2 to 3 min
Scallops	1 lb	Medium for 5 to 6 min/lb	2 to 3 min
Shrimp	1 lb	High for 4 to 6 min/lb	1 to 2 min
Lobster Tails	1½ lb	High for 4 to 6 min/lb	1 to 2 min
Salmon Steaks	1½ to 2 lb	Medium for 5 to 6 min/lb	2 to 3 min

Baked Stuffed Whole Fish

What a catch! Serves 2

1½ pounds whole fish
3 tablespoons melted butter or margarine
1 teaspoon salt

1 cup herb seasoned croutons
⅓ cup boiling water
3 tablespoons finely chopped celery
1 tablespoon minced onion
1 teaspoon poultry seasoning

Paprika

1. Wash dressed fish and wipe dry with a paper towel. Brush interior of fish with half of melted butter; then sprinkle with salt.

2. Toss together croutons, water, celery, onion and seasoning. Loosely fill cavity of fish. Fasten with woodenpicks.

3. Place fish in a 12x7½-inch glass dish. Brush fish exterior with remaining butter; sprinkle with paprika. Cover dish with plastic film; pierce serveral holes in the film to allow steam to escape. Microwave on High for 6½ to 7½ minutes, or until fish can be flaked with a fork. Let stand for 2 to 3 minutes.

Tips: *If whole fish is too long for the dish, remove the head.*

To cook two fish in the same dish, place the heads at opposite ends. Almost double the recipe for stuffing and microwave time.

Baked Cod In Lime Sauce

Serve 4 with this tasty dish

1 pound cod fillets

1 tablespoon butter or margarine

½ teaspoon salt

¼ teaspoon powdered ginger

⅛ teaspoon white pepper

$1/16$ teaspoon crumbled bay leaf

¼ cup lime juice

2 green onions, thinly sliced

1. Place cod fillets in a 12x7½-inch glass dish.

2. Place butter in a small bowl. Microwave on High for 30 seconds or until melted. Stir in remaining ingredients. Pour mixture over fillets. Cover dish with plastic film; pierce 2 or 3 holes in the film to allow steam to escape.

3. Microwave on High for 6 to 7 minutes. Let stand for 1 to 2 minutes before serving.

Tip: *Serve with lime slices or wedges.*

Flounder In Herbs

Cooks in a cream/herb sauce; serves 3 or 4

1 pound flounder fillets, thawed

1 small onion sliced, separated into rings

1 tablespoon butter or margarine

⅔ cup light cream

1 teaspoon salt

½ teaspoon garlic salt

½ teaspoon monosodium glutamate

½ teaspoon oregano

¼ teaspoon thyme

1 bay leaf

Dash pepper

1. Place fillets in a 12x7½-inch glass dish. Top with onion rings.

2. Combine remaining ingredients in a glass bowl to make a sauce. Microwave on High for 1½ minutes. Stir well. Pour over fillets.

3. Microwave on High, uncovered, for 6 to 7 minutes.

Fish Fillet Oriental

4 servings to start early in the day and marinate

1 package (1 lb) fish fillets, thawed

2 tablespoons brown sugar
3 tablespoons orange juice
2 tablespoons oil
2 teaspoons soy sauce
¼ teaspoon ginger

1. Arrange fillets in a 12x7½-inch glass dish.

2. Mix remaining ingredients in a small bowl. Pour over fillets. Cover dish with plastic film; refrigerate for several hours.

3. Pour off marinade. Cover fillets with plastic film; pierce holes in the film for steam to escape. Microwave on High for 6 minutes. Let stand, covered, for 1 to 2 minutes to complete cooking.

Cold Poached Salmon Steaks

Marinated salmon with cucumber sauce to serve 4

2 cups water
½ lemon, sliced
½ onion, sliced
1 stalk celery, cut into pieces
Few sprigs parsley
3 tablespoons vinegar
2 tablespoons lemon juice
1½ teaspoons salt
6 whole cloves
1 bay leaf

4 salmon steaks (about 2 lbs)

1 large cucumber, peeled, seeded and grated
½ cup heavy cream, whipped
1 teaspoon salt
½ teaspoon dry dill seed
$1/16$ teaspoon black pepper

1. Combine first 10 ingredients in a 12x7½-inch glass dish. Microwave on High, uncovered, for 5 minutes.

2. Submerge salmon steaks in marinade. Microwave on High, uncovered, for 5 minutes. Lift steaks from stock and carefully remove skin and bones. Chill at least 3 hours before serving.

3. Prepare cucumber sauce while salmon chills. Drain cucumber in a sieve. Whip heavy cream; fold in salt, dill, pepper, and cucumber. Chill and serve with cold salmon. Makes about 2 cups of sauce.

Tangy Red Snapper

6 servings baked in an orange-nutmeg sauce

2 pounds red snapper fillets, cut into serving pieces

1 teaspoon grated orange peel
¼ cup orange juice
2 tablespoons oil
1 teaspoon salt
⅛ teaspoon nutmeg
Dash pepper

1. Arrange fillet pieces in a 12x7½-inch glass dish.

2. Combine remaining ingredients; pour mixture over fillets. Cover dish with plastic film; pierce a few holes for steam to escape. Microwave on High for 10 to 12 minutes.

Sauterne Baked Sole

Baked in a creamy wine sauce; serves 4

Pictured on page 146

1 package (1 lb) frozen sole fillets, thawed

2 tablespoons butter or margarine
2 tablespoons flour
½ cup milk
¼ cup cream
¼ cup Sauterne or dry white wine
1 teaspoon lemon juice
¼ teaspoon salt
2 tablespoons minced onion
3 tablespoons grated Parmesan cheese

1. Thaw fillets. See instructions on page 220.

2. Place butter in a 1½-quart glass casserole. Microwave on High for 30 seconds or until melted. Add flour, milk, cream, Sauterne, lemon juice, and salt. Blend together, using a wire whisk. Add onion. Microwave on High, uncovered, for 3 minutes. Stir every 30 seconds. Blend in cheese.

3. Arrange fillets in a 12x7½-inch glass dish. Spread sauce over top. Cover dish with plastic film; pierce a few holes in the film for steam to escape. Microwave on High for 6 to 7 minutes.

Stuffed Trout with Herb Sauce

Mouth-watering good; serves 2

2 trout (½ lb each)
1 cup seasoned stuffing

1 cup dairy sour cream
1 teaspoon parsley flakes
1 scallion, chopped, including greens
¾ teaspoon salt
½ teaspoon thyme
½ teaspoon tarragon
⅛ teaspoon pepper

1. Stuff each trout with ½ cup dressing. Secure with woodenpicks. Place fish in a 12x7½-inch glass dish. Microwave on High, uncovered, for 6 minutes.

2. Meanwhile, combine remaining ingredients in a small bowl. Spread over trout just before serving.

Turbot Fillets

4 easy servings

1 pound turbot fillets, thawed
2 tablespoons lemon juice
⅛ teaspoon Beau Monde seasoned salt
⅛ teaspoon pepper
1 tablespoon chopped parsley
Paprika
Butter or margarine

1. Arrange fillets in a 12x7½-inch glass dish. Pour lemon juice over fillets; season with salt and pepper. Sprinkle with parsley and paprika. Dot with butter.

2. Microwave on High for 6 to 7 minutes.

Crabmeat Delight

6 servings; green pepper and sharp Cheddar give it a bite

1 cup finely chopped green pepper
1 tablespoon butter or margarine

2 cups shredded sharp Cheddar cheese
¾ cup tomato juice
2 tablespoons flour
¼ teaspoon dry mustard
¼ teaspoon salt
Dash pepper

1 egg, slightly beaten
¾ cup milk, scalded
2 cans (7½ oz each) crabmeat, drained and flaked

1. Place green pepper and butter in a 1½-quart glass casserole. Microwave on High, uncovered, for 3 minutes. Stir halfway through microwave time.

2. Mix in 1⅓ cups cheese, tomato juice, flour, mustard, salt and pepper.

3. Stir in egg. Microwave on High, uncovered, for 2 minutes. Add milk and crabmeat; mix well. Microwave on High for 2 minutes longer.

4. Stir and sprinkle remaining cheese on top. Microwave on High, uncovered, for 2 minutes. Let stand for 5 minutes before serving.

Tip: *Delicious served in patty shells, over toast or rice.*

Crab-Shrimp Bake

Delicious, delicate seafood combination to serve 4

1 cup cooked shrimp
1 can (7½ oz) crabmeat, drained and flaked
¼ cup chopped onion
1 cup mayonnaise
½ teaspoon salt
1 teaspoon Worcestershire sauce
Dash pepper

1 cup soft bread crumbs
1 tablespoon butter or margarine

1. Cut large shrimp in half lengthwise. Combine shrimp, crabmeat, onion, mayonnaise, salt, Worcestershire sauce, and pepper in a 1-quart glass casserole. Mix well.

2. Combine bread crumbs and butter in a 1-cup glass measure. Microwave on High for 30 seconds or until butter is melted. Mix until crumbs are well coated with butter. Sprinkle crumbs over top of casserole.

3. Microwave on High, uncovered, for 7 to 8 minutes.

Hot Crab Salad and Avocado

An elegant luncheon for 6 to 8

1 medium green pepper, chopped
1 small onion, chopped
1 cup diced celery
3 cans (6½ oz each) crabmeat, drained and flaked
1 cup mayonnaise
½ teaspoon salt
Dash pepper
1 teaspoon Worcestershire sauce

1. Combine first 8 ingredients in a 3-quart glass casserole. Cover with plastic film; pierce a hole in the film for steam to escape.

2. Microwave on Medium for 10 minutes, stirring once.

3. Microwave on High for 2 minutes longer.

1 avocado
Lemon juice

4. Slice avocado and brush with lemon juice. Arrange on casserole; serve at once.

Tips: *As a variation, serve hot crab salad in avocado halves, topped with toasted croutons.*

To save time, prepare early in the morning and refrigerate. Microwave on High until reheated.

Quick Seafood Newburg

Spoon over rice or English muffins to serve 4

1 can (10½ oz) condensed cream of shrimp soup
1 tablespoon minced green pepper
1 tablespoon finely chopped onion
1 tablespoon Worcestershire sauce

1. Combine soup, green pepper, onion, and Worcestershire sauce in a 1½-quart glass casserole. Microwave on High for 2 minutes, stirring once.

1 can (5 oz) lobster, crab, or shrimp, drained (or 1 cup cooked)
1 can (4 oz) sliced mushrooms, drained
¼ cup coffee cream

2. Flake seafood into casserole. Add mushrooms and cream. Stir well. Cover with plastic film; pierce holes for steam to escape. Microwave on High for 3 to 4 minutes.

3. Serve in patty shells, over rice, or on toasted English muffins.

Scalloped Corn and Oysters

Made with butter crackers; serves 6

2 cups crumbs from round butter crackers
2 tablespoons butter or margarine, melted

1 pint oysters
1 can (17 oz) cream-style corn

1. Add ½ cup crumbs to melted butter. Set aside.

2. Reserve up to ½ cup oyster liquid. Wash oysters, checking for shell. In a 1½-quart glass casserole, layer half of corn, dry crumbs, and oysters. Layer remaining ingredients, beginning with corn and ending with oysters. Pour oyster liquid over top.

3. Microwave on Medium, covered, for 10 minutes.

4. Rotate dish. Microwave on Medium, covered, for 3 minutes longer.

5. Spread buttered crumbs over oyster mixture. Microwave on High, uncovered, for 2 minutes.

6. Let stand, covered, for 5 minutes before serving.

Salmon Ring

A ring, or loaf, for 5 or 6 to enjoy

1 can (1 lb) salmon, drained and flaked
2 eggs, beaten
1 cup soft bread crumbs
½ cup chopped green pepper or celery
¼ cup chopped green stuffed olives
¼ cup light cream
2 tablespoons instant minced onion
1 tablespoon parsley flakes
¼ teaspoon Beau Monde seasoning salt
1 tablespoon lemon juice

1. Combine all ingredients in a medium-size bowl.

2. Place an empty small custard cup or juice glass, upright, in the center of a 1½-quart glass casserole. Spoon mixture into the casserole around the cup.

3. Cover with waxed paper. Microwave on Medium for 16 to 18 minutes. Rotate dish halfway through microwave time.

4. Let stand 3 minutes; then unmold and serve hot.

Salmon Stuffed Green Peppers

Colorful, flavorful; makes 6 servings

6 medium green peppers

1. Wash peppers; cut off tops; remove seeds and membranes; set aside. Cut stem out of center of green pepper tops; finely chop remaining green pepper.

1 can (1 lb) salmon, drained and flaked
1 cup soft bread crumbs
½ cup finely chopped celery
⅓ cup mayonnaise
1 egg
2 tablespoons lemon juice
2 tablespoons prepared mustard
2 tablespoons soft butter or margarine
1 tablespoon minced onion
¼ teaspoon salt
⅛ teaspoon hot pepper sauce

2. Combine all ingredients except paprika and cheese. Add chopped peppers to salmon mixture. Stuff pepper shells, and arrange in a circle in a 3-quart glass casserole.

Paprika

3. Sprinkle paprika over the salmon stuffing of each pepper. Microwave on Medium, covered, for 10 minutes.

4. Rotate dish. Microwave on Medium, covered, for 5 to 7 minutes longer.

2 slices Cheddar or American cheese, cut into 12 strips

5. Cross two strips of cheese over top of each pepper. Microwave on High, covered, for 1 minute to melt the cheese.

Lobster Tails

Pictured facing page 1

1 package (10 oz) frozen lobster tails, thawed

1. With scissors make a cut lengthwise down back through hard shell of each tail. Hold tail in both hands, and open flat. Turn tails, meat side up, in a 10x6-inch glass dish.

2 tablespoons melted butter or margarine
1 teaspoon lemon juice

2. Brush lobster meat with butter and lemon juice mixture. Microwave on High for 2½ to 3 minutes. Be careful not to overcook lobster; it will toughen if cooked too long.

3. Let stand for 1 to 2 minutes before serving.

Fresh Cooked Shrimp

Use in your favorite dish

2½ pounds fresh shrimp in shell
4 cups boiling water
½ cup vinegar
1 teaspoon salt
2 bay leaves
6 cloves

1. Place shrimp in a 3-quart glass casserole. Add boiling water and remaining ingredients.

2. Microwave on High, covered, for 5 minutes.

3. Drain; rinse shrimp in cold tap water for easier handling. Remove shell and vein. Shrimp is now ready to use in your favorite dish.

Tip: *Allow 2 to 2½ pounds shrimp in shell for about 1 pound cooked, cleaned shrimp.*

Shrimp Creole

A New Orleans favorite; makes 4 or 5 servings

2 slices bacon

1. Place bacon in a 3-quart glass casserole; cover with a paper towel. Microwave on High for 2 minutes or until bacon is crisp. Remove bacon slices, and set aside to drain.

1 cup chopped onion
¾ cup chopped green pepper
¾ cup chopped celery
¼ cup chopped parsley

2. To bacon fat add onion, green pepper, celery, and parsley. Microwave on High, uncovered, for 4 minutes.

1½ tablespoons flour
1 can (14½ oz) tomatoes

3. Stir flour into vegetables. Add tomatoes and liquid; mix well. (Cut whole tomatoes into pieces.) Microwave on High, uncovered, for 6 minutes, stirring halfway through microwave time.

1 clove garlic, minced
1 teaspoon sugar
1 teaspoon salt
¼ teaspoon crushed red pepper
⅛ teaspoon white pepper
Dash thyme
1 pound raw or frozen shrimp, shelled and cleaned

4. Add garlic, sugar, salt, red pepper, white pepper, thyme. Crumble bacon slices and stir into mixture. Add shrimp. Microwave on High, covered, for 6 minutes, or until shrimp is cooked.

Hot rice

5. Let stand for 3 minutes before serving over hot rice.

Shrimp Kabobs

Use wooden skewers; serves 5

1 pound cooked large shrimp
1 pound fresh mushrooms, stems removed
1 can (20 oz) pineapple chunks, drained
2 green peppers, cut into squares
1 large dill pickle, cut in ¼-inch slices

⅓ cup melted butter or margarine
2 tablespoons Worcestershire sauce
1 tablespoon minced onion

Salt
Pepper
Garlic powder

1. Alternate ingredients on ten 10-inch wooden skewers using 4 shrimp, 4 mushroom caps, 2 pineapple chunks, 2 green pepper squares, and 1 pickle slice per kabob.

2. Combine melted butter, Worcestershire sauce, and onion. Brush over kabobs. Allow to marinate for 20 minutes.

3. Place 5 kabobs crosswise on a 12x7-inch glass dish. Sprinkle each kabob with salt, pepper, and garlic powder just before cooking.

4. Microwave on High for 4 minutes. Turn kabobs. Microwave on High for 4 minutes longer.

5. Repeat steps 3 and 4 with remaining 5 kabobs.

Tips: *For easier threading, pierce foods first with a metal skewer; then slide onto a wooden skewer.*

Serve 2 kabobs over a bed of rice per person.

Easy Shrimp-Lobster Newburg

Makes about 4 cups to serve over toast or as a dip

2 tablespoons butter or margarine
1 can (4 oz) sliced mushrooms, drained

1 can (7 oz) lobster
2 cans (10¾ oz each) condensed cream of shrimp soup
1 teaspoon prepared mustard
⅛ teaspoon pepper
Dash garlic salt

2 tablespoons chopped green onion, including tops

1. Place butter and mushrooms in a 1½-quart glass casserole. Microwave on High for 2 minutes.

2. Drain lobster; remove cartilage. Add lobster, soup, mustard, and seasonings to casserole. Cover with glass lid or plastic film; pierce a hole in the film for steam to escape. Microwave on High for 7 minutes.

3. Add onion; stir. Let stand for 5 minutes before serving.

Oriental Shrimp

Shrimp, pea pods, water chestnuts over rice; serves 3 or 4

¾ cup chicken broth
1 tablespoon cornstarch
¼ cup sliced green onion with tops
2 tablespoons soy sauce
⅛ teaspoon ground ginger

1. Combine chicken broth and cornstarch in a 1½-quart glass casserole. Stir in onion, soy sauce, and ginger. Microwave on High, uncovered, for 3 minutes or until thickened and bubbly. Stir after each minute.

1 package (6 oz) frozen pea pods
2 cups cooked shrimp
½ cup sliced water chestnuts
1 small tomato, peeled and cut into wedges
¼ cup sliced ripe olives

2. Rinse pea pods in strainer under hot water tap. Add pea pods, shrimp, water chestnuts, tomato wedges, and olive slices to broth mixture. Microwave on High, covered, for 2 minutes or until hot.

Hot cooked rice

3. Serve over rice.

Hot Seafood Salad

Quick, budget luncheon dish for 4 to 6

1 can (10¾ oz) condensed cream of shrimp soup
¼ cup milk
¼ pound process cheese spread
1 can (7 oz) tuna, drained and flaked in large pieces
1 cup chopped celery
¼ cup chopped onion
¼ cup chopped green pepper

1. Combine all ingredients in a 1½-quart glass casserole. Mix well.

2. Microwave on Medium, covered, for 6 minutes. Stir halfway through microwave time. Microwave on High for 1 minute longer.

Tip: *Serve over cooked rice, noodles, or toast.*

Fish 'n' Chips

A tuna/potato-chip casserole to serve 4

1 can (10¾ oz) condensed cream of celery soup
⅓ cup light cream
1 can (3 oz) sliced mushrooms, undrained

1 bag (2 oz) potato chips, crushed
1 can (7 oz) tuna, drained

1. Mix together soup, cream, and mushrooms with liquid.

2. Arrange layers of crushed chips, flaked tuna, and soup mixture in a 1½-quart glass casserole, beginning and ending with crushed chips.

3. Microwave on Medium, covered, for 10 minutes.

4. Microwave on High for 1 to 2 minutes longer.

Creamy Lemon Sauce

1½ cups to serve with fish

2 tablespoons butter or margarine
2 tablespoons flour
½ teaspoon salt

1 egg yolk
½ cup light cream

1 cup fish broth
¼ cup lemon juice
2 tablespoons chopped parsley
Dash hot pepper sauce

1. Place butter in a 1-quart glass casserole. Microwave on High for 30 seconds or until melted. Stir in flour and salt.

2. Beat egg yolk into cream. Pour into flour mixture. Mix well. Microwave on High for 45 seconds. Stir every 15 seconds.

3. Mix in remaining ingredients. Microwave on High for 2 minutes. Stir every 30 seconds.

White Clam Sauce for Spaghetti

For pasta and seafood lovers; 4 servings

1 medium onion, chopped
1 to 2 cloves garlic, minced
¼ cup oil
¼ cup butter or margarine

2 cans (10 oz each) whole baby clams
3 tablespoons chopped fresh parsley
1½ teaspoons salt

Cooked spaghetti
Parmesan cheese

1. Combine onions, garlic, oil, and butter in a 1½-quart glass casserole. Microwave on High, uncovered, for 3 minutes.

2. Drain clams, reserving ⅓ cup liquid. Add clams, liquid, parsley and salt to onion mixture. Microwave on High, covered, for 5 minutes.

3. Let stand, covered, for 2 to 3 minutes before serving. Serve over spaghetti. Sprinkle with Parmesan cheese.

Rice, Pastas, and Cereals

Rice, pasta, and cereal all are essential to a well-rounded diet. They belong to the Bread Group of the four basic food groups; you can substitute any of them for a serving of bread. As you look over the selection of recipes in this chapter, you will find many tasty dishes that your family will enjoy.

Rice

Rice is a nutritious dish. Try serving it many ways. Here are a few suggestions:

- As a side dish: fluffed plain rice; rice combined with other ingredients. (See the many recipes in this chapter.)
- In an entree: stuffed cabbage rolls; in a casserole; a bed of rice under seafood, shish kabobs, sweet and sour meatballs. (See other chapters for complete recipes.)
- In a dessert. (See *Deserts*.)
- In a soup. (See *Soups*.)

Microwave time for cooking (rehydrating) rice is about the same as conventional time. Although time is not a factor, you may still find it more convenient to microwave rice. You can use in the microwave oven some glass and poultry dishes that are not designed for conventional surface cooking. Once the rice is cooked, simply serve from the same dish as is; or add other ingredients, finish according to the recipe, and serve from the same dish.

To reheat rice, microwave on High, covered, until steaming. Stir once if the rice has been refrigerated.

Packaged Rice Mix

An easy, one-dish quickie

Water (see package for amount)

1 package rice mix

1. Place water in glass casserole. Microwave on High, covered, until boiling.

2. Stir in rice and seasonings. Microwave on Low, covered, until tender.

Fluffy Orange Rice (page 163)

Rice

Basic recipe for packaged rice

Water (see chart)
1 tablespoon butter or
    margarine
1 teaspoon salt

Rice (see chart)

1. Combine water, butter, and salt in casserole.

2. Microwave on High, covered, until boiling.

3. Stir in rice.
   - If uncooked, microwave on Low, covered, as specified.
   - If precooked (Minute® Rice, for instance), do not microwave; continue with step 4.

4. Let stand, covered, for 5 minutes. Fluff with fork and serve.

Rice, packaged	Yield, cooked	Glass Casserole, covered	Water	Microwave Instructions	
				High to boil water	Low to cook rice
Long Grain White 1 cup	3 cups	2 qt	2 cups	4 to 5 min	14 to 17 min
Brown 1 cup	4 cups	3 qt	3 cups	6 to 7 min	30 to 35 min
Long Grain White and Wild Mix 6 oz	3 cups	2 qt	2½ cups	5 to 6 min	25 to 30 min
Precooked 1 cup	2 cups	1 qt	1 cup	3 to 4 min	Let stand, covered, for 5 to 10 min*

*Do not microwave precooked rice. Simply stir into boiling water, cover, and let stand.

Quick Spanish Rice

6 spicy Spanish servings

4 slices bacon

1 can (16 oz) tomatoes
¾ cup water
½ cup frozen chopped onion
1 package (6 oz) Spanish rice
    mix

1. Place bacon in a 2-quart glass casserole; cover with paper towel. Microwave on High for 4 to 5 minutes. Remove bacon, and set aside.

2. In the same casserole, combine 2 tablespoons of tomatoes, water, onion, and Spanish rice mix. Microwave on High, covered, for 8 minutes, stirring after 4 minutes.

3. Let stand, covered, for 5 minutes.

4. Crumble bacon over top and serve.

Fiesta Rice

A colorful, tasty dish; 4 servings

1 cup packaged precooked rice

½ cup chopped onion
¼ cup chopped green pepper
2 tablespoons vegetable oil

¼ cup catsup
1 teaspoon salt
½ teaspoon chili pepper
⅛ teaspoon pepper

1. Prepare rice as directed on facing page. Let stand.

2. Place onion, green pepper, and oil in a 2-quart glass casserole. Microwave on Medium, uncovered, for 4 minutes.

3. Stir in catsup. Add spices, then rice. Mix well.

4. Microwave on Medium, covered, for 6 minutes. Stir once.

Parsleyed Rice

Dairy products combine with rice for 4 to 6 nutritious servings

2 cups cooked rice
½ pound shredded American cheese
1 tablespoon instant minced onion
1 clove garlic, minced
½ teaspoon salt
⅛ teaspoon pepper

¼ cup vegetable oil
2 eggs
2 cups milk

1 tablespoon parsley flakes

1. Combine rice, cheese, onion, garlic, salt and pepper in a 1½-quart glass casserole.

2. Beat oil with eggs and milk. Stir into rice mixture.

3. Microwave on Medium, covered, for 20 to 25 minutes, rotating dish every 10 minutes.

4. Sprinkle with parsley flakes. Fluff with fork and serve.

Fluffy Orange Rice

An easy way to dress up ordinary rice; serves 4

Pictured on page 160

1 cup chopped celery
¼ cup chopped onion
¼ cup butter or margarine

1¼ cups water
2 tablespoons orange juice concentrate
½ teaspoon salt

1⅓ cups packaged, precooked rice

1. Place celery, onion, and butter in a 1½-quart glass casserole. Microwave on High for 5 minutes or until celery is soft.

2. Stir in water, concentrate, and salt. Microwave on High, covered, for about 7 minutes or until boiling.

3. Stir in rice. Let stand, covered, for 5 to 10 minutes. Fluff with fork and serve.

Pastas

More than just spaghetti, pastas include a variety of sizes, textures, and shapes of macaroni products. Try some of these serving ideas:

- In a salad: with elbow macaroni; with sea shells. (Start with the basic cooking chart in this chapter.)

- As a side dish: buttered noodles; macaroni and cheese. (See the recipes in this chapter.)

- In a soup: chicken noodle soup; minestrone. (See *Soups.*)

- As an entree: spaghetti, lasagna; in a casserole; a bed of noodles under beef tips or stroganoff. (See this and other chapters for complete recipes.)

Microwave time for cooking pasta is about the same as conventional time. However, you may find it convenient to microwave pasta. Use glass and pottery dishes, even the lasagna-size 12x7½-inch glass dish, to cook the pasta and to finish according to the recipe. Then simply serve from the same dish.

To microwave pasta add the pasta to boiling water that has a small amount of oil in it; oil helps prevent boilovers. Use plenty of water; be sure that the water completely covers the pasta throughout microwave time for evenly tender results.

To reheat pasta microwave on Medium, covered, until steaming. Stir once if the pasta has been refrigerated.

Pastas

*Basic recipe
for packaged pasta*

Water (see chart)
1 tablespoon cooking oil
1 teaspoon salt

Pasta (see chart)

1. Combine water, oil, and salt in a glass casserole.

2. Microwave on High, covered, until boiling.

3. Stir in pasta. Microwave on Low, covered, as specified. Taste to judge tenderness.

4. Drain; rinse with hot water. Serve or combine with other ingredients, as desired.

Pasta, uncooked	Yield, cooked	Glass Casserole, covered	Water	Microwave Instructions	
				High to boil water	**Low to cook pasta**
Spaghetti 8 oz	4 cups	3 qt	4 cups	8 to 10 min	11 to 13 min
Macaroni 3 cups	4 cups	3 qt	3 cups	7 to 9 min	11 to 13 min
Egg Noodles 2 cups	2½ cups	2 qt	3 cups	7 to 9 min	9 to 11 min
Lasagna Noodles 8 oz	4 cups	12x7½ baking dish	6 cups	11 to 13 min	14 to 16 min
Macaroni & Cheese Mix, 7¼ oz	3 cups	2 qt	2 cups	4 to 5 min	15 to 17 min

Canned Spaghetti or Macaroni And Cheese

1 can (14 to 15 oz) spaghetti or macaroni and cheese

1. Empty contents of can into a 1-quart glass casserole.

2. Microwave on Medium, covered, for 5 to 7 minutes, stirring once.

Packaged Pasta Mix

An easy, one-dish quickie

Water (see package for amount)

1 package pasta mix

1. Place water in a glass casserole. Microwave on High, covered, until boiling.

2. Stir in pasta and seasonings. Microwave on Low, covered, until tender.

Quick Spaghetti with Olives

From the shelf to the table; serves 4

4 cups water

1 package (19½ oz) spaghetti dinner

1 tablespoon butter or margarine

6 stuffed green olives, sliced

1. Place water in a 3-quart glass casserole. Microwave on High, covered, for 8 minutes or until boiling.

2. Add spaghetti. Microwave on Low, covered, for 11 minutes or until tender.

3. Drain. Add butter and stir. Pour container of meat over spaghetti. Microwave on Medium, covered, for 2 to 3 minutes.

4. Sprinkle package of grated Parmesan cheese on top, and garnish with olives.

Noodles au Gratin

A cheesy, creamy dish to serve 4

2 cups uncooked noodles

½ pound Cheddar cheese, grated
1 teaspoon poppy seeds

1 pint dairy sour cream
Paprika

1. Cook noodles as directed on facing page.

2. Mix noodles, cheese, and poppy seeds together. Place half of the noodle mixture in an 8x8x2-inch glass baking dish.

3. Spread half of sour cream over noodles; then add the remainder of the noodles. Top with another layer of sour cream. Sprinkle with paprika.

4. Microwave on Medium, covered, for 14 to 16 minutes, rotating dish every four minutes.

Easy Lasagna

A quick dinner for 4

1 box lasagna dinner
⅓ cup warm water

1 pound ground beef

1 jar (2½ oz) sliced
  mushrooms with liquid
½ cup cold water

1. Blend package of seasonings with ⅓ cup water. Set aside.

2. Crumble beef into a 2-quart glass casserole. Microwave on High, uncovered, for 5 to 6 minutes or until beef is no longer pink, stirring once.

3. Add sauce mix, mushrooms with liquid, and water. Stir. Microwave on Medium, covered, for 8 to 10 minutes or until sauce simmers.

4. Stir in noodles. Microwave on Low, covered, for 5 minutes. Stir.

5. Add seasoning mix. Stir. Microwave on Low, covered, for 5 minutes. Let stand for 5 minutes.

Tip: *If you have a Frigidaire Browning Skillet accessory, use this method for step 2. Preheat on High for 4 minutes. Brown ground beef on High for 2 minutes, stirring after one minute. Continue with steps 3, 4, 5.*

Macaroni Medley

4 to 6 will sing about this side dish

3 cups cooked macaroni

1 can (10¾ oz) condensed
  cream of onion soup
1 cup grated mild process
  cheese
¼ cup chopped onion
¼ cup minced green pepper
½ cup milk
1 tablespoon butter or
  margarine
1 tablespoon Worcestershire
  sauce
1 teaspoon salt
¼ teaspoon pepper

¼ cup grated mild process
  cheese
1 teaspoon dried parsley

1. Prepare macaroni as directed on page 164. Set aside.

2. Blend next nine ingredients in a 1½-quart glass casserole. Microwave on Medium for 5 minutes.

3. Add cooked macaroni. Stir. Microwave on Medium, covered, for 10 minutes, stirring after 5 minutes.

4. Top with grated cheese and parsley.

Cereals

We've often heard that breakfast is the most important meal of the day. How about a bowl of hot cereal to get you and your family started in the morning! It's a healthy alternative to the sugar-coated dry cereals.

You can prepare hot cereal for breakfast quickly and easily in the microwave oven—and have time to be creative. Add raisins, peach slices, or nuts to everyone's bowl; and serve a taste-tempting, nutritious breakfast.

The microwave oven allows you to prepare individual servings of hot cereal directly in cereal bowls. This is especially convenient if everyone wants a different variety of hot cereal, or if each family member gets up and eats at a different time.

Of course, you can prepare a family-size quantity of hot cereal in the microwave oven. Stir it once or twice during microwave time.

Microwave time for cooking cereal is about the same as conventional time. Mix instant cereal with water; then microwave it on High, uncovered, for the time specified on the package. If the cereal is not quick-cooking, bring the water to boil; then microwave the cereal on High, covered, for the time specified on the package.

Generally let all hot cereals stand, covered, for a few minutes before serving.

Quick-cooking Oatmeal

A no-fuss breakfast for one

¾ cup water
⅓ cup quick-cooking oats
⅛ teaspoon salt

1. Measure water, cereal, and salt into cereal bowl. Mix well.

2. Microwave on High, uncovered, for 1¼ to 1¾ minutes.

3. Stir. Let stand, covered, for 1 to 2 minutes before serving.

Tip: *Microwave two individual bowls at one time on High for 2 to 2½ minutes.*

Oatmeal with Raisins

A healthy way to start the day; serves 4 to 6

1½ cups quick-cooking oats

3 cups water
¾ teaspoon salt
⅓ cup raisins

1. Add rolled oats to a 2-quart glass casserole.

2. Stir in water, salt, and raisins.

3. Microwave on High, uncovered, for 4 to 5 minutes, stirring after 3 minutes.

4. Let stand for 1 to 2 minutes before serving.

Quick Cream of Wheat

A nutritious breakfast for one

¾ cup water
3 tablespoons quick-cooking cream of wheat
⅛ teaspoon salt

1. Measure water, cereal, and salt into a suitable cereal bowl. Mix well.

2. Microwave on High, covered, for 1½ to 2 minutes.

3. Stir. Let stand, covered, for 1 to 2 minutes before serving.

Tip: *Microwave two individual bowls at one time for 2½ to 3 minutes.*

Quick Grits

Southern style breakfast treat for 6

1 cup quick grits
1 teaspoon salt
4 cups boiling water

1. Measure grits and salt into a 2-quart glass casserole. Stir in boiling water.

2. Microwave on High, uncovered, for 5 minutes, stirring halfway through microwave time.

3. Cover; let stand for 5 minutes.

Butter or margarine

4. Top with butter or margarine, and serve.

Grits au Gratin

Serve in place of potatoes; makes 6 servings

1 cup quick grits (white)
4 cups boiling water
1 teaspoon salt

1. Measure grits, water, and salt into a 2-quart glass casserole.

2. Microwave on High, uncovered, for 5 minutes stirring halfway through microwave time.

3. Cover; let stand for 3 minutes.

¼ cup butter or margarine
1 package (4 oz) shredded Cheddar cheese
¼ teaspoon garlic powder, optional

4. Add butter, cheese, and garlic powder; stir until melted.

2 eggs, beaten
¾ cup water

5. Stir in beaten eggs and water. Microwave on Medium, uncovered, for 5 munutes.

1 cup crisp rice cereal, crushed

6. Stir, Sprinkle with crushed cereal. Microwave on Medium for 5 minutes longer.

7. Serve warm.

Cornmeal Mush

6 servings of a Southern favorite

1 cup white or yellow cornmeal

4 cups water
1½ teaspoons salt

1. Place cornmeal in a 3-quart glass casserole.

2. Add water and salt. Stir well.

3. Microwave on High, uncovered, for 5 minutes.

4. Stir. Microwave on High for 5 minutes longer.

5. Stir well. Let stand, covered, for 3 to 5 minutes before serving.

Polenta

6 portions to make ahead

3 cups cornmeal mush
1 package (4 oz) shredded Cheddar cheese
⅛ teaspoon paprika
Dash cayenne

1. To casserole dish of mush, mix cheese, paprika, and cayenne.

2. Microwave on Medium for 2 minutes. Let stand, covered, for 5 minutes.

3. Pour into greased 8x8x2-inch dish. Cover with waxed paper; refrigerate overnight.

Flour
Vegetable oil
Syrup

4. At serving time, cut into serving pieces, coat with flour. Saute in a small amount of vegetable oil on a conventional surface unit. Serve with syrup, if desired.

Sandwiches

Whether you want to serve sandwiches for a quick lunch or at a make-it-yourself buffet, you'll find recipes in this chapter to give you ideas. But don't stop here. Choose from an array of breads, buns, rolls, meats, cheeses, vegetables, and leftovers. Make your own Dagwood creation, heat, and enjoy!

Ingredients. Start with your choice of sliced bread, buns, hard and soft rolls, or submarine loaves. Some breads do not become as soggy as others; these include day-old or toasted white bread/buns, firmly textured breads such as whole wheat and rye, and rich-dough breads made with eggs and shortening.

Bread gets tough and rubbery when overcooked in the microwave oven. To guard against this yet still obtain hot fillings, use several thin pieces of meat rather than one thick one. If the filling is frozen, defrost it before you assemble the sandwich. You don't have to thaw the bread first.

Microwave instructions. Place the sandwich on a paper plate; or wrap it in a paper towel or napkin. The paper will absorb some of the moisture as it leaves the sandwich; this humidity control helps to prevent a soggy bottom. Moreover, a paper wrapper tends to hold some of the heat in the sandwich.

Actual time required depends on the filling. Microwave all sandwiches on High until the filling is hot, even though the bread feels only warm. Add cheese toward the end of microwave time, and allow it to melt.

Serve these sandwiches immediately.

Make sandwiches ahead, and refrigerate or freeze as desired. This works well for sandwiches with dry fillings, such as submarines. To thaw the sandwich, microwave it on High for 1 to 2 minutes; then let it stand for temperatures to equalize. Once the filling is defrosted, microwave the sandwich on High until heated.

For wet filling sandwiches, such as Sloppy Joes, freeze the filling separately to prevent the bread from becoming soggy. To prepare, thaw the filling first; then assemble the sandwich and heat it.

Hot Dogs

The All-American sandwich

Wieners
Hot dog buns

1. Place wieners in split hot dog buns. Wrap each bun loosely in paper napkin or paper towel.

2. Microwave on High until wiener feels warm:

1 hot dog	½ to ¾ minute
2 hot dogs	¾ to 1 minute
4 hot dogs	1¼ to 1½ minutes
6 hot dogs	1¾ to 2 minutes

3. Let stand a minute or two before serving.

Tips: *Or arrange wieners in buns on paper plate or paper towel in oven.*

For wieners without buns, arrange in glass dish; microwave for the minimum times shown above.

Tuna Boats (page 175)

Hamburgers

Makes 4 quarter-pound burgers

1 pound ground beef
1 teaspoon salt
½ teaspoon pepper

Barbecue sauce or cheese slices

1. Mix ground beef with salt and pepper. Shape into four patties.

2. Place patties in a 12x7½-inch glass dish. Cover dish with a paper towel.

3. Microwave on High for 2 minutes. Drain fat and turn patties over.

4. Top patties with barbecue sauce or cheese slices. Microwave on High, covered, for 2 to 3 minutes. Let stand 2 to 3 minutes before serving.

Tip: *Microwave one hamburger on High for 2 to 2 ½ minutes. Turn after 1 minute.*

Sloppy Joes

6 servings of a lunchtime favorite

1 pound ground beef
1 small onion, chopped

½ cup chopped green pepper
½ cup catsup
2 tablespoons brown sugar
2 tablespoons vinegar
1 teaspoon salt
1 teaspoon chili powder
1 teaspoon Worcestershire sauce

6 hamburger buns

1. Crumble ground beef into a 1½-quart glass casserole. Add onion. Microwave on High, uncovered, for 5 to 6 minutes or until meat has lost its pink color. Stir to break into pieces. Drain fat.

2. Add remaining ingredients except buns. Microwave on High, covered, for 10 minutes, or until simmering. Stir twice.

3. Spoon into hamburger buns. Serve immediately.

Tip: *If sauce is too thick for your taste, add several tablespoons of water.*

Magic Beef Barbecue

Makes 20 sandwiches, or spaghetti sauce base, or casserole beginnings

3 pounds ground chuck
2 medium onions, chopped
1 bottle (12 oz) catsup
1 bottle (14 oz) chili sauce
¼ cup pickle relish (optional)

Buns or toast

1. Crumble ground chuck into a 3-quart glass casserole. Mix in remaining ingredients.

2. Microwave on High, uncovered, for 15 minutes, stirring twice.

3. Serve hot over buns or toast.

Tip: *Refrigerate leftover mixture. Later, use as desired—in sandwiches; as base for spaghetti sauce; in casserole with pasta and cheese.*

Round-up Sandwich

Serves 6 hungry "cowhands" when they come in from the backyard

1 pound ground beef
¼ cup chopped green pepper
¼ cup onion

1 cup bottled barbecue sauce

6 hot dog buns, split
6 slices process American cheese, cut in halves

1. Combine meat, green pepper, and onion; mix lightly. Shape into 6 patties to fit hot dog buns. Place patties in a 12x7½-inch glass dish. Microwave on High for 6 minutes. Turn twice, and pour off excess juice.

2. Add sauce; cover with plastic film. Microwave on High for 4 minutes; rotate dish halfway through microwave time. Set aside.

3. Cover top half of each bun with 2 pieces of cheese. Arrange on paper or glass plate. Microwave on High for 1 to 1¼ minutes or until cheese melts. Place meat patties in buns and serve.

Reuben Sandwich

A colorful and flavorful treat for one

Rye bread
Thousand Island dressing

Thinly sliced corned beef
Sauerkraut
Swiss cheese

1. Place bread slice on paper or glass plate; spread with dressing.

2. Top with layer of corned beef, drained sauerkraut, and slice of cheese. Top with slice of rye.

3. Microwave on High for about 45 seconds or until cheese melts.

Bacon, Cheese, and Tomato Sandwiches

5 openface sandwiches

5 slices bacon

5 slices bread, toasted
¼ cup mayonnaise or salad dressing
2 medium tomatoes, sliced
5 slices Swiss, Cheddar or American cheese

1. Arrange bacon between layers of paper towels in shallow glass baking dish.

2. Microwave on High for 4 to 5 minutes or until crisp; set aside.

3. Spread each piece of toast with mayonnaise. Arrange on paper-lined glass platter. Top with tomato and cheese slices. Crumble a slice of bacon onto each sandwich.

4. Microwave on High for 2 to 2½ minutes or until cheese melts.

Hot Swiss Chicken Salad Sandwiches

Made from yesterday's bird; serves 8

1 cup diced cooked chicken
⅔ cup chopped celery
½ cup cubed natural Swiss cheese
¼ cup mayonnaise or salad dressing
½ teaspoon lemon juice
¼ teaspoon salt

8 hamburger buns

1. Combine all ingredients except buns; mix well.

2. Fill each split hamburger bun with ¼ cup of mixture. Place four sandwiches on a glass plate.

3. Microwave on High for 2½ to 3 minutes.

Tip: *Microwave one sandwich on High for 45 seconds. Refrigerate the remaining mixture until others come in for lunch.*

Turkey in Buns

Tasty after-holiday sandwiches for 4

4 hamburger buns, toasted

1 cup chopped, cooked turkey
1 tablespoon instant minced onion
1 teaspoon instant minced parsley
¼ cup chopped salted peanuts
1 hard-cooked egg, chopped
½ cup mayonnaise
⅓ cup shredded sharp Cheddar cheese
Salt
Pepper

1. Line glass plate with paper towels. Arrange bottom halves of buns on plate.
2. Combine remaining ingredients. Season to taste with salt and pepper.

3. Spread mixture on the bottom half of 4 buns. Add tops.
4. Microwave on High for 3 minutes or until heated.

Tuna Boats

Sail through a luncheon with 4 tuna-cheese combos

Pictured on page 170

1 can (6½ oz) tuna, drained
1 cup cubed American or Cheddar cheese
⅓ cup mayonnaise or salad dressing
¼ cup sweet pickle relish
2 tablespoons chopped green onion
½ teaspoon prepared mustard

4 hot dog buns
Sliced green olives

1. Combine first 6 ingredients; mix well.

2. Fill buns with tuna mixture; garnish with olives. Arrange buns in an 8x8x2-inch glass dish.
3. Microwave on Medium, uncovered, for 3 to 4 minutes or until cheese begins to melt.

Sauces and Toppings

What better way to perk up an ordinary meal—or to add gusto to a special meal—than with a sauce! Choose a sauce to pour over meat, seafood, vegetables, even dessert. Choose a creamy one, or a fruity one. Choose a sweet one, a spicy one, or a delicate one. The choice is yours.

You may prefer to microwave the sauce in the serving utensil if appropriate for microwave use. To guard against boilovers, be sure the utensil is large enough to hold double the amount of sauce.

Microwave most sauces on High. However, for egg/butter sauces microwave on Medium or Low to prevent spatters; these lower settings also result in a smoother sauce. For spicy sauces, microwave on High until boiling point; then switch to Low to simmer the sauce, allowing the flavors to develop.

Watch sauces carefully. Sauces with milk tend to boil over rapidly once hot. Stir sauces during microwave time, as specified in the recipe, to prevent separation or lumps. If sauce starts to separate or curdle, it is overcooked; remove it and improve its consistency with an electric mixer or blender.

Store leftover sauce, covered, in the refrigerator. Microwave on Medium, uncovered, to reheat the sauce.

Basic White Sauce

1 cup of creamy white sauce (thin)

See Tip for variations

1 tablespoon butter or margarine

1 tablespoon flour
½ teaspoon salt
1 cup milk

1. To melt butter in a 1-quart glass bowl or casserole, microwave on High for 30 seconds.

2. Stir in flour and salt to make a smooth paste. Blend in milk gradually.

3. Microwave on High for 3 minutes, stirring every 30 seconds.

Tip: *This recipe makes a thin white sauce. For variations:*

Medium: Use 2 tablespoons of butter and flour for each cup of milk.

Thick: Use 4 tablespoons of butter and flour for each cup of milk.

Cheese sauce: Add ½ cup shredded Cheddar or Swiss cheese to the Basic White Sauce.

Ginger Cheese Pie (page 95) with Melba Sauce (page 181)

Hollandaise Sauce

½ cup to serve with vegetables or fish

¼ cup butter or margarine

¼ cup light cream
2 egg yolks
1 tablespoon lemon juice
½ teaspoon dry mustard
½ teaspoon salt
Dash hot pepper sauce

1. To melt butter in a 4-cup glass measure or medium bowl, microwave on High for 1 minute.

2. Stir in remaining ingredients. Microwave on High for 1 minute, stirring every 15 seconds.

3. Stir briskly with a wire whisk until light and fluffy.

Rich Mushroom Sauce

1½ cups to spoon on meat

3 tablespoons butter or margarine

1½ tablespoons flour
¼ teaspoon salt
¾ cup half and half, or light cream
1 teaspoon soy sauce

1 can (4 oz) mushrooms, drained

1. Place butter in a 1-quart glass measure. Microwave on High for 1 minute or until butter is melted.

2. Stir in flour and salt until smooth. Gradually add half and half and soy sauce. Stir until well blended.

3. Microwave on High for 2 minutes, stirring every 30 seconds.

4. Stir in mushrooms. Microwave on High for 30 seconds or until heated.

Barbecue Sauce

Great on the grill; makes 3 cups

1 bottle (14 oz) catsup
¾ cup packed brown sugar
½ cup vinegar
¼ cup water
½ teaspoon celery seed
½ teaspoon salt
⅛ teaspoon pepper
Bay leaf

1. Combine ingredients in a 4-cup glass measure. Microwave on High for 5 minutes or until mixture boils.

2. Microwave on Low for 15 minutes longer. Remove bay leaf before using.

Mustard Sauce

Makes 1¼ cups of sauce for egg rolls

3 tablespoons sugar
1½ tablespoons cornstarch
3 teaspoons dry mustard
1 cup chicken broth or bouillon
1 tablespoon butter or margarine
Dash pepper

1. Combine sugar, cornstarch and dry mustard in a 2-cup glass measure. Stir in chicken broth. Top with butter and pepper.

2. Microwave on High, uncovered, for 3 to 4 minues or until mixture boils and is smooth and thickened. Stir every minute.

Hot Vanilla Sauce

1 cup to spoon onto desserts

3 tablespoons soft butter or margarine
½ cup sugar

2 egg yolks, slightly beaten
Dash salt
½ cup boiling water

1 teaspoon vanilla

1. Cream together butter and sugar in a 1-quart glass casserole.

2. Beat in egg yolks and salt. Gradually stir in hot water.

3. Microwave on High, uncovered, for 2 minutes. Stir every 30 seconds. Be careful not to overcook.

4. Stir in vanilla. Serve hot.

Rich Butterscotch Sauce

1½ cups of a creamy, dessert topping

1¼ cups packed light brown sugar
2 tablespoons cornstarch
½ cup half and half, or light cream
2 tablespoons light corn syrup
¼ cup butter or margarine
⅛ teaspoon salt

1 teaspoon vanilla

1. Blend sugar and cornstarch in a 1-quart glass measure. Add half and half, syrup, butter, and salt. Stir until well blended.

2. Microwave on Medium, uncovered, for 6 to 7 minutes. Stir every 3 minutes.

3. Add vanilla and stir until smooth. Serve warm or cold.

Tip: *For variation, substitute 1 teaspoon maple flavoring for vanilla. Add ⅓ cup chopped nuts, if desired.*

Apple-Raisin Sauce

1½ cups to serve with baked ham or over spice cake

2 tablespoons brown sugar
1 tablespoon cornstarch
⅛ teaspoon salt
⅛ teaspoon allspice

1 cup apple juice

¼ cup seedless raisins

½ cup diced apples

1. Combine brown sugar, cornstarch, salt, and allspice in a 1-quart glass casserole.

2. Blend in apple juice. Microwave on High, uncovered, for 2 to 2½ minutes. Stir halfway through microwave time.

3. Mix in raisins. Microwave on High for 2 minutes, stirring twice.

4. Add apples just before serving.

Bing Cherry Sauce

1½ cups to spoon onto desserts, or to make Cherries Jubilee

1 can (1 lb) bing cherries
¾ cup cherry juice

2 tablespoons sugar
1 tablespoon cornstarch
Dash salt

1 teaspoon butter
½ teaspoon lemon juice

1. Drain cherries and reserve juice. Measure juice and, if necessary, add water to make ¾ cup.

2. Combine sugar, cornstarch, and salt in a 1-quart glass dish or measuring cup. Stir in reserved cherry juice.

3. Microwave on High, uncovered, for 2 to 3 minutes or until sauce is thick and clear. Stir after each minute.

4. Stir in butter, lemon juice, and cherries. Microwave on High for 45 seconds.

Tips: *Serve warm or cold over cake, pudding, or ice cream.*

To make Cherries Jubilee Sauce substitute 1 tablespoon brandy for lemon juice.

Dessert Lemon Sauce

Makes 1 cup

½ cup sugar
1 tablespoon cornstarch
1 cup water

2 tablespoons butter or margarine
½ teaspoon grated lemon peel
1½ tablespoons lemon juice
Dash salt

1. Combine sugar and cornstarch in a 1-quart glass casserole. Stir in water.

2. Microwave on High, uncovered, for 3 minutes or until thickened and clear, stirring every minute.

3. Blend in butter, lemon peel, lemon juice, and salt.

Tip: *Serve warm or cold.*

Melba Sauce

Delicious over ice cream, custard, fruit, or cake; 1½ cups

Pictured on page 176

1 package (10 oz) frozen raspberries

½ cup sugar
2 tablespoons cornstarch
½ cup currant or apple jelly
1 teaspoon lemon juice

1. Place frozen raspberries in a 1-quart glass casserole. Microwave on Low, uncovered, for 2 to 3 minutes.

2. Blend sugar and cornstarch. Stir sugar mixture into raspberries. Break up currant jelly and add with lemon juice.

3. Microwave on High for 3 minutes. Stir. Microwave on High for 2 to 3 minutes longer, or until jelly is melted and sauce is thickened and clear.

4. Strain if desired; then cool.

Peach Sauce

Makes 1¼ cups of topping for cake, gingerbread or pancakes

See Tip for Apricot Sauce

¼ cup sugar
1 tablespoon cornstarch
⅛ teaspoon salt
½ cup milk

½ cup peach preserves
2 tablespoons lemon juice
1 tablespoon butter or margarine

1. Mix sugar, cornstarch, and salt together in a 4-cup glass measure. Stir in milk.

2. Blend in peach preserves and lemon juice. Add butter.

3. Microwave on High, uncovered, for 3 to 4 minutes or until mixture boils and is smooth. Stir every minute.

Tip: *For variation, substitute apricot preserves.*

Hot Fudge Sauce

Makes 1 cup to pour over ice cream, of course

1 package (6 oz) semisweet chocolate pieces
½ cup evaporated milk

1. Mix chocolate pieces and milk together in a 2-cup glass measure.

2. Microwave on Medium for 2 minutes or until chocolate pieces are melted. Stir with a wire whisk until well blended.

Soups

Ranging from low-calorie broths to hearty complete-meal combinations, soups are traditionally good. Here are a few recipe ideas for the many times you will want to serve soup.

- A quick bowl of canned Chicken Noodle Soup for lunch.
- A family-size bowl of Vegetable Beef Soup or Chili for dinner.
- A tureen of Crab Bisque for indoor entertaining.
- A tureen of Frosty Tomato Soup or Cold Zucchini Soup for patio entertaining.
- Individual cups of French Onion Soup or Egg Drop Soup as a first course at a sitdown dinner.

With your microwave oven you can quickly prepare a cup of soup without messing up the kitchen. Or prepare a from-scratch soup the morning or day before and refrigerate it; later, simply heat and serve.

Choose a glass or china utensil (cup, bowl, casserole, tureen) that is suitable for microwave use and is large enough for the soup to boil. Cover the soup to steam it and to prevent spatters. Use waxed paper, plastic film, a saucer, or any appropriate glass cover. If you use plastic film, pierce a few holes in it before microwave time.

Microwave the soup as you would the individual ingredient. For instance, microwave vegetable soups on High; broths on High; creamed soups on Low. For soups that should simmer, microwave on Low. Stir the soup during the microwave time to distribute the ingredients and to equalize the temperatures.

Generally allow a brief standing time, covered, for the flavors to develop. Then serve.

Store leftover soup, covered, in the refrigerator. Later ladle out a cup or as much as desired; microwave on High, covered, until reheated.

Canned Soup

A quick lunch

1 can of soup

1 can of water or milk (see label)

1. Pour soup in a 1½-quart glass casserole.
2. Add liquid, if required. See instructions on soup can.
3. Microwave, covered, until hot. See chart.
4. Stir. Let stand, covered, for 3 minutes before serving.

Canned Soup	Yield	Add liquid	Microwave Instructions
Condensed (10¾ oz)			
Broth	2 servings	Water	High for 3 to 4 min
Cream of Mushroom	2 servings	Milk	Medium for 7 to 8 min
Most others	2 servings	Water or milk	High for 5 to 6 min
Condensed (26 oz)	5 servings	Water or milk	High for 8 to 9 min
Ready-to-eat strength (10¾ oz)	1 serving	None	High for 2½ to 3½ min
Ready-to-eat strength (19 oz)	2 servings	None	High for 5 to 7 min

Russian Borscht (page 185)

Dehydrated Soup Mix

Water (see chart)

Soup mix

1. Pour water into appropriate container.
2. Read package instructions; see chart. Either add soup mix to water; or boil water, covered, first.
3. Microwave soup and water, covered, as specified in the chart.
4. Let stand, covered, for 5 minutes before serving.

Dehydrated Soup Mix	Yield	Glass container, covered	Water	Microwave Instructions
Instant Mix for One Cup ($1\frac{1}{2}$ oz pkg with 4 single-serving envelopes)				
1 envelope	1 serving	1 mug or soup bowl	$\frac{2}{3}$ cup	Soup and water: High for 2 to $2\frac{1}{2}$ min
2 envelopes	2 servings	2 mugs or soup bowls	$\frac{2}{3}$ cup each	Soup and water: High for 3 to $3\frac{1}{2}$ min
Soup Mix with Rice or Noodles ($3\frac{1}{2}$ oz pkg with 2 family-size envelopes)				
1 envelope	4 servings	2-qt casserole	3 cups	Water: High for 7 to 8 min Soup and water: Low for 5 to 6 min
Soup Mix without Rice or Noodles ($2\frac{3}{4}$ oz pkg with 2 family-size envelopes)				
1 envelope	4 servings	2-qt casserole or pitcher	4 cups	Water: High for 8 to 10 min Soup and water: High for 4 to 5 min
Soup Mix (5 oz pkg to prepare all at once)	5 servings	2-qt casserole	5 cups	Water: High for 9 to 10 min Soup and water: Low for 10 to 12 min

Hearty Bean Soup

6 servings for a cold winter's day

3 slices bacon

1. Place bacon strips in a large glass casserole or ceramic Dutch oven. Microwave on High, covered with paper towel, for 3 to 4 minutes or until crisp. Remove bacon, crumble, and set aside.

½ cup celery, chopped
½ cup onion, chopped

2. To bacon drippings, add celery and onion. Microwave on High, covered, for 3 to 4 minutes or until onion is transparent.

4 frankfurters, cut in ½-inch pieces
1 can (1 lb, 5 oz) pork and beans
1 can (1 lb) stewed tomatoes
2 cups water
2 beef bouillon cubes
1 teaspoon Worcestershire sauce
1 teaspoon parsley flakes
1 teaspoon sugar
1 bay leaf
Dash cayenne

3. Add bacon and remaining ingredients to casserole. Microwave on High, covered, for 5 minutes.

4. Stir. Microwave on Low, covered, for 30 minutes or until flavors have blended. Remove bay leaf and serve.

Russian Borscht

Short-cut beet soup; serves 4

Pictured on page 182

2 tablespoons butter
½ cup finely chopped onion

1. Place butter and onion in a 2-quart glass casserole. Microwave on High, uncovered, for 2½ minutes.

1 can (1 lb) diced or Julienne cut beets

2. Empty can of beets with juice into an electric blender. Add onions. Blend until smooth.

1 cup hot water
3 beef bouillon cubes
¼ teaspoon salt
Dash hot pepper sauce

3. Return vegetable pulp to casserole; add hot water, bouillon cubes, salt, and hot pepper sauce. Microwave on High, covered, for 5 minutes or until hot.

1 tablespoon lemon juice
Sour cream

4. Stir in lemon juice. Top each serving with a spoonful of sour cream.

French Onion Soup

A classic appetizer for 5 to 6 to enjoy

3 medium onions, chopped
¼ cup butter or margarine

2 tablespoons instant beef bouillon
2 tablespoons soy sauce
1 tablespoon Worcestershire sauce
½ teaspoon paprika
Dash pepper
5 cups water

1. Combine onion and butter in a 3-quart glass casserole. Microwave on High, covered, for 9 to 11 minutes or until onions are transparent.

2. Stir in remaining ingredients. Microwave on High, covered, for 8 to 10 minutes or until hot.

Tip: *Top each serving with a slice of toasted French bread; sprinkle with Parmesan cheese.*

Split Pea Soup

Hearty soup for 6 to 8

1 pound (2 cups) dry split green peas
1 carrot, diced
1 small potato, cubed
1 small onion, chopped
1 ham bone
1 pound smoked ham, cubed
2 quarts boiling water

1. Place all ingredients except salt and pepper in a 4-quart glass casserole. Stir together.

2. Microwave on High, covered, for 30 minutes, stirring twice.

3. Microwave on Low, covered, for 20 minutes or until peas are tender.

4. Remove bone and pieces of ham; set aside.

5. Blend soup in an electric blender until creamy.

Salt and pepper

6. Return pieces of ham to soup. Add salt and pepper to taste.

7. To serve, Microwave in a glass casserole until soup is hot.

Frosty Tomato Soup

Beautiful for patio entertaining; makes 6 bowls

1 cup chopped onions
6 medium, ripe tomatoes, chopped
2 tablespoons vegetable oil

1 can (10½ oz) condensed beef broth
¼ cup catsup

1 tablespoon dry dill weed
1 teaspoon salt
Dash hot pepper sauce
3 cups crushed ice

½ cup heavy cream, whipped

1. Place onion, tomatoes, and oil in a 3-quart glass casserole. Microwave on High for 4 minutes, or until vegetables are cooked. Stir once.

2. Stir in broth and catsup. Microwave on High for 2 minutes longer.

3. Pour into an electric blender, and blend until smooth. Return mixture to casserole.

4. Stir in seasonings. Add ice, and refrigerate until chilled.

5. To serve, blend with rotary beater. Top each serving with a spoonful of whipped cream.

Cold Zucchini Soup

4 cups of chilled soup for a hot day

2 pounds zucchini, cut in ¼-inch slices
½ cup water

2½ chicken bouillon cubes
2 tablespoons butter or margarine
1 tablespoon flour (optional)
⅛ teaspoon garlic powder
⅛ teaspoon nutmeg
2 to 3 dashes hot pepper sauce

Sour cream

1. Place zucchini and water in a 2-quart glass casserole. Microwave on High, covered, for 14 minutes, or until tender.

2. Place zucchini and liquid in a blender container. Add remaining ingredients.

3. Blend on high speed until smooth. Chill.

4. Serve with dollops of sour cream.

Chicken Vegetable Soup

4 to 6 quick servings

1 can (19 oz) chunk style chicken soup
1 can (19 oz) chunk style vegetable soup
1 can (13¾ oz) chicken broth
1 teaspoon parsley flakes

1. Combine all ingredients in a 1½-quart glass casserole.

2. Microwave on Medium, covered, for 8 to 10 minutes or until hot.

Cheesy Chicken Soup

Soup combo for 3 to 5

1 can (10¾ oz) condensed cream of chicken soup
1 soup can water
¼ pound mild process cheese, shredded
2 tablespoons sherry, optional
¼ teaspoon Worcestershire sauce
¼ teaspoon garlic salt

1. Combine all ingredients in a 1-quart glass casserole. Microwave on Low, covered, for 5 minutes. Stir with wire whisk.

2. Microwave on Low for 3 minutes longer. Stir. Let stand for 5 minutes.

Speedy Minestrone

A vegetable soup with meat and macaroni; serves 8 to 10

2 cups cubed cooked beef, pork, or chicken
1 can (16 oz) tomatoes, undrained
1 can (10¾ oz) condensed tomato soup
1 can (15½ oz) kidney beans, undrained
1 can (12 oz) French style sliced green beans, undrained
½ cup uncooked elbow macaroni
2 cups shredded cabbage
⅓ cup chopped onion
1 cup water
1 tablespoon Worcestershire sauce
½ teaspoon salt
½ teaspoon garlic salt
¼ teaspoon pepper

1. Combine all ingredients except cheese in a 3-quart glass casserole. Mix well.

2. Microwave on High, covered, for 20 minutes. Stir once.

Parmesan cheese (optional)

3. Microwave on Low, covered, for 15 minutes. Sprinkle with Parmesan cheese, if desired.

Vegetable Beef Soup

Flavor improves the second day; makes 3 quarts

1 pound ground beef
½ cup chopped onion

1. Crumble ground beef in a 4-quart glass casserole or ceramic Dutch oven. Add onion. Microwave on High, covered, for 5 to 6 minutes, or until beef is no longer pink, stirring once.

8 cups hot water
1 cup diced potatoes
1 cup shredded cabbage
½ cup chopped celery
½ cup diced carrots
½ cup frozen peas or green beans
1 can (#303) tomatoes (2 cups)
1 tablespoon chopped fresh parsley (or 1 teaspoon dried parsley flakes)
1 tablespoon salt
¼ teaspoon pepper

2. Add remaining ingredients except noodles; mix well. Microwave on High, covered, for 10 to 15 minutes or until boiling.

3. Microwave on Low, covered, for 30 minutes, stirring once.

1 cup medium noodles

4. Add noodles. Microwave on Low, covered, for 30 minutes longer or until noodles are done and vegetables are tender. Serve immediately; or cool and refrigerate or freeze.

5. To thaw, microwave on Low.
To reheat, microwave on High.

Egg Drop Soup

A hot, appetizing cocktail for 5 to 6

3 cups chicken stock, fresh or canned

1. Pour chicken stock into a 4-cup glass measure. Microwave on High for 5 to 6 minutes or until boiling.

1 tablespoon cornstarch
2 tablespoons water
½ teaspoon salt

2. Mix water and cornstarch. Stir into chicken stock. Add salt. Microwave on High for 1 to 2 minutes, stirring twice.

1 egg, slightly beaten
1 scallion, including greens, finely chopped

3. Slowly pour in beaten egg and stir gently. Garnish with chopped scallion.

Chili

Adjust the hotness to suit your taste; 5 or 6 servings

1 pound ground beef
1 medium onion, chopped
1 medium green pepper, chopped

1 can (28 oz) tomatoes, undrained
1 can (15½ oz) kidney beans, undrained
1 can (8 oz) tomato sauce
1 tablespoon sugar
1 tablespoon Worcestershire sauce
2 to 3 teaspoons chili powder
1 teaspoon salt

1. Crumble ground beef into a 3-quart glass casserole. Add onion and green pepper. Microwave on High, covered, for 5 to 6 minutes or until meat is no longer pink, stirring once.

2. Drain fat. Add remaining ingredients. Mix well.

3. Microwave on High, covered, for 5 minutes.

4. Stir. Then microwave on Medium for 15 minutes or until flavors are blended, stirring once.

Crab Bisque

Elegantly topped with whipped cream and chives; serves 5 to 6

1 can (10¾ oz) condensed cream of asparagus soup
1 can (10¾ oz) condensed cream of mushroom soup
1½ cups milk
1 cup light cream
1 cup (6½ oz can) crabmeat, flaked

1. Combine soups, milk, and cream in a 2-quart glass casserole. Stir in flaked crabmeat.

2. Microwave on Medium, covered, for 8 to 10 minutes or until almost boiling, stirring several times.

¼ cup cooking sherry, optional
Salted whipped cream, optional
Minced chives

3. Just before serving, stir in sherry. Top with fluffs of salted whipped cream; sprinkle with minced chives.

New England Clam Chowder

Hearty, hot, serves 4; see Tip for Manhattan variation

3 slices bacon

1. Place bacon in a 2-quart glass casserole; cover with paper towel. Microwave on High for 2 to 3 minutes or until crisp.

1 can (8 oz) minced clams

2. Remove bacon; crumble, and set aside. Drain clam liquid into bacon drippings. Set clams aside.

2 potatoes, peeled and cubed
½ cup chopped onion
½ cup water

3. Add potatoes, onion, and water to bacon drippings. Microwave on High, covered, for 10 minutes or until potatoes are tender. Stir once.

2 tablespoons flour
1⅓ cups milk
1 teaspoon salt
Dash of pepper

4. Blend flour with small amount of milk to dissolve. Add to cooked mixture. Add milk, salt, pepper, and minced clams.

Parsley

5. Microwave on Low, covered, for 10 minutes, stirring once. Let stand for 5 minutes. Garnish with crumbled bacon and parsley, if desired.

Tip: *For Manhattan Clam Chowder, add 1 cup diced carrots and ½ cup diced celery to step 3. Substitute 1 cup undrained tomatoes for flour and milk in step 4. Increase step 5 microwave time to 13 minutes.*

Oyster Stew

3 to 4 creamy servings

½ pint oysters, with liquid

1. Drain oysters, reserving liquid. Set oysters aside.

1½ cups milk
½ cup cream
¼ cup butter or margarine

2. Combine oyster liquid, milk, cream, and butter in a 2-quart glass casserole.

3. Microwave on Medium, covered, for 5 minutes or until almost boiling.

½ teaspoon salt
⅛ teaspoon paprika
½ teaspoon Worcestershire sauce
2 drops liquid hot pepper seasoning

4. Add oysters and seasoning. Microwave on Medium, uncovered, for 2 to 3 minutes or until edges of oysters begin to curl. Do not boil.

Butter or paprika

5. Ladle stew into serving bowls; top with a dot of butter or paprika. Serve.

Vegetables

If you have been trying to get your family to eat more vegetables, microwave cooking may be the answer. The flavor, tenderness, and color of microwave vegetables are far superior to conventionally cooked vegetables. In addition, since you use less water to microwave vegetables, the nutrients remain in the serving dish instead of being poured down the drain.

The charts and recipes in this chapter are designed for specific vegetable dishes. Generally, however, these simple guidelines will help you prepare any vegetable whether fresh, frozen, or canned.

Preparation. Carefully arrange vegetables in the oven. Place thicker ends (stalks) toward the outside of the dish. Keep thinner ends toward the inside. (See page 11.)

Arrange dense vegetables, such as baking potatoes, in a circle with at least one inch separating them. (See page 11.)

Add a small amount of moisture to steam most vegetables and to keep them from drying out. Starchy vegetables require more water than others to prevent drying out. However, too much moisture tends to make any vegetable soggy and to increase microwave time.

Pierce holes in the outer skins of vegetables such as potatoes, acorn squash, etc. This allows steam to escape during microwave time. (See page 10.)

Season vegetables after microwave time. Vegetables will get a spotted appearance if salt is sprinkled on them before microwave time. Moreover, salt tends to draw the natural moisture out of the vegetables during microwave time.

Cover most vegetables—either with a tight-fitting lid or with plastic film. As moisture is retained in the dish, the vegetables will cook quicker and more evenly. Moisture also retains flavor.

Microwave instructions. Microwave all fresh and frozen vegetables on High. Actual time required depends on many variables: the moisture content of the vegetables, age, freshness, brand, temperature before cooking, as well as personal preferences. Adapt microwave times accordingly.

Stir or turn the vegetables halfway through microwave time to help distribute the heat evenly. Or rotate the dish.

Remove vegetables while still slightly underdone. Let stand from 2 to 5 minutes, depending on the density of the vegetables. The vegetables will continue to cook during this standing time. If vegetables are overcooked, they become dehydrated and tough.

Fresh Cauliflower (page 195) with Cheese Sauce (page 177); Twice Baked Potatoes (page 211); Fresh Broccoli (page 194).

Fresh Vegetables

1. Place vegetables in a glass casserole.
2. Add water as specified in chart. Cream or butter may also be added for moisture.
3. Microwave on High, covered, stirring halfway through microwave time.
4. Let stand, covered, for about 3 minutes before serving.
5. Season, as desired.

Fresh Vegetables		Amount	Microwave on High, covered (approx min)	Special Instructions
Artichokes		2 med	5 to 7	Add ¼ cup water
Asparagus, 4-inch pieces		15	5 to 7	Add ¼ cup water Discard tough ends
Beans,	Green Wax	1 lb	7 to 9	Snap or French cut beans Add ¼ cup water
	Lima	1 lb (2 cups shelled)	6 to 8	Add ½ cup water
		2 lb (4 cups shelled)	9 to 11	Add ½ cup water
Beets,	whole	4 med	15 to 17	Barely cover with water
	sliced	4 med	12	Add ½ cup water
Broccoli		1 small bunch (1½ lb)	7 to 9	Cut away tough part of stalk Split tender ends Add ½ cup water
Brussels Sprouts		½ lb (2 cups)	4 to 6	Add 2 tbsp water
		1 lb (4 cups)	5 to 7	Add 3 tbsp water
Cabbage,	chopped	1 small head	10 to 12	Add 2 tbsp water
	whole	1 med head	12 to 15	Add 2 tbsp water

Chart continued on next page

Fresh Vegetables, *continued*

Fresh Vegetables		Amount	Microwave on High, covered (approx min)	Special Instructions
Carrots, sliced		4 med	4 to 6	Add 2 tbsp water
		6 med	6 to 8	Add 2 tbsp water
Cauliflower,	whole	1 small head	5 to 7	Add ½ cup water
	flowerets	1 med head	9 to 11	Add ½ cup water
Celery, coarsely chopped		4 cups	7 to 9	Add ¼ cup water
Corn, kernels		1½ cups	3 to 5	Add ¼ cup water
Corn on the Cob (Also see recipe page 207)		2 ears	4 to 6	Place in glass dish; pour melted butter over corn; cover dish
		4 ears	8 to 10	Turn ears 2 or 3 times during microwave time
Eggplant, cubed		1 med (4 cups)	4 to 6	Peel and dice Add 2 tbsp water
Mushrooms		½ lb	4 to 5	Add 2 tbsp water
Okra		1 lb	5	Add 2 tbsp water
Onions, quartered		2 large	5 to 7	Add ½ cup water
		4 large	7 to 9	
Parsnips		4 med	7 to 9	Add ¼ cup water
Peas, Green		2 lb (2 cups shelled)	4 to 6	Add 2 tbsp water
		4 lb (4 cups shelled)	9 to 10	Add 2 tbsp water

Chart continued on next page

Fresh Vegetables, *continued*

Fresh Vegetables		Amount	Microwave on High, covered (approx min)	Special Instructions
Potatoes, baked				See recipe, page 210
Potatoes, new boiled in jackets		4 med	12 to 14	Slice potatoes Add 2 tbsp butter, ¼ cup water Stir after 5 min
		6 med	17 to 19	
Potatoes, Red boiled		6 med (2 lb)	12 to 15	Peel, cut in half Add ¼ cup water Stir once after 6 min
Rutabaga, cubed or sliced		3 cups	7 to 9	Wash, peel, cube, or slice Add ½ cup water, 3 tbsp butter
Spinach		4 cups (1 lb)	6 to 7	Wash. Microwave with water that clings to the leaves
Squash, Acorn Butternut		1 med	4 to 6	Pierce skin with sharp knife in several places Place whole squash on paper towel
		2 med	8	
Sweet Potatoes,	baked			See recipe, page 213
	boiled	4 med	8 to 10	Peel, cut in half lengthwise Add ¼ cup water
		6 med	12 to 14	
Swiss Chard		¾ lb	7 to 8	Add ¼ cup water
Tomatoes, baked		2 med	3	Add 2 tbsp water
Turnips, cubed or sliced		2 or 3 med (1 lb)	7 to 9	Peel, and cube or slice Add 3 tbsp water
Yellow Squash, sliced Zucchini, sliced		2 med (3 cups)	7	Add ¼ cup water

Frozen Vegetables

For boil-in-the-bag vegetables, see next page

1. Place contents of one package (approximately 10 ounces) of frozen vegetables in a 1-quart glass casserole.
2. Add water as specified in the chart.
3. Microwave on High, covered, stirring halfway through microwave time.
4. Season, as desired.

Tip: *For two packages, use a 1½-quart casserole dish. Microwave time will be almost doubled.*

Frozen Vegetables (one package, approx 10 oz)		Microwave on High, covered (approx min)	Special Instructions
Artichokes		5 to 6	Ice side up. Separate pieces after 3 min
Asparagus, green spears		5 to 6	Ice side up. Separate spears after 3 min
Beans,	Green Wax	7½ to 8½	If solid pack, place ice side up. If loose pack, add 2 tbsp water
	Green French cut	7 to 8	Add 2 tbsp water
	Lima	8½ to 9½	Add ¼ cup water
Broccoli		8½ to 9½	Ice side up. Separate pieces after 5 min
Brussels Sprouts		7	Add ¼ cup water
Carrots		8 to 10	Add 2 tbsp water
Cauliflower		5 to 6	Add 2 tbsp water
Corn, whole kernels		4 to 5	Add ¼ cup water
Corn on the Cob		5 to 6	Add ¼ cup water; turn after 3 min
Mixed Vegetables		6½ to 7½	Add ¼ cup water
Okra		6 to 7	Add 2 tbsp water
Peas, Black-eyed		10 to 12	If solid pack, place ice side up. If loose pack, add ¼ cup water
Peas, Green		4½ to 5½	If solid pack, place ice side up. If loose pack, add 2 tbsp water
Peas and Carrots		5 to 6	If solid pack, place ice side up. If loose pack, add 2 tbsp water
Spinach		4½ to 5½	Ice side up
Squash, Hubbard		4 to 6	Add 2 tbsp water

Boil-in-the-bag Frozen Vegetables

A meal accompaniment, complete in itself

1 package (approx 10 oz) frozen vegetables in boilable plastic bag

1. Using a sharp knife, cut an X in the plastic bag, slitting from corner to diagonal corner. Invert the package, X side down, into a glass dish.

2. Microwave on High, rotating the dish halfway through microwave time. Check package instructions for microwave time. If none is given, microwave on High for ⅓ of conventional boiling time.

Canned Vegetables

From the shelf to a serving dish in a moment's notice

1 can vegetables

1. Empty vegetables and a small amount of liquid into a glass casserole. Drain off excess liquid and save, if desired.

2. Microwave on High, covered, until heated. Allow approximately 2 minutes for each cup of vegetables.

Seasonings, as desired

3. Add seasonings and serve.

Tip: *Refrigerate excess liquid for later use in casseroles, soups, etc.*

Glazed Acorn Squash

Tender and tasty for 4 to enjoy

2 acorn squash

1. Pierce skin of squash with sharp knife in several places. Microwave on High for 6 minutes.

¼ cup butter or margarine
¼ cup brown sugar
Cinnamon

2. Cut squash in half lengthwise; remove seeds and stringy portions. Place in a shallow glass baking dish. Place butter and brown sugar in the center of squash. Sprinkle with cinnamon.

3. Microwave on High for 4 to 5 minutes, or until tender.

Apple-Acorn Squash

4 hearty servings, easy to make with pie filling

2 acorn squash, cooked

1 can (20 oz) apple pie filling
1 teaspoon cinnamon
½ teaspoon nutmeg

1 tablespoon butter or margarine

1. Cook squash as described on page 196. Cut in half, lengthwise. Remove seeds and stringy portions.

2. Place ¼ cup apple pie filling in center of each half. Sprinkle with cinnamon and nutmeg. Place on a flat glass plate.

3. Microwave on High for 4 to 8 minutes or until well heated. Dot with butter and serve.

Asparagus Vinaigrette

A tangy vegetable for 3; use sauce for other vegetables too

3 tablespoons sweet pickle relish
2 tablespoons fresh snipped parsley
¾ teaspoon sugar
1 teaspoon salt
¼ cup cider vinegar
¾ cup vegetable oil

1 package (10 oz) frozen asparagus

1. Mix together all ingredients except asparagus. Puree in a blender, if desired. Set aside.

2. Place asparagus in a 1½-quart glass casserole. Microwave on High, covered, for 5 minutes.

3. Pour ⅓ cup sauce over asparagus. Microwave on Low, covered, for 5 minutes.

4. To serve hot, first let stand for several minutes. To serve cold, refrigerate for several hours; then drain and serve.

Tip: *Use sauce for broccoli, carrots, or zucchini.*

Baked Beans

Gingersnaps added for flavor; serves 6

4 slices bacon

2 cans (1 lb each) pork and beans
¼ cup dark corn syrup
¼ cup catsup
2 tablespoons chopped onion
¾ cup finely crushed gingersnaps

1. Cut bacon in small pieces. Place in a 1½-quart glass casserole or bean pot. Microwave on High for 4 minutes. Stir halfway through microwave time.

2. Stir in remaining ingredients. Microwave on High for 10 minutes. Stir every 4 minutes.

Green Beans with Onion Rings

Serves 4 to 6

2 packages (10 oz each) frozen green beans
½ teaspoon salt
1 can (10¾ oz) condensed cream of celery soup

1 can French fried onion rings

1. Place beans in a 1½-quart glass casserole. Sprinkle with salt. Spread soup over beans. Microwave on High, covered, for 5 minutes.

2. Break up beans with fork; stir. Place onion rings on top. Continue to microwave on High, covered, for 8 minutes.

Green Beans and Mushrooms

5 to 6 servings in a creamy sauce

1 pound fresh green beans
¼ cup water
1 can (3 to 4 oz) sliced mushrooms, drained

1 cup dairy sour cream
1 tablespoon brown sugar
1 tablespoon flour
½ teaspoon salt
Dash pepper

1. Rinse and drain beans. Trim ends. Snap beans in two. Place in a 1½-quart glass casserole with water. Microwave on High, covered, for 8 minutes. Let stand for 2 minutes. Drain. Stir in mushrooms.

2. Mix remaining ingredients. Stir into beans and mushrooms. Microwave on High, covered, for 3 to 4 minutes.

3. Stir. Let stand, covered, for 5 minutes before serving.

Dilled Beans

Use green or wax beans for 4 good servings

1 package (9 oz) frozen French-cut green beans
2 tablespoons boiling water

¼ cup dairy sour cream
¼ teaspoon dill weed
Salt and pepper

1. Place frozen beans in a 1-quart glass casserole. Add water. Microwave on High, covered, for 6 minutes.

2. Drain beans. Mix in remaining ingredients. Salt and pepper to taste.

4-Bean Pot

12 hearty servings for a backyard supper; freezes well

8 slices bacon

1 cup chopped onion

1 can (1 lb) green beans, drained
1 can (1 lb) lima beans, drained
1 can (1 lb) pork and beans, drained
1 can (1 lb) kidney beans, drained
¾ cup packed brown sugar
½ cup vinegar
½ teaspoon garlic salt
½ teaspoon dry mustard
⅛ teaspoon pepper

1. Cut bacon into small pieces. Microwave on High, covered, until brown and crisp. Remove meat and reserve.

2. To saute onions in bacon fat, microwave on High for 3 minutes. Stir halfway through microwave time.

3. Combine all ingredients in a 3-quart glass casserole. Microwave on High, covered, for 15 minutes. Serve hot or cold.

Tip: *Before microwave time divide mixture into two 1½-quart casseroles. Freeze one for later use. For today's casserole, microwave on High for 7 to 9 minues. For the frozen casserole, see page 228.*

Harvard Beets

4 colorful servings

2 cups cooked, sliced beets and juice

1 tablespoon cornstarch
¼ cup sugar
½ teaspoon salt
¼ cup cider vinegar

1 tablespoon butter

1. Cook beets. See page 194. Reserve ⅓ cup beet juice.

2. To a 2-quart glass casserole add dry ingredients. Stir in vinegar and reserved beet juice. Microwave on High, covered, for 4 to 5 minutes.

3. Add beets and stir. Dot with butter. Microwave on High, covered, for 5 minutes. Let stand for several minutes before serving.

Beet Tops

Cooked greens a family of 6 will enjoy

2 bunches fresh beet tops

1. Wash leaves well, removing stems. Shake off excess water. Place leaves in a 2-quart glass casserole. Microwave on High, covered, for 8 to 10 minutes. Set aside.

¾ cup frozen chopped onions
2 tablespoons butter or margarine
½ teaspoon salt
Dash pepper

2. Place onions, butter, salt, and pepper in a 1-quart glass casserole. Microwave on Medium, covered, for 3 to 4 minutes.

3. Drain beet tops. Chop up coarsely. Add sauteed mixture, and stir together. Microwave on High, covered, for 4 to 5 minutes.

Tip: *Sprinkle with cider vinegar or lemon juice, if desired.*

Spicy Beets

Serve cold or hot at a picnic

1 pound beets, cooked and drained

1. Skin and slice beets. Place in a 1½-quart glass casserole.

½ cup orange juice
½ cup orange marmalade
2 teaspoons cornstarch
½ teaspoon allspice
½ teaspoon ground cloves
¼ teaspoon salt

2. Blend juice, marmalade, cornstarch, spices, and salt in a 2-cup glass measure. Microwave on High for 2 to 3 minutes.

1 tablespoon butter or margarine

3. Pour mixture over beets. Dot with butter. Microwave on High, covered, for 3 to 5 minutes.

Cheddar Creamed Broccoli

Serves 6 to 8; made with condensed soup and almonds

2 pounds fresh broccoli

½ cup water

1 can (10¾ oz) condensed Cheddar cheese soup
¼ cup milk
½ cup slivered almonds
2 green onions, including tops, finely chopped
1 tablespoon chopped parsley

1. Remove large leaves and tough part of broccoli stalks. Rinse well. Cut large stalks into strips for easier serving. Make deep cuts in stalk ends.

2. Place broccoli and water in a 3-quart glass casserole. Microwave on High, covered, for 16 to 18 minutes, or until fork tender. Let stand, covered.

3. Mix soup and milk in a small glass bowl until smooth. Add almonds, onions, and parsley. Microwave sauce on High, uncovered, for 3 to 3½ minutes. Stir halfway through microwave time.

4. Drain broccoli. Pour sauce over broccoli. Serve.

Red Cabbage with Apples

6 sweet-sour servings

1 medium head red cabbage, shredded
2 tart apples, peeled and chopped
1 cup boiling water
½ cup apple cider vinegar
3 tablespoons butter or margarine
3 tablespoons sugar
½ teaspoon salt
1 stick cinnamon

1. Combine ingredients in a 3-quart glass casserole. Stir together.

2. Microwave on High, covered, for 10 to 12 minutes or until cabbage is tender. Stir every 4 minutes. Let stand for 5 to 10 minutes.

Scalloped Cabbage au Gratin

A nutritious vegetable treat for 8

1 head coarsely shredded cabbage (8 cups)
¼ cup water
1 teaspoon salt

3 tablespoons butter or margarine
3 tablespoons flour
1 teaspoon salt
⅛ teaspoon pepper

1½ cups milk
¾ cup shredded cheese

½ cup shredded cheese
Cracker crumbs (optional)

1. Place cabbage, water, and salt in a 3-quart glass casserole. Microwave on High, covered, for 10 minutes, stirring lightly after 5 minutes. Drain; set aside.

2. Place butter in a 1-quart glass dish. Microwave on High to melt. Blend in flour, salt, and pepper.

3. Add milk to flour paste. Microwave on High for 5 to 6 minutes, or until thickened, stirring every minute. Stir in ¾ cup cheese.

4. Add sauce to drained cabbage, mixing gently. Top with ½ cup cheese and cracker crumbs, if desired.

5. Microwave on High, covered, for 5 to 6 minutes, or until cheese is melted and hot. Rotate dish halfway through microwave time.

Spicy Carrots

Adds color and taste to your meal for 4

1 bunch carrots, pared
2 tablespoons butter or margarine

2 tablespoons brown sugar
1 teaspoon dry mustard
2 drops hot pepper sauce
¼ teaspoon salt
Dash pepper

1. Cut carrots in 2-inch strips. Rinse in cold water; drain. Place in a 2-quart glass casserole with butter. Microwave on High, covered, for 5 minutes. Stir halfway through microwave time.

2. Combine remaining ingredients. Pour over carrots. Microwave on High, covered, for 5 minutes, or until tender. Stir halfway through microwave time.

Cauliflower with Oriental Sauce

This whole-head vegetable serves 6

1 medium head cauliflower

½ cup chopped onion
½ cup diced celery
3 sprigs parsley, chopped
1 tablespoon butter or margarine

1 beef or chicken bouillon cube
1 cup hot water
1 tablespoon cornstarch
1 tablespoon soy sauce
Dash pepper

1. Wash cauliflower; remove outer green stalks. Place whole head in a 2-quart glass casserole. Cover with glass lid or with plastic film. Microwave on High, covered, for 10 minutes. Drain. Set aside, covered.

2. In a 1-quart casserole, place onion, celery, parsley, and butter. Microwave on High, uncovered, for 5 minutes. Stir halfway through microwave time.

3. Dissolve bouillon cube in water. Blend in cornstarch, soy sauce, and pepper. Pour into onion mixture. Microwave on High for 2 minutes. Stir every 30 seconds.

4. Place cooked cauliflower head on a serving dish. Top with sauce.

Tip: *For an easy sauce, mix ½ cup salad dressing or mayonnaise with 1 teaspoon prepared mustard. Pour over cooked cauliflower; sprinkle with shredded Cheddar cheese.*

Far East Celery

With water chestnuts and almonds in a creamy sauce; serves 4 to 6

4 cups celery, cut in 1-inch pieces
¼ cup water
½ teaspoon salt

1 can (5 oz) water chestnuts

1 can (10¾ oz) condensed cream of chicken soup
¼ cup chopped pimento
¼ cup slivered almonds

½ cup soft bread crumbs
1 tablespoon melted butter or margarine

1. Combine celery, water and salt in a 1½-quart glass casserole. Microwave on High, covered, for 7 to 9 minutes. Drain and set aside.

2. Drain water chestnuts, and cut into thin slices. Mix chestnuts into celery.

3. Mix together soup, pimento, and almonds. Stir into celery mixture.

4. Mix crumbs and butter until crumbs are well coated. Sprinkle crumbs over celery mixture. Microwave on High, covered, for 4 minutes or until hot.

Corn in the Husk

Always a favorite

Pictured on facing page and on front cover

2 or 4 ears of corn

1. Remove outer husks, but leave inner husk on corn. Carefully remove silk, if desired. Replace husks and fasten with string or rubber band. Arrange in shallow glass dish.

2. Microwave on High, turning ears halfway through microwave time.

2 ears	4 to 6 minutes
4 ears	8 to 10 minutes

Melted butter

3. Serve with melted butter.

Corn Pudding Souffle

Creamy souffle serves 8

1 tablespoon butter or margarine
2 tablespoons sugar
3 tablespoons flour
1 teaspoon salt

1. Place butter in a 4-cup glass measure. Microwave on High for 15 seconds or until melted. Stir in sugar, flour, and salt.

1½ cups milk
4 egg yolks

2. Combine milk and egg yolks. Beat until well blended. Gradually add to the flour mixture, stirring with a wire whisk.

3. Microwave on High, uncovered, for 4 to 5 minutes. Stir every minute with a whisk.

1 can (1 lb) cream style corn
4 egg whites, beaten to soft peaks

4. Combine sauce and corn in a 12x7½-inch glass dish. Blend well. Fold in egg whites. Microwave on High, uncovered, for 7 to 9 minutes. Rotate dish twice during microwave time.

5. Let stand, covered with plastic film, for 3 to 5 minutes before serving.

Eggplant Casserole

Bubbly, tasty; made with fresh garden tomatoes; serves 4 to 6

⅓ cup butter or margarine
2 medium onions, sliced
1 eggplant (1½ lb) pared and cut in ½-inch cubes

1. Place butter in a 3-quart glass casserole. Microwave on High until melted. Add onion and eggplant.

2. Microwave on High, covered, for 10 minutes, stirring once.

1 teaspoon salt
3 medium tomatoes, sliced or cut in wedges
1 cup shredded cheese

3. Mix in salt. Arrange tomatoes on top; sprinkle with cheese. Microwave on High, covered, for 5 to 6 minutes or until cheese bubbles, rotating dish once.

Corn in the Husk (this page)

Eggplant Italiano

Bakes with tomato sauce and cheeses; serves 4 to 6

1 medium eggplant

2 cans (8 oz each) tomato sauce

2 teaspoons oregano

½ cup shredded sharp cheese

1 package (6 oz) Mozzarella cheese, sliced

1. Pare eggplant; cut in ⅛-inch thick slices.

2. Spread 2 tablespoons tomato sauce in bottom of a 2-quart glass casserole. Layer half of eggplant, 1 can tomato sauce, 1 teaspoon oregano, and ¼ cup of sharp cheese. Repeat layers.

3. Top with Mozzarella cheese. Microwave on High, covered, for 17 to 19 minutes. Rotate dish twice during microwave time.

Tarragon Mushrooms

Serve as a vegetable or over rice; serves 4

1 pound fresh mushrooms

1 green onion, including tops, finely chopped

¼ cup butter or margarine

½ teaspoon Beau Monde seasoned salt

½ teaspoon tarragon

⅛ teaspoon garlic salt

Dash pepper

1. Rinse mushrooms, and cut off woody end of stems. Combine mushrooms and onion in a 1½-quart glass casserole.

2. Combine remaining ingredients in a 1-cup glass measure. Microwave on High for 30 seconds or until melted.

3. Pour butter mixture over mushrooms. Microwave on High, covered, for 5 to 6 minutes or until mushrooms are tender.

French Onion Casserole

Delicious and outstanding vegetable; serves 6 to 8

4 medium onions, sliced

3 tablespoons butter or margarine

2 tablespoons flour

Dash pepper

¾ cup beef bouillon

¼ cup dry sherry

1½ cups plain croutons

2 tablespoons melted butter or margarine

½ cup shredded process Swiss cheese

3 tablespoons grated Parmesan cheese

Paprika

1. Separate onion slices into rings, and place with 3 tablespoons butter in a 3-quart glass casserole. Microwave on High, covered, for 7 minutes or until slightly tender.

2. Blend in flour and pepper. Stir in bouillon and sherry. Microwave on High for 3 minutes or until thickened, stirring once.

3. Toss croutons with melted butter. Spoon onto onion mixture. Sprinkle with cheeses, and then paprika. Microwave on High for 2 to 3 minutes or until cheese is melted.

Peas in Butter-Nut Sauce

Serves 4

2 pounds fresh peas (2 cups shelled)
2 tablespoons water

½ cup chicken stock or bouillon
¼ cup minced green onion, including tops
2 tablespoons chopped parsley
⅓ cup finely chopped walnuts
1 teaspoon paprika
½ teaspoon salt

1. Place peas and water in a 1-quart glass casserole. Microwave on High, covered, for 5 minutes. Drain, and set aside.

2. Combine remaining ingredients in a 2-cup glass measure. Microwave on High for 1 minute or until hot.

3. Pour mixture over peas; stir. Microwave on High, covered, for 1 to 2 minutes or until heated.

Chinese Peas

4 servings of an oriental favorite

1 package (7 oz) frozen Chinese peas (edible pod peas)
1 tablespoon butter or margarine
½ cup chicken stock or broth

½ cup thinly sliced water chestnuts

2 teaspoons cornstarch
2 tablespoons cold water or chicken stock

Salt

1. Place peas, butter, and chicken stock in a 1-quart glass casserole. Microwave on High, covered, for 7 minutes, stirring halfway through microwave time.

2. Stir in chestnuts. Push vegetables to one side of the dish.

3. In a separate cup or small bowl, combine cornstarch and water. Tilt vegetable casserole so liquid drains out of vegetables; add cornstarch mixture to vegetable liquid. Stir vegetables and liquid together, mixing well.

4. Microwave on High, uncovered, for 3 minutes, stirring once. Add salt to taste.

New Potatoes and Peas in Cream

4 servings; good flavor combination!

1 package (10 oz) frozen peas

1. Place peas in a 1-quart glass casserole. Microwave on Low, covered, for 5 minutes to defrost. Drain and set aside.

1 pound small new potatoes

2. Scrub potatoes. Cut off band of skin around middle of each. Pierce each potato twice with a fork. Put potatoes in a 2-quart glass casserole. Microwave on High, covered, for 8 minutes. Drain.

2 tablespoons butter or margarine
1 tablespoon flour
½ teaspoon salt
⅛ teaspoon pepper
½ cup light cream

3. Place butter in a 2-cup glass measure; microwave on High for 30 seconds or until melted. Add flour, salt, pepper. Blend in cream gradually. Microwave on High for 1½ minutes or until thickened. Stir every 30 seconds.

⅓ cup chopped onion

4. Combine peas, onions, and sauce. Mix well. Add to cooked potatoes. Stir to coat all. Microwave on High, covered, for 3 minutes or until heated.

Baked Potatoes

Make as many as your family can eat

Baking potatoes, medium (7 ounces each)

1. Select uniform size potatoes. Scrub potatoes and dry.

2. Pierce each potato all the way through with a large fork. Arrange potatoes in a circle on a paper towel, about 1 inch apart. Avoid placing 1 potato in center, surrounded by other potatoes. (See page 11.)

3. Microwave on High, turning potatoes about halfway through microwave time.

1 potato	4 to 6 minutes
2 potatoes	7 to 9 minutes
4 potatoes	13 to 15 minutes
6 potatoes	16 to 18 minutes

Microwave times are approximate. Actual time required depends on the size and variety of potatoes.

> Do not overcook; extreme dehydration may result in smoking or fire.

4. Remove while slightly firm, and let stand for 2 minutes. Potatoes will finish cooking during this standing time.

Twice Baked Potatoes

6 to 8 servings to keep on hand, frozen

Picture on page 192

6 medium potatoes

3 tablespoons butter
1 teaspoon salt
1 teaspoon chopped chives
⅛ teaspoon pepper
¼ cup sour cream
⅔ cup milk
½ cup shredded cheese

1. Pierce skin of potatoes with fork. Place on a paper towel. Microwave on High for 17 minutes, or until just tender. Turn potatoes over halfway through microwave time. Let stand for 10 minutes.

2. Cut potatoes in half lengthwise. Scoop out pulp into bowl, being careful not to tear shells. Mash potatoes well.

3. Beat in remaining ingredients except cheese. Spoon into potato shells. Top with cheese. Wrap tightly and freeze.

4. Before serving, place frozen potatoes in a 12x7½-inch glass dish; cover with waxed paper. Microwave on High for 10 minutes. Then microwave on Medium for 7 minutes, or until heated through.

Quick Scalloped Potatoes

2 easy servings made with frozen hash browns

6 ounces frozen hash browns

1 teaspoon instant minced onion
1 tablespoon butter
½ cup milk
¼ teaspoon salt
Dash pepper
Paprika

1. Place frozen potatoes in a 1-quart glass casserole. Microwave on High, covered, for 4 minutes.

2. Mix in onion, butter, milk, salt, and pepper. Sprinkle with paprika.

3. Microwave on High, covered, for 4 to 5 minutes, or until liquid is absorbed and potatoes are tender.

Scalloped Potatoes

5 to 6 from-scratch servings

5 to 6 medium potatoes, peeled and sliced, uncooked

4½ tablespoons flour
1¼ teaspoons salt

1½ cups milk

3 tablespoons butter or margarine
Paprika

1. Arrange half of sliced potatoes in the bottom of a 3-quart glass casserole.

2. Combine flour with salt. Sprinkle half of this mixture on potatoes. Repeat steps 1 and 2 with remaining ingredients.

3. Pour milk in a 2-cup glass measure. Microwave on High for 2 to 3 minutes, or until scalded and almost boiling.

4. Pour milk over potatoes. Dot with butter. Sprinkle generously with paprika. Microwave on High, covered, for 18 to 20 minutes, or until potatoes are tender, rotating the dish several times.

Whipped Potatoes

Baked with cream cheese and onion dip; serves a party of 8

8 to 10 potatoes, peeled
½ cup water

1 package (8 oz) cream cheese, softened
1 carton (8 oz) prepared French onion dip
½ cup milk
1½ teaspoons salt
⅛ teaspoon pepper
Garlic salt (optional)

2 tablespoons butter or margarine
Paprika
Sprigs of parsley

1. Halve and quarter potatoes. Combine potatoes and water in a 3-quart glass casserole. Microwave on High, covered, for 20 minutes. Drain.

2. Blend together cream cheese and onion dip in a large mixing bowl with an electric beater. Add hot potatoes, several pieces at a time. Add milk, beating until light and fluffy. Stir in salt, pepper, and garlic salt.

3. Spoon into a 3-quart glass casserole. Dot with butter. Microwave on High, covered, for 10 minutes, stirring halfway through microwave time. Sprinkle with paprika and parsley.

German Potato Salad

6 hot servings

4 cups sliced cooked potatoes

6 slices bacon

½ cup chopped onion

2 tablespoons flour
2 tablespoons sugar
1½ teaspoons salt
½ cup vinegar

1 teaspoon celery seed
Parsley

1. Bake potatoes. Cool, peel and slice. Set aside.

2. Cut bacon into small pieces. Place in a 1½-quart glass casserole. Microwave on High, covered, for 5 minutes. Stir halfway through microwave time.

3. Stir in onion. Microwave on High, covered, for 2 minutes.

4. Stir in flour, sugar, and salt. Mix thoroughly. Slowly stir in vinegar. Microwave on High for 3 minutes, stirring twice.

5. Blend in potatoes and celery seed. Toss lightly. Garnish with parsley. Serve hot.

Baked Sweet Potatoes

Delicious with lots of butter

Sweet potatoes or yams, medium (7 to 8 ounces each)

1. Select uniform size potatoes. Scrub and dry.

2. Pierce each potato all the way through with a large fork. Arrange potatoes in a circle on a paper towel, about 1 inch apart. Avoid placing 1 potato in center, surrounded by other potatoes. (See page 11.)

3. Microwave on High, turning potatoes about halfway through microwave time.

2 potatoes	8 to 11 minutes
4 potatoes	15 to 18 minutes

Microwave times are approximate. Actual time required depends on the size and variety of potatoes.

> Do not overcook; extreme dehydration may result in smoking or fire.

4. Remove while slightly firm, and let stand for 2 minutes. Potatoes will finish cooking during this standing time.

Candied Sweet Potatoes

4 servings to go with baked ham

3 to 4 large sweet potatoes

¼ cup butter or margarine
½ cup packed brown sugar
1 tablespoon flour
2 tablespoons cream or milk
½ teaspoon salt

1. Wash sweet potatoes. Pierce each potato with fork; place on paper towel in oven. Microwave on High for 8 to 10 minutes, or until almost tender. Peel and cut in ½-inch thick slices.

2. Combine remaining ingredients in a 9-inch round glass dish. Microwave on High, uncovered, for 2 to 3 minutes or until thickened. Stir halfway through microwave time.

3. Add potatoes to syrup, coating all sides. Microwave on High, uncovered, for 5 minutes. Rotate dish halfway through microwave time, and spoon syrup over top.

Creamed Spinach

3 to 4 servings with an onion-mushroom flavor

1½ pounds fresh spinach

½ cup dairy sour cream
3 tablespoons dry onion-mushroom soup mix

1. Remove stems from spinach. Rinse spinach leaves, and place in a 2-quart glass casserole. (Leave excess moisture on spinach.) Microwave on High, covered, for 6 to 7 minutes.

2. Combine sour cream and soup mix. Stir into spinach. Microwave on High, covered, for 2 minutes.

Tomato Casserole

Flavored with Cheddar; serves 6

¼ cup butter or margarine
2 tablespoons chopped onion

2 cans (1 lb each) tomatoes, drained
½ cup cracker crumbs
1 egg, beaten
½ cup cubed Cheddar cheese
1 tablespoon sugar
1 teaspoon salt
¼ teaspoon paprika
Dash chili powder

1. Place butter and onion in a 1½-quart glass casserole. Microwave on High, uncovered, for 2 minutes.

2. Combine tomatoes, crumbs, egg, cheese, sugar, salt, and spices with onion mixture. Microwave on High, covered, for 5 minutes. Stir halfway through microwave time.

Stewed Tomatoes

4 to 6 servings made from scratch

3 medium tomatoes

1 tablespoon minced onion
2 teaspoons sugar
1 teaspoon salt
⅛ teaspoon pepper
2 tablespoons butter or margarine

1 cup soft bread cubes

1. To easily peel tomatoes, first pierce skins. Then microwave on High for 1 to 1½ minutes. Peel tomatoes. Cut in fourths.

2. Combine tomatoes, onion, seasonings, and butter in a 1½-quart glass casserole. Microwave on High, covered, for 3 minutes. Stir once.

3. Stir in bread cubes. Microwave on High, covered, for 2 to 3 minutes.

Turnip Medley

Celery and green pepper complete this vegetable trio; for 6 to 8

6 cups sliced white turnips
½ cup water
½ teaspoon salt

2 cups diced celery
¾ cup chopped green pepper

2 tablespoons butter or margarine
Salt
Pepper

1. Place turnips in a 3-quart glass casserole. Add water and salt. Microwave on High, covered, for 10 minutes.

2. Add celery and green pepper to turnips. Stir. Microwave on High, covered, for 5 to 7 minutes longer, or until vegetables are tender.

3. Stir in butter. Add additional salt and pepper to taste. Let stand, covered, for 2 to 3 minutes before serving.

Yellow Squash

With onions for taste; serves 4 to 6

2 medium yellow squash, thinly sliced
2 medium onions, sliced
¼ cup water

2 tablespoons butter or margarine
2 tablespoons flour
½ teaspoon salt
⅛ teaspoon pepper
1 tablespoon soy sauce
1 cup milk

1. Combine squash, onion, and water in a 2-quart glass casserole. Microwave on High, covered, for 9 minutes or until tender. Drain. Let stand, covered.

2. Place butter in a 2-cup glass measure. Microwave on High for 30 seconds or until melted. Stir in flour, salt, pepper, and soy sauce. Gradually stir in milk using a wire whisk.

3. Microwave sauce on High for 3 to 3½ minutes, or until thickened. Stir with whisk every 30 seconds.

4. Pour sauce over squash and onions, and serve.

Tip: *Substitute ½ teaspoon dill for soy sauce, if desired.*

Zucchini Casserole

6 to 8 creamy, cheesy servings

4 cups thinly sliced zucchini
¼ cup hot water

¾ cup shredded sharp cheese
1 egg
½ cup dairy sour cream
1 tablespoon flour

3 slices bacon, cooked and crumbled
¼ cup browned bread crumbs

1. Place zucchini in a 1½-quart glass casserole with water. Microwave on High, covered, for 7 minutes. Drain.

2. Mix cheese, egg, sour cream and flour. Stir into zucchini. Microwave on High, covered, for 3 minutes. Stir.

3. Combine bacon and bread crumbs. Sprinkle over casserole. Microwave on High, covered, for 2 minutes.

Zucchini Boats

8 stuffed halves contain about 64 calories each, go well with poultry

4 small zucchini

2 cups crumbled herb-seasoned stuffing mix
1 tablespoon butter
¼ teaspoon salt

1 egg, slightly beaten
2 tablespoons grated Parmesan cheese

1. Cut zucchini in half lengthwise. Scoop out center, using spoon, leaving ¼-inch shell. Reserve shells.

2. Chop scooped-out pulp, and place in glass mixing bowl. Add stuffing mix, butter and salt. Mix lightly. Microwave on High, covered, for 4 minutes, or until stuffing is moistened.

3. Stir in egg. Spoon into zucchini shells. Place on large serving platter. Sprinkle with Parmesan cheese.

4. Cover with waxed paper. Microwave on High for 8 minutes, or until zucchini is tender.

Tip: *A grapefruit spoon is handy for scooping out zucchini.*

Defrosting Foods

The microwave oven— the perfect complement to your freezer

Frozen foods are definitely a part of our lifestyle. You probably have a refrigerator with a separate freezer compartment. You may even have a freestanding freezer. And no wonder! You recognize all the conveniences of having frozen foods on hand—uncooked foods to defrost and prepare as desired; commercially frozen convenience foods to defrost and reheat; and your frozen homemade make-ahead creations to defrost and reheat.

Until now, your choices for defrosting foods were limited:

● Let the food slowly thaw in the refrigerator— perhaps for a few days as with the holiday turkey.

● Let the food stand in room temperature. This could be risky for some foods. The outer edges could be subject to bacterial growth long before the center of the food is thawed.

Now with your microwave oven, you can remove foods from the freezer and thaw them in the microwave oven, taking minutes instead of hours or days. The microwave oven speeds defrosting, cooking, and reheating time and relieves you of time spent in the kitchen, allowing you to schedule other activities close to the dinner hour.

Since defrosting varies with the type and size of food, no single procedure can work with all foods. Here's where to look in this book to find the defrosting procedure for the following food types:

● **Bread dough.** See page 43 for thawing and proofing commercially frozen bread dough in the microwave oven. Bake the bread in a conventional oven.

● **Fruits.** See page 83 for defrosting commercially frozen fruits. Serve while still icy.

● **Vegetables.** See page 197. Vegetables can be cooked directly from the frozen state. A separate thawing procedure is not needed.

● **Uncooked meats, poultry, and seafood.** See this chapter, pages 218 to 221.

● **Commercially frozen convenience foods,** including a la carte items, individual dinners, ingredients and mixtures, and baked goods. See this chapter, pages 222 to 227.

● **Home prepared frozen casseroles.** See this chapter, pages 222 to 223, 228 to 229.

Defrosting uncooked meats, poultry, fish, seafood

Meats, poultry, and fish are convenient to keep in the freezer, ready to be defrosted and prepared as needed. Since the food is uncooked, you can prepare it as desired once thawed. Be as creative as your time and menu allow!

When you purchase commercially frozen food, rush it to your home freezer. No need to rewrap it unless the food package is damaged.

When you purchase fresh food, rewrap it in a suitable material before freezing. Check manufacturer's instructions to see if the material is suitable for the freezer. Consider using a material that is also suitable for the microwave oven. Freezer materials include:

- Moistureproof, vaporproof materials prevent evaporation and provide best protection for the foods. Some examples are rigid plastic, glass, and metal freezer containers.
- Moisture-resistant, vapor-resistant materials can retain food quality satisfactorily if properly used. Some examples are plastic film, plastic bags, and freezer paper. Follow manufacturer's instructions; some materials are satisfactory for long-term storage, others for short-term storage.

Freeze foods as soon as possible. For best results, storage temperatures should range from 0° to -5° F. Microwave times in this chapter are based on foods held at this temperature range.

A few food handling techniques are important to defrosting uncooked meats, poultry, and fish, as explained on the next few pages. Become familiar with these techniques; then use the step-by-step instructions and the charts which follow.

Place the wrapped food package in a glass dish

To retain moisture and natural juices, thaw foods in the original freezer wrap if such a wrap is suitable for use in the microwave oven. However, pierce a few holes in the wrap to allow steam to escape.

Remove metal ties; use string instead.

If food is wrapped in foil, remove the foil. Rewrap the food in paper, plastic, or other material that is suitable for microwave use.

Place the wrapped food package in a glass dish or other suitable container. This dish will catch any juice or moisture that may drain out of the package during the defrosting time. Use a spoon or baster to remove this moisture as it accumulates.

Later you can cook the food in the same dish.

Microwave on Low, and allow two standing times

For most uncooked meats, poultry, and fish, the defrosting procedure includes four periods of time:

- Microwave on Low for $2/3$ of microwave time.
- Let stand.
- Microwave on Low for remaining $1/3$ of microwave time.
- Let stand.

During the two standing times, temperatures equalize. Those portions of food that have absorbed the most microwave energy conduct their heat to the colder portions of the food, allowing defrosting to continue.

These standing times are essential for evenly thawed food. Don't eliminate them in an effort to speed up the defrosting process. If you do, the microwaves will not penetrate the ice barrier. The outer/thinner portions of the food will continue to cook; the inner/thicker portions will remain frozen.

Occasionally stir, turn the food, etc

In addition to standing time, another group of food handling techniques helps to equalize the thawing of foods. Depending on the food, you may:

- Stir the food.
- Separate the pieces.
- Turn the food over.
- Rotate the dish.
- Remove thawed portions (especially helpful with ground meat, mixed pieces of chicken).

These techniques help in achieving an evenly thawed food item because they redistribute the foodload within the pattern of microwaves. They also .mix colder portions of food with warmer portions, helping to equalize temperatures.

Remove the food before it is completely thawed

For best results, the food should be slightly icy at the end of microwave time. It will continue to defrost during the last standing time. Prepare the food and cook it when a few ice cystals remain in the center of the food.

If you allow too much microwave time, you may be unsatisfied with the results:

- The food may dry out.
- The edges may begin to cook before the center thaws completely.
- Microwave time for the cooking process will be different than specified in the recipe.
- The food may cook unevenly, requiring more handling (stirring, turning, etc) than normal.
- The food may overcook.

For these reasons, defrost the food only for as long as necessary. Prepare food and start to cook it while it is cool to the touch and still has ice crystals in its center.

Frozen Uncooked Foods

*Meats,
Poultry,
Fish,
Seafood*

*Review text on
pages 218-219*

How to defrost uncooked meats, poultry, fish, seafood

1. Place the wrapped food in a glass dish. Be certain the wrap is suitable for microwave use. If not, re-wrap accordingly.

2. Determine total microwave time (pounds x 5 = minutes).

3. Microwave on Low, covered, for ⅔ of total microwave time. Turn or stir the food occasionally.

4. Let stand, covered, for temperatures to equalize. In general, this standing time varies from three to fifteen minutes, depending on the weight of food. See *Basic Time Guide,* on the next page.

5. After standing time: remove thawed portions, separate pieces, turn food over, rotate the dish, stir—as applicable.

6. Microwave on Low, covered, for the remaining ⅓ of microwave time, turning or stirring occasionally.

7. Allow another standing time for temperatures to equalize, as specified in the *Last Standing Time* charts.

   ● Meats, including Variety Meats: Let stand, covered, in room temperature.

   ● Fish or poultry: Immerse the food package in cold water, and let stand as specified in the chart.

   If original wrapping is not watertight or properly sealed, first place food in a plastic bag. Squeeze out as much air as possible; close the bag with a wire tie. Then immerse the food package.

8. Prepare the food for cooking, as desired.

Tip: *If poultry weighs over 10 pounds, you may speed up the defrosting. Substitute this method for step 3, above. Microwave on Medium, wrapped, for 20 minutes, turning bird on its other side after 10 minutes. Switch to Low, and microwave until ⅔ of microwave time is up. Next continue with step 4 above.*

(Charts are continued on next page.)

Basic Time Guide for Defrosting
Uncooked Meats, Poultry, Fish, and Seafood

Weight of Food	Total Microwave Time (pounds x 5)	Microwave on Low (⅔ microwave time)	First Standing Time	Microwave on Low (⅓ microwave time)	Last Standing Time
1 pound	5 minutes	3 minutes	3 minutes	2 minutes	
2	10	6	3	4	
3	15	10	5	5	
4	20	15	5	5	See separate charts below
5	25	17	10	8	
6	30	20	10	10	
7	35	23	15	12	
8	40	27	15	13	
9	45	30	15	15	
10	50	33	15	17	
15	75	50	15	25	

Last Standing Time for Defrosting Uncooked Meats

Weight	Standing Time in Room Temperature		
	Patties	Chops, Steaks, Ribs, Variety Meats	Roasts, Bulk Ground Meat
1 pound	5 to 10 min	10 to 15 min	10 to 20 min
2	5 to 10	10 to 20	15 to 30
3	—	10 to 20	45 to 60
4	—	20 to 30	45 min to 1¼ hr

Last Standing Time for Defrosting Uncooked Poultry

Weight	Standing Time in Cold Water	
	Pieces	Whole
1 pound	5 to 10 min	5 to 10 min
2	5 to 10	10 to 15
3	10 to 20	15 to 20
4	15 to 20	15 to 20
5	—	20 to 30
6	—	20 to 30
7	—	30 to 40
10	—	50 to 60
15	—	1 to 1½ hr

Last Standing Time for Defrosting Uncooked Fish and Seafood

Weight	Standing Time in Cold Water
1 pound	3 to 5 min
2	10 to 15

Defrosting and reheating prepared foods

Convenience is truly the key word to this grouping of foods. Take them from the freezer, pop them into the microwave oven, and serve them piping hot! This, of course, is an oversimplification; but the convenience of having fully prepared food on hand is definitely a time- and worksaver.

A freezer well-stocked with prepared foods complements your microwave oven. You can put a meal on the table in less time and with much less effort than if you had to start from scratch.

Choose from a large array of convenience foods in your grocer's freezer case:

- Foods to serve hot—vegetables, entrees, sauces, complete dinners, sandwiches.
- Foods to thaw and then prepare according to directions—egg mixtures, pancake batters.
- Foods to thaw and serve—cakes and other baked good, coffee lighteners, whipped toppings.

Or prepare your own convenience foods. Make casseroles in advance, and freeze them to eat within three months. Many of the food preparation and freezing techniques have already been discussed. (See *Food Handling Techniques*, page 13; *Casseroles*, page 45.) Thawing and reheating instructions are in this chapter.

A few food handling techniques are important to defrosting and reheating commercially prepared and home prepared foods, as explained on this page. Become familiar with these techniques; then use the step-by-step instructions and the charts which follow.

Select a suitable utensil

Frozen convenience foods and your frozen homemade casseroles may or may not be packaged in a utensil that is suitable for microwave use. Let's quickly review the more common packages and their special considerations. (See pages 4 to 7.)

Boilable plastic bags. Pierce several holes in the top surface of the bag. Place the bag in a glass dish. Steam will escape through the holes, but the sauce will not spill out. (If you remove food from the plastic bag, cover the dish to speed the heating process.)

Foil containers. Remove foods from foil trays, shells, etc. Transfer the food to a suitable dish. Select a dish that is approximately the same length and width as the original container. A dish that is too large will allow sauces to flow outward, where they will absorb more microwave energy and evaporate. The dish should be deep enough to allow stirring and boiling, if applicable.

Casserole dishes. Choose one that is large enough to allow stirring. Be sure it does not have metal trim, metal parts, or invisible metallic content.

Plastic freezer containers. Microwave only until the food can easily be removed from the plastic container. Then transfer the food to a glass or ceramic dish. Plastic containers in general do not withstand the heat of the food; they may become distorted, and/or melt.

Glass freezer jars. Remove the metal lid. Microwave until the food can be removed. Then transfer the food to a glass or ceramic dish. Freezer jars are too small to allow stirring and boiling.

Microwave according to the prepared food

Covered or uncovered. Check the charts to see whether the dish should be covered or uncovered. In general, use a cover to prevent spatters or to hold in the heat/steam. Leave the dish uncovered if the food should have a crisp exterior (fried chicken, fish sticks, etc).

Microwave time. The length of time needed to thaw and reheat the food varies. Brands and size of package, sizes and types of food items, thickness of sauces, and starting temperature of the frozen food all affect the required microwave time. Check the package for microwave time; if none is given, use the charts in this chapter. Adjust time as needed.

Low, Medium, or High. In general, to thaw large volume, dense, or sensitive foods, microwave on Low or Medium. Switch to High while ice crystals still remain, and continue to microwave until hot.

Microwave on Medium those foods that contain a large amount of mushrooms, cheese, sour cream, eggs.

Many frozen prepared foods can be defrosted and reheated on High. Check the charts for specific microwave instructions.

Occasionally stir, turn the food, etc

To help equalize thawing and reheating, practice these techniques during microwave time:

- Stir the food.
- Separate the pieces.
- Turn the pieces over.
- Rotate the dish.

These techniques help in achieving an evenly thawed and reheated food because they distribute the food-load within the pattern of microwaves. They also mix colder portions of food with warmer portions, helping temperatures to equalize more readily.

Commercially Frozen Convenience Foods

A la carte items
Ingredients and Mixtures
Individual Dinners
Baked Goods

Review text on pages
222-223

1. Open the package and place the food in the suggested dish.
   - If the food is in a metal container, transfer the food to a glass dish (see chart).
   - If the food is in a boilable plastic bag, pierce holes in the top of the bag. Place the bag of frozen food in the suggested dish, uncovered.
   - If you remove the food from the boilable plastic bag, place the food in the suggested dish, covered.
2. Check package for microwave instructions. If none are given, microwave as specified in the charts, stirring the food or rotating the dish occasionally.
3. Stir the food before serving, if applicable.

A la carte Items to Serve Hot		
Food Item	**Utensil, Special Instructions**	**Microwave Instructions**
Beef Stew, 10 oz	1-qt glass casserole, uncovered if in boilable bag*	High for 5 to 7 min
Beef Stroganoff 9¾ oz	1-qt glass casserole, uncovered if in boilable bag*	High for 5 to 6 min
Cabbage Rolls, 14 oz	1-qt glass casserole, covered	Medium for 6 min; then High for 6 min
Chicken a la King, 9½ oz	1-qt glass casserole, uncovered if in boilable bag*	Medium for 5 min; then High for 3 min
Chicken Divan, 8½ oz	1-qt glass casserole, covered	Medium for 8 min
Corn Souffle, 12 oz	1½-qt glass casserole, covered	Medium for 5 min; then High for 5 min
Creamed Chipped Beef, 11 oz	1½-qt glass casserole, uncovered if in boilable bag*	High for 6 to 7 min
Egg Rolls, 6 oz	8x8x2-inch dish, uncovered; arrange rolls in rows	High for 3 to 4 min

*If you remove the food from the boilable plastic bag before microwave time, cover the cassserole.
**Pierce film after microwave time. Wait for steam to escape; then remove the film and serve the food.

Chart continued on next page

Food Item	Utensil, Special Instructions	Microwave Instructions
A la carte Items to Serve Hot *continued*		
Enchiladas, 22 oz	10x6-inch dish; cover with plastic film**	Medium for 10 min; then High for 5 min; let stand for 2 to 3 min
Escalloped Chicken and Noodles, 11½ oz	1½-qt glass casserole, uncovered	High for 8 to 9 min
Fish Sticks, 8¾ oz	8x8x2-inch dish; uncovered	Medium for 5 to 6 min
Fried Chicken, 32 oz	12x7½-inch dish, uncovered	Medium for 10 min; then High for 5 min
Fried Fish Fillet, 8 oz	8x8x2-inch dish, uncovered	Medium for 7 to 8 min
Green Peppers, Stuffed, 14 oz	1-qt glass casserole, covered	Medium for 5 min; then High for 7 min
Lasagna, 21 oz	1½-qt glass casserole, covered	Medium for 10 min then High for 5 min
Macaroni & Cheese, 8 oz	1-qt glass casserole, covered	Medium for 5 min; stir; then High for 3 min
Potatoes au Gratin, 11½ oz	1½-qt glass casserole, covered	High for 6 to 7 min
Potatoes, Baked, Stuffed, 10 oz	Glass plate	Medium for 10 min; then High for 1 to 2 min
Potatoes, Scalloped, 12 oz	1½-qt glass casserole, covered	Medium for 5 min; then High for 5 to 6 min
Salisbury Steak & Gravy, 32 oz	12x7½-inch glass dish; cover with plastic film**	Medium for 10 min; then High for 10 to 12 min
Sandwiches, 9 oz	Paper plate; cover with paper towel	Medium for 3 to 4 min
Scrambled Eggs & Sausage, 6¼ oz	Dinner plate; cover with plastic film loosely	Medium for 5 min

*If you remove the food from the boilable plastic bag before microwave time, cover the cassserole.

**Pierce film after microwave time. Wait for steam to escape; then remove the film and serve the food.

Chart continued on next page

A la carte Items to Serve Hot *continued*		
Food Item	**Utensil, Special Instructions**	**Microwave Instructions**
Shrimp Newburg, 6½ oz	1-qt glass casserole, uncovered if in boilable bag*	High for 4 to 5 min
Sliced Beef & Barbecue Sauce, 5 oz	1-qt glass casserole, uncovered if in boilable bag*	High for 3 to 4 min
Soup, 8 oz	1-qt glass casserole, uncovered; remove from plastic bag after 2 min; stir before serving	High for 5 to 6 min
Spaghetti with Meat Sauce, 14 oz	1½-qt glass casserole, uncovered if in boilable bag*	High for 7 min
Swiss Fondue, 10 oz	1-qt glass casserole, uncovered if in boilable bag*	Medium for 7 to 8 min
Tuna Noodle Casserole, 11½ oz	1½-qt glass casserole, covered	High for 8 to 9 min
Welsh Rarebit, 10 oz	1½-qt glass casserole, covered	Medium for 6 to 7 min; let stand for 2 min; stir

*If you remove the food from the boilable plastic bag before microwave time, cover the casserole.
**Pierce film after microwave time. Wait for steam to escape; then remove the film and serve the food.

See basic instructions on page 224

Ingredients and Mixtures to Thaw Before Using		
Food Item	**Utensil, Special Instructions**	**Microwave Instructions**
Egg Mixture, 8 oz	Open carton	Low for 3 to 5 min; let stand for 2 to 3 min
Pancake Batter, 1 pt	Open carton	Low for 5 to 6 min; let stand for 2 to 3 min; stir
Coffee Creamer, 1 pt	Open carton	Low for 5 to 6 min; let stand for 2 to 3 min
Whipped Topping, 9 oz, 13½ oz	Open carton	Low for 2 min (9 oz) or for 3 min (13½ oz); let stand for 5 min; stir

See basic instructions on page 224

Individual Dinners to Serve Hot

Food Item	Utensil, Special Instructions	Microwave Instructions
Chicken Chow Mein Dinner, 11 oz	Dinner plate; cover loosely with plastic film	Medium for 8 to 10 min
Mexican Dinner, 1 lb	Dinner plate; cover loosely with plastic film	Medium for 10 min; then High for 2 min
Swiss Steak, 10 oz	Dinner plate; cover loosely with plastic film	Medium for 10 to 12 min
Turkey Dinner, 11½ oz	Dinner plate; cover loosely with plastic film	Medium for 10 to 12 min
Large Size Dinner, 15 oz	Dinner plate; cover loosely with plastic film	Medium for 10 min; then High for 2 min

See basic instructions on page 224

Baked Goods to Thaw and Serve

Food Item	Utensil, Special Instructions	Microwave Instructions
Bread, 1-lb loaf	Remove tie; leave bread in plastic bag	Medium for 2 to 3 min; let stand for 2 to 3 min
Brownies, 13 oz	Paper plate, uncovered	Low for 2 min
Buns, Sandwich, 13 oz	Remove tie; leave buns in plastic bag	Medium for 2 to 3 min; let stand for 2 to 3 min
Cake, 18 oz	Plate, uncovered	Low for 3 min; center may be icy; let stand for 5 min
Coffeecake, 11¼ oz	Plate, uncovered	Medium for 3 to 4 min or until warm
Cupcakes, 10 oz	Plate, uncovered	Low for 2 min; let stand for 3 to 5 min
Donuts, Mini, 10 oz	Place paper towel on plate; stack donuts; cover with paper towel	Medium for 2 min
French Toast, 10 oz	Plate, uncovered	Medium for 3 to 5 min
Waffles, 9 oz	Plate, uncovered	Medium for 3 to 5 min

Frozen Home Prepared Casseroles

Review text on pages 222 to 223

1. Prepare the food and utensil for microwave use. Remove foil; remove metal ties; pierce the plastic bag; etc.

2. Microwave on Low, covered, to start defrosting the casserole. (See chart.)

   At the end of this defrost period, food should have ice crystals in its center and be only partially thawed.

3. To finish the defrosting process and to reheat the casserole, microwave on Medium or High, covered. (See chart.)

   • Microwave on Medium those casseroles that contain a large quantity of meat, cheese, eggs, cream, or other sensitive food.

   • Microwave on High those casseroles that contain mostly starchy foods—rice, pasta, potatoes, etc—or other nonsensitive foods.

   • See individual recipes in appropriate sections of this book for specific Medium or High guidelines.

4. Halfway through reheat time, separate the pieces, stir the food, rotate the dish, etc—as applicable.

5. Continue reheating on Medium or High until hot. If desired, use a thermometer during the last half of reheat time (see page 13). Normal serving temperatures range from 130° to 140° F.

6. Let stand, covered, for temperatures to equalize. (See chart.)

Tip: *To reheat individual servings, follow steps 1 through 3. Then portion out as much food as desired onto a dinner plate. Microwave on High, covered with a paper towel, until hot. Immediately refrigerate the unused portion of the casserole.*

Guide for Home Prepared Casseroles			
Covered Casserole, ⅔ full	**Microwave Instructions**		**Special Instructions**
	To Defrost	**To Reheat**	
1 qt	Low for 8 min	Medium for 14 to 22 min; or High for 12 to 18 min	Let stand, covered, for a few minutes before serving.
1½ qt	Low for 10 min	Medium for 24 to 36 min; or High for 16 to 24 min	Stir halfway through reheating time. Let stand, covered, for 5 min before serving.
2 qt	Low for 12 min	Medium for 32 to 44 min; or High for 22 to 30 min	Stir halfway through reheating time. Let stand, covered, for 5 to 10 min before serving.
3 qt	Low for 14 min	Medium for 42 to 54 min; or High for 28 to 40 min	

Appendix

Four Basic Food Groups

For a balanced daily diet, eat some servings from each of the four basic food groups.

Food Group	Foods	Daily Servings
Milk	Milk Cheese Ice Cream	3 or more for children 4 or more for teens 2 or more for adults
Meats	Meat Fish Poultry Eggs Dry Beans* Peas* Nuts*	2 or more *Alternates
Fruits and Vegetables	Fruits Vegetables	4 or more Choose citrus fruit or tomatoes Choose green or yellow vegetables
Breads and Cereals	Breads Cereals Pastas Rice	4 or more Choose enriched or whole grain foods

Standard and Metric Measures

The Standard English System
Abbreviations used in this book

tsp = teaspoon
tbsp = tablespoon
c = cup
pt = pint
qt = quart
gal = gallon
oz = ounce
lb = pound
°F = degree Fahrenheit
min = minutes
hr = hour

Equivalents

3 tsp = 1 tbsp
16 tbsp = 1 c
2 c = 1 pt
2 pt (4 c) = 1 qt
4 qt = 1 gal
16 oz = 1 lb
60 min = 1 hr

The Metric System
Abbreviations

l or L = litre
ml = millilitre
g = gram
kg = kilogram
m = metre
cm = centimetre
°C = degree Celsius

Conversions
(approximate)

Fluid measure (capacity)

1 tsp = 5 ml
1 tbsp = 15 ml
1 c = 240 ml
1 c = .24 L
1 pt = .47 L
1 qt = .95 L
1 gal = 3.79 L
1 L = 2.1 pt
1 L = 1.06 qt
1 L = .26 gal

Dry measure (weight)

1 oz = 28.3 g
1 lb = .45 kg
1 g = .035 oz
1 kg = 2.2 lb

Length

1 inch = 2.54 cm
1 ft = .305 m
1 cm = .39 inch
1 m = 3.28 ft

Temperature

212° F = 100° C Water boils
68° F = 20° C Room temperature
32° F = 0° C Water freezes
0° F = −18° C ⎫ Recommended range
−5° F = −20° C ⎭ for frozen foods

Substitutions and Equivalents

Food Item	Substitution or Equivalent
Baking powder, 1 teaspoon	⅓ teaspoon baking soda, plus ½ teaspoon cream of tartar
Bread crumbs, ⅓ cup	1 slice
Butter or margarine, ½ cup	8 tablespoons, or 1 stick
Cheese, 2½ cups freshly grated	½ pound
Cream Cheese, 3 ounces	6 tablespoons
Chives, 1 tablespoon chopped	1 teaspoon freeze-dried
Chocolate, 1 square (1 ounce)	3 tablespoons cocoa, plus 1 tablespoon fat
Cornstarch, 1 tablespoon	2 tablespoons flour
Cracker crumbs, ¾ cup	1 cup bread crumbs
Cream, heavy, 1 cup	2 to 2½ cups whipped
Eggs, 6 medium whole	about 1 cup
10 to 11 medium whites	about 1 cup
13 to 14 medium yolks	about 1 cup
Flour, 1 cup sifted all-purpose	1 cup minus 2 tablespoons unsifted all-purpose
1 cup sifted cake	1 cup minus 2 tablespoons sifted all-purpose
Garlic, 1 small clove	⅛ teaspoon garlic powder, or ⅛ teaspoon minced garlic
Ginger, 1 tablespoon candied, washed of sugar	1 tablespoon raw ginger, or ⅛ teaspoon powdered ginger
Green pepper, 2 tablespoons fresh	1 tablespoon dried flakes
Herbs, 1 teaspoon dried leaf	¼ teaspoon powdered

Chart continued on next page

Substitutes and equivalents, *continued*

Food Item		Substitution or Equivalent
Horseradish, 1 tablespoon fresh		2 tablespoons bottled
Lemon,	1 whole	2 to 3 tablespoons juice, plus 2 teaspoons peel
	1 teaspoon grated peel	½ teaspoon dried peel
	1 teaspoon juice	½ teaspoon vinegar
Macaroni, 1 cup uncooked		2 to 2¼ cups cooked
Milk,	1 cup whole	½ cup evaporated, plus ½ cup water or 4 tablespoons powdered milk, plus 1 cup water
	1 cup buttermilk or sour milk	1 tablespoon vinegar or lemon juice, plus milk to make 1 cup
Mushrooms, 1 pound fresh		6 ounces canned
Noodles, 1 cup uncooked		1¼ cups cooked
Onion, ¼ cup chopped		1 tablespoon instant minced, or 1 tablespoon instant flaked, or ¼ cup frozen chopped, or 1 teaspoon powder, or about 1 small onion, chopped
Orange,	1 medium	6 to 8 tablespoons juice, plus 2 to 3 tablespoons peel
	1 teaspoon grated peel	½ teaspoon dried peel
Parsley, 1 tablespoon fresh snipped		1 teaspoon dried flakes
Raisins, 1 pound		2¾ cups seedless whole
Rice, 2½ cups uncooked		8 cups cooked
Sugar,	1 cup packed brown	1 cup granulated sugar
	1 cup powdered	1 cup granulated sugar
Yogurt, 1 cup		1 cup buttermilk

Index